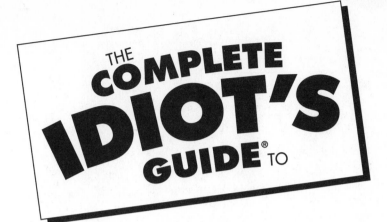

THE COMPLETE IDIOT'S GUIDE® TO

The College Diet Cookbook

by Shelly Vaughan James

ALPHA

A member of Penguin Group (USA) Inc.

To all the excellent cooks in my life, who taught me everything I know about cooking and living well.

ALPHA BOOKS

Published by the Penguin Group

Penguin Group (USA) Inc., 375 Hudson Street, New York, New York 10014, USA

Penguin Group (Canada), 90 Eglinton Avenue East, Suite 700, Toronto, Ontario M4P 2Y3, Canada (a division of Pearson Penguin Canada Inc.)

Penguin Books Ltd., 80 Strand, London WC2R 0RL, England

Penguin Ireland, 25 St. Stephen's Green, Dublin 2, Ireland (a division of Penguin Books Ltd.)

Penguin Group (Australia), 250 Camberwell Road, Camberwell, Victoria 3124, Australia (a division of Pearson Australia Group Pty. Ltd.)

Penguin Books India Pvt. Ltd., 11 Community Centre, Panchsheel Park, New Delhi—110 017, India

Penguin Group (NZ), 67 Apollo Drive, Rosedale, North Shore, Auckland 1311, New Zealand (a division of Pearson New Zealand Ltd.)

Penguin Books (South Africa) (Pty.) Ltd, 24 Sturdee Avenue, Rosebank, Johannesburg 2196, South Africa

Penguin Books Ltd., Registered Offices: 80 Strand, London WC2R 0RL, England

Copyright © 2007 by Shelly Vaughan James

All rights reserved. No part of this book shall be reproduced, stored in a retrieval system, or transmitted by any means, electronic, mechanical, photocopying, recording, or otherwise, without written permission from the publisher. No patent liability is assumed with respect to the use of the information contained herein. Although every precaution has been taken in the preparation of this book, the publisher and author assume no responsibility for errors or omissions. Neither is any liability assumed for damages resulting from the use of information contained herein. For information, address Alpha Books, 800 East 96th Street, Indianapolis, IN 46240.

THE COMPLETE IDIOT'S GUIDE TO and Design are registered trademarks of Penguin Group (USA) Inc.

International Standard Book Number: 978-1-59257-680-7
Library of Congress Catalog Card Number: 2007924623

09   08   07   8   7   6   5   4   3   2   1

Interpretation of the printing code: The rightmost number of the first series of numbers is the year of the book's printing; the rightmost number of the second series of numbers is the number of the book's printing. For example, a printing code of 07-1 shows that the first printing occurred in 2007.

Printed in the United States of America

Note: This publication contains the opinions and ideas of its author. It is intended to provide helpful and informative material on the subject matter covered. It is sold with the understanding that the author and publisher are not engaged in rendering professional services in the book. If the reader requires personal assistance or advice, a competent professional should be consulted.

The author and publisher specifically disclaim any responsibility for any liability, loss, or risk, personal or otherwise, which is incurred as a consequence, directly or indirectly, of the use and application of any of the contents of this book.

Most Alpha books are available at special quantity discounts for bulk purchases for sales promotions, premiums, fundraising, or educational use. Special books, or book excerpts, can also be created to fit specific needs.

For details, write: Special Markets, Alpha Books, 375 Hudson Street, New York, NY 10014.

Publisher: *Marie Butler-Knight*
Editorial Director: *Mike Sanders*
Managing Editor: *Billy Fields*
Acquisitions Editor: *Michele Wells*
Senior Development Editor: *Christy Wagner*
Production Editor: *Kayla Dugger*

Copy Editor: *Amy Borrelli*
Cartoonist: *Richard King*
Cover Designer: *Kurt Owens*
Book Designers: *Kurt Owens /Trina Wurst*
Indexer: *Angie Bess*
Layout: *Ayanna Lacey*

Contents at a Glance

Contents

What the recipe symbols mean:

Blender

Grill

Broiler

Microwave

Electric grill

Oven

Electric skillet

Slow cooker

Electric wok

Stovetop

Introduction

When you decided to see what recipes you could find in this cookbook, you were probably looking for a few delicious dishes you felt were easy enough for you to make. I've included dozens of appetizing recipes, all of them aimed at cooks who might still be learning their way around the kitchen. But I believe the best test of a great cookbook is if you, the reader, can take away what you've learned and put into practice the methods you need to live a more healthful life full of great taste.

I've tried to share recipes made with the foods I think you love, as well as to intrigue your taste buds with new flavors and combinations. Beyond the mouthwatering recipes, I've shared basic information you need to know to become a confident cook. Equipped with this essential information, you can cook and eat in your independence. You might think about food choices differently, being mindful of health benefits. But you should never feel restricted in your ability to put together a tasty meal.

Here's to your health and your passion for learning!

How This Book Is Organized

This book is divided into six parts:

Part 1, "Cooking 101," provides indispensable information on the basics you need to know to handle foods and work with assurance in the kitchen you set up. You'll learn how to read a recipe, as well as a nutrition facts panel and a recipe analysis.

Part 2, "Morning, Noon, or Night," features tempting recipes for breakfasts, sandwiches, soups, and salads. These foods carry the familiar flavors your stomach is happy to have anytime of the day.

Part 3, "Main Courses," highlights your need for main dish recipes to anchor your meals. You'll find everything from fish and seafood, chicken and turkey, beef and pork, and even meatless meals.

Part 4, "Studying Abroad," offers foods from around the globe. You can perk up your tired taste buds with Mexican, Italian, Asian, and Mediterranean cooking.

Part 5, "Great Go-Withs," is packed with recipes for all your favorite sides—salads, veggies, noodles, and grains. These are the recipes you need to make your meals complete.

Part 6, "Something More," pleases your sweet tooth and cures your attack of the munchies. You'll find snacks to study with, sweet treats to gobble up, scrumptious desserts to end a meal with, and beverages to sip with pleasure.

Garnishes

You'll see many sidebars throughout the book that offer you a little something extra. Here's what to look for:

Class Notes
These boxes give definitions of helpful cooking vocab.

Lecture Hall
Warnings in these boxes tell you how to avoid possible problems.

Of Higher Learning
Facts given in these boxes impart extraneous information you can use to impress your friends.

Learning Curve
These boxes contain valuable information to help you in the kitchen and with specific recipes.

Acknowledgments

Although only one name appears on the cover of this cookbook, I am all too aware of the contributions made by many others to make this book possible.

I would like to thank my family for their patience, for picking up some of the slack at home, for their baby-sitting services, and for their willingness to taste-test everything (and clearing space in my fridge so I could cook some more).

Thank you, Michele Wells, my acquisitions editor at Alpha, whose guidance helped shape this book into the best it could be. I thank my development editor Christy Wagner, production editor Kayla Dugger, and copy editor Amy Borrelli for pruning my manuscript for accuracy and readability. I would also like to thank JoAnna M. Lund, whose direction and confidence in my abilities launched me into a new career.

Special Thanks to the Technical Reviewer

The Complete Idiot's Guide to the College Diet Cookbook was reviewed by an expert who double-checked the accuracy of what you'll learn here, to help us ensure that this book gives you everything you need to know about cooking and eating well in college. Special thanks are extended to John Carbone.

John is a doctoral student in the Nutritional Sciences Department at the University of Connecticut. In addition to working toward his Ph.D. in nutritional biochemistry, John will soon complete all the requirements needed to become a registered dietitian. During the academic year, he also teaches an undergraduate laboratory on food composition and preparation.

Trademarks

All terms mentioned in this book that are known to be or are suspected of being trademarks or service marks have been appropriately capitalized. Alpha Books and Penguin Group (USA) Inc. cannot attest to the accuracy of this information. Use of a term in this book should not be regarded as affecting the validity of any trademark or service mark.

Part

Cooking 101

Cooking, like any endeavor, requires a foundation of certain knowledge. Learning what you need to know to start is easy. Cooking doesn't have to result in Pan-Seared Scallops and Oyster Mushroom Sweet Potato Salad with Cilantro Ginger Vinaigrette to be impressive and taste delicious. So relax!

Whether you're in an apartment with a full kitchen or sharing a dorm room with a microwave and minifridge, with the information in Part 1, you'll be able to set up kitchen quarters and find recipes to fit your needs. You may be responsible for your meals for the first time ever, and you can eat well—little room, little money, little experience, and all.

"Well, one of us is going to have to learn how to cook."

Prerequisites: What Every Cook Needs to Know

In This Chapter

- ◆ Understanding cooking measurements and how to measure properly
- ◆ Keeping you and your food safe
- ◆ Making substitutions when you have to

Every cook needs to know the basics of how to handle foods and how to use cooking tools. Plus, he or she needs to know how to do it all safely. Once you learn the fundamentals, you can move on to the pleasure of cooking foods that will satiate. Do your homework, and you can be eating great by dinnertime!

Measuring Up

Without measurements, you have one of my grandmother's recipes: a little of this, and then add that until it looks right. That might work for an experienced cook like Grandma, but for the rest of us, measuring is important to cooking and essential to baking. Knowing how to measure correctly may mean the difference between success and failure of a recipe. The principles are simple, but you need to learn them.

Measuring How-Tos

Liquid measuring cups are made of clear glass or plastic and, as you can imagine, are used to measure liquid ingredients. You'll likely find them in 1-cup, 2-cup, or 4-cup sizes. If the measurements are marked on the outside of the measuring cup, you'll need to read the amounts at eye level. Set the measuring cup flat on the counter and bend down to the cup's level to get an accurate reading. The meniscus, or edge of the liquid, should be touching your desired measurement line.

Because cooks grew weary of bobbing up and down to pour and then check for an accurate measurement, you'll now find liquid measuring cups with the measurements marked on the inside of the measuring cup, at a slant you can easily read while standing straight.

You can find dry measuring cups in plastic or stainless-steel sets, with ¼-, ⅓-, ½-, and 1-cup measures; some sets may have ⅛-, ⅔-, or 2-cup measures as well. To use, spoon light ingredients, such as flour or sugar, into the appropriate measuring cup, mounding above the edge. Move the flat side of a butter knife across the top of the measuring cup, scraping off the excess amount so your ingredient is level with the top of the cup. This provides the most accurate measurement.

Measuring spoons also are available in plastic or stainless-steel sets. You can use these to measure small amounts of dry or wet ingredients. Standard measures are ¼, ½, and 1 teaspoon and 1 tablespoon. Some sets have ⅛-teaspoon and ½-tablespoon measures, too.

Of Higher Learning

When brown sugar is called for in a recipe, it should be firmly packed into the measuring cup, unless otherwise indicated. Just spoon the brown sugar into the measure and press down with the back of the spoon until the cup is tightly filled. When you release properly measured brown sugar into your mixing bowl, it should retain the shape of the measuring cup.

Learning Curve

When measuring thick, sticky liquids—honey, molasses, corn syrup, etc.—lightly coat the measure first with nonstick cooking spray for easy release and cleanup.

Measurement Abbreviations

Various abbreviations are used in most cookbooks and recipes to designate standard measurements and sizes. The following table lists the abbreviations used in this cookbook.

Abbreviation	Amount
lb.	pound
oz.	ounce
pkg.	package
TB.	tablespoon
tsp.	teaspoon

Measurement Equivalents

Knowing equivalent measurements can help you size up a recipe or substitute another measure for a dirty or missing one. Following are some common substitutions you might find handy.

This ...	Equals This ...
½ tablespoon	1½ teaspoons
1 tablespoon	3 teaspoons
4 tablespoons	¼ cup
5 tablespoons + 1 teaspoon	⅓ cup
16 tablespoons	1 cup
2 tablespoons	1 fluid ounce
1 cup	8 fluid ounces
2 cups	1 pint
2 pints	1 quart
4 quarts	1 gallon

Safety Matters

When my daughter was a toddler, practically every day I chanted, "The stairs are no place to play." I'm going to have to stress the same warning for the kitchen. Becoming lackadaisical in the kitchen is so easy to do. But it's very important that you be aware of what you're doing. It's essential for your health and well-being.

Keep It Clean

Cleanliness, in addition to being next to godliness, is the best way to avoid the hospital or your school's health center. Cross-contamination of microscopic bacteria is a real threat, even if unseen. Make the following tips your habits:

- Always wash your hands in warm, soapy water before you begin to cook.

- Always wash your hands in warm, soapy water after handling raw meats, poultry, and fish—before you touch anything else.

- Wash all kitchen surfaces, appliances, utensils, and dishes with hot, soapy water after each use, especially any that touched raw meats, poultry, and fish.

- Wash kitchen towels, dishcloths, and sponges often. Run sponges through the dishwasher or microwave them for a minute one or more times a week, but still replace them often.

- If spills occur, wipe them up immediately to prevent bacterial growth.

Careful Food Handling

How you manage your food purchases directly correlates with your probability of staying healthy. Every time you come in contact with food, remember the following procedures:

- Shop in a supermarket that has good product turnover, making sure refrigerated foods feel cold, frozen foods are solid, and canned items are dent-free.

- Check the best-by, sell-by, and use-by dates on all foods before buying.

- Go directly home from the supermarket, storing perishable foods in the refrigerator or freezer immediately. Carry a cooler in your car trunk to keep foods cold during hot weather or long drives.

◆ Keep the refrigerator below 40°F, using a thermometer to check if necessary.

◆ Thaw, as well as marinate, foods in the refrigerator, not at room temperature.

◆ Don't return cooked foods to the same plate or cutting board that held the foods while raw.

◆ Cool hot foods before refrigerating. Divide large amounts in small containers to cool more quickly.

◆ Discard any perishable foods held at room temperature for longer than 2 hours (1 hour if outside at 90°F or hotter).

Sharp Knife Tips

Every home in America is filled with dangerous weapons. This fact is easy to forget, as kitchen knives are such useful, frequently used tools. The hazards are indisputable though. Ask around, and you'll find nearly everyone has a knife-related story to tell. I don't want you to have a tragic kitchen knife story to tell—or worse yet, not to tell. Keep the following knife safety tips in mind:

◆ Buy the best-quality knives your budget allows.

◆ Don't store a knife in the same space with other utensils you'll be reaching for (including in the sudsy sink for washing).

◆ Firmly hold foods to be cut by your fingertips, and be sure to curl them away from the knife.

◆ Scrape foods from a cutting board with the back side of the knife to preserve the blade's sharpness.

◆ Keep your knives sharp. Dull knives are far more dangerous. Invest in a sharpening steel, and follow the package directions to keep your knives at top performance.

◆ Carry a knife pointing down with the blade facing away from you.

◆ Lay down a knife when not in use. Don't answer the phone, go to the door, or let the dog out while still carrying the knife.

Recommended Cooking Temperatures

Foods must be cooked thoroughly to destroy all harmful bacteria that may be present. Use a food thermometer to verify a food's doneness. The tip of the thermometer should be inserted into the center of the thickest part of the food. Here's a quick cheat sheet to be sure your food is done.

Food	Temperature
Poultry	
Whole chicken or turkey	180°F
Thighs, wings, or legs	180°F
Breasts or roasts	170°F
Ground chicken or turkey	165°F
Meat	
Ground beef, pork, or veal	160°F
Beef	
Medium rare	145°F
Medium	160°F
Well done	170°F
Pork	
Medium	160°F
Well done	170°F
Ham	
Fresh	160°F
Precooked	140°F
Stuffing	165°F
Egg dishes	160°F
Leftovers	165°F

Ingredient Substitutions

Keeping a well-stocked pantry and making careful grocery lists should put all the ingredients you need at the ready. Still, after reading through a recipe and gathering the called-for items, you might discover that your roommate helped herself to your yogurt for breakfast. Or you might be looking for a new, interesting recipe to try when you find one that you have all the ingredients for except hot pepper sauce. Utilizing some substitutions can save the dish—and a trip to the market. The following table gives you several common substitutions that can get you out of a pinch.

When You Need ...	Try Substituting ...
Baking powder (1 tsp.)	¼ tsp. baking soda + ½ tsp. cream of tartar
Breadcrumbs	Equal amount matzo meal or cracker crumbs
Broth (1 cup)	1 bouillon cube dissolved in 1 cup water
Brown sugar (1 cup)	1 cup granulated sugar + 2 TB. molasses
Cayenne (⅛ tsp.)	3 to 4 drops hot pepper sauce
Cod	Halibut, ocean perch, or trout
Dry mustard (1 tsp.)	1 TB. prepared yellow mustard
Egg (1 whole)	2 egg whites
Fat-free milk (1 cup)	Nonfat powdered milk, prepared
Granulated sugar (1 cup)	Brown sugar (1 cup)
Hot pepper sauce (1 tsp.)	¾ tsp. cayenne + 1 tsp. vinegar
Instant tapioca (1 TB.)	1 TB. flour
Lemon juice	Equal amount lime juice
Lemon peel (1 tsp. grated)	½ tsp. lemon extract
Ricotta cheese	Equal amount cottage cheese
Sour cream	Equal amount plain yogurt
Soy sauce	Equal parts Worcestershire sauce and water
Tomato juice (1 cup)	½ cup tomato sauce + ½ cup water
Tomato sauce	Half tomato paste + half water
Vinegar	Equal amount lemon juice

With the proper equipment, high-quality ingredients (or at least a good substitute), and kitchen know-how, nothing's stopping you. Let's get cooking!

The Least You Need to Know

◆ Liquid ingredients are measured in liquid measuring cups, while dry ingredients are measured in dry measuring cups.

◆ Small amounts of any ingredient can be measured with measuring spoons.

◆ Baking success depends on precise measurement.

◆ Kitchen safety—for the cook, for the food, for the equipment—is essential.

◆ When you're caught without an ingredient, the recipe may succeed with an appropriate substitution.

Chapter 2

Required Reading

In This Chapter

- ◆ A close look at a recipe
- ◆ Deciphering a food label
- ◆ Understanding nutrition

A little reading can provide a lot of knowledge. Studying the nutrition facts panel on the foods you buy and watching the nutrition analyses that accompany these recipes will make you an educated eater. After that, reading the recipe and knowing what the directions are telling you to do will keep you eating well.

Reading a Recipe

Each time you consider preparing a recipe, it's imperative that you read through the entire recipe before measuring any ingredients or turning on a burner. You don't want to be in the middle of making a recipe only to find you're missing a vital ingredient or don't have the right pan. You can probably scan through a familiar recipe just to be certain you haven't forgotten something, but it's best to read through a new recipe twice.

What's What in a Recipe

When you look at a recipe, the first information you'll notice is the recipe's title. This should give you some indication of what type of recipe it is, what some of the ingredients are, maybe a hint of the taste, and perhaps the ease of preparation.

In this cookbook, you'll also see a symbol representing the recipe's preparation method(s)—microwave, slow cooker, stovetop, etc. For a complete listing of the methods and symbols, turn to the introduction.

Next, you'll see dollar signs. Each recipe in the book is rated on a one (*$*) to four (*$$$$*) scale. One dollar sign means the ingredients should be inexpensive, especially in conjunction with the number of servings you'll get. You might want to reserve four-dollar-sign recipes for special occasions if you're shopping on a tight budget.

Of Higher Learning

> Some produce is more affordable in season. Take advantage of these foods, such as tomatoes and green bell peppers, when they're plentiful. Not only will the dishes be more delicious with in-season produce, they'll also be much more budget-friendly. And don't forget, everything's on sale sometime.

Under the recipe title, you'll find text that offers extra information about the dish. When I was the editor of a cooking magazine, we called it "romance copy." This information isn't crucial to the recipe, but it's nice to have. Look here for comments on serving ideas, food textures, ease of preparation, and more.

A recipe's ingredient list lets you know what items you need and in what quantities. Some ingredients will need to be prepared before you start the recipe. When you see "¼ cup sliced mushrooms," you can measure out the sliced mushrooms you brought home from the supermarket. If you have whole mushrooms in the crisper, you'll need to trim and slice them for the recipe. Watch for directives that follow an ingredient entry, too. When you see "1 (15-oz.) can black beans, rinsed and drained," you'll want to rinse and drain the beans before you begin the recipe.

Learning Curve

Don't forget to watch for these sidebar boxes alongside the recipes because they provide useful information.

Following the ingredient list are step-by-step directions, instructing you on how to prepare the called-for ingredients into an edible dish. Make certain you understand what you're directed to do. If you need to better understand a cooking term, take the time to look it up (see Appendix A).

Other recipe information you'll want to check out is the recipe's yield and the serving size. These numbers are provided alongside the prep time and cook time. You may also see chill time, freeze time, set time—whatever the recipe needs to be completed.

Several recipes also include a variation. If you see a cooking appliance symbol there, the variation tells you how to prepare the recipe using a different method. Other variations may offer ingredient substitutions or alternative serving suggestions.

Let's Get Cooking!

When you're ready to make a recipe—after you've read it all—the next step is to gather everything you'll need. Set out the ingredients, the appropriate measuring cups and spoons, necessary containers or cookware, and called-for cooking appliances as needed. Get your ingredients ready as indicated in the ingredient list (chopped, rinsed, etc.). Now you're ready to start cooking.

Lecture Hall _____

Of course, cooking takes longer if you're simultaneously talking on the phone, unloading the dishwasher, and cleaning out the refrigerator. When you're starting out in the kitchen, limit other distractions so you can focus on the food and the cooking.

As you work your way through the recipe's directions, you'll be working in the prep time and the cook time given. I've tried to be a bit generous with the prep time, as much of this may be new to you. Rest assured, though, that if cooking isn't a familiar task, the more you do it, the more natural it becomes. You'll soon find yourself working more quickly and smoothly.

Understanding a Food Label

When you pick up a packaged food, you'll probably see a very appetizing photo sprinkled with health claims (some regulated by the Food and Drug Administration, others not—at least not yet). To get down to the nitty-gritty, turn the package to the nutrition facts panel. This is where you'll learn just what the food is made of.

Learning Curve

When you're comparing two foods, ensure that a quick comparison is fair. If the serving sizes differ, you'll need to find a common denominator. A 1-cup serving size with 5 grams fat is lower in fat than a 6-ounce serving size with 4 grams fat.

Serving size is the base information you need to know to size up any food. All the information that follows is built on this amount. So if you'll typically treat yourself to two servings, double everything—good (calcium), bad (sodium), and ugly (trans fat).

Calories indicate the energy provided by the food. Each gram of protein and carbohydrate supplies 4 calories, while each fat gram equals 9 calories. How many calories you need each day depends on your gender, age, height, and activity level. You'll need to cut back 3,500 calories to lose 1 pound.

Calories from fat breaks down the number of total calories supplied from the food's fat content.

Total fat gives the number in grams. Fat is then subdivided into saturated fat, trans fat, polyunsaturated fat, and/or monounsaturated fat. Try to limit the saturated and trans fats you consume. Your body needs some fat to function properly, so for optimal health, try to get it in unsaturated forms.

Cholesterol is produced in your body and found in animal products. The current recommendation for healthy adults is to consume no more than 300 milligrams a day.

Sodium is necessary for fluid balance in the body, but Americans consume well in excess of need. Current dietary guidelines recommend only 1,500 milligrams for African Americans and middle-aged and older Americans. Other healthy adults should limit their daily intake to 2,300 milligrams.

Carbohydrate will be listed in grams and broken down into dietary fiber and sugars. Most Americans don't get the recommended 25 grams fiber, which is more prevalent in foods such as whole grains, beans, vegetables, and fruits.

Protein is the building block of your muscles and a fundamental component of each and every cell in your body. The dietary recommendation ranges from 44 to 63 grams per day, depending on body weight.

Vitamins and minerals are listed near the bottom of the nutrition facts panel only in percentages. Percent Daily Values are typically based on a 2,000-calorie diet. These numbers may or may not be applicable to you. Generally, the higher the percentages for vitamin A, vitamin C, calcium, iron, and any additional nutrients listed, the better.

Navigating the Nutrition Analysis

A nutrition analysis is provided for each recipe in this cookbook. With a quick glance, you can see what a serving of any recipe contains. The serving size and the total number of servings the recipe makes are given; if the number of servings is only one, the serving size is omitted, as the entire recipe is the serving.

When a recipe offers an alternative ingredient, it's not considered in the nutrition analysis. The ingredient listed first is used in the calculation. Likewise, any suggested serving accompaniments aren't taken into account, as you may or may not choose to follow these suggestions.

The analyses provided in this cookbook offer the following information:

Calories   The number of calories you should consume in a day is based on your gender, age, height, and physical activity level. You'll also want to consider your weight goal, either losing, gaining, or maintaining. Consult your doctor or nutritionist if you're beginning a weight-loss program. Visit www.mypyramid.gov to create a personal food pyramid.

Calories from fat   Fat provides the most calories per gram at 9. Protein and carbohydrate contain 4 calories per gram.

Total fat   Your total fat shouldn't exceed 65 grams per day if you eat a 2,000-calorie diet. Monounsaturated and polyunsaturated fats should be favored.

Saturated fat   Only 10 percent or less of your daily calories should come from saturated fat. For a 2,000-calorie diet, that calculates to 22 grams.

Protein   The daily recommendation ranges from 44 to 63 grams, depending on body weight.

Carbohydrates   The 2,000-calorie diet recommendation is 300 grams a day.

Please use these nutrition analyses as guidelines. Differences in your exact ingredients and preparation methods may result in altered nutrient amounts. A food's nutritional values can vary by season, grower, and location. Thereby, the provided figures cannot be considered exact. Still, you can trust that the numbers are close and use them for tracking your intake.

Of Higher Learning

Cooking, like any other activity, has its own lingo. The good news is many terms are of the common vernacular. The better news is that you can easily look up any unfamiliar cooking-related terms in this book's glossary (see Appendix A).

You're now a well-versed scholar of food. You can choose your ingredients, you can decipher what nutrients you're eating, and you can prepare your recipes. Celebrate this matriculation with a delicious, healthful meal!

The Least You Need to Know

◆ Always read through a recipe—maybe twice—before you start cooking.

◆ Check the nutrition facts panel on all foods so you're an informed eater.

◆ A recipe's nutrition analysis provides information you can use to make smart food choices.

Chapter 3

Setting Up Your Kitchen Quarters

In This Chapter

◆ Kitchen appliance extravaganza

◆ Cooking tools, cookware, and containers: stocking up

◆ Avoiding bare cupboards

You might be looking at a full kitchen with plenty of storage space or puzzled by where you can fit your microwave without insisting that your roommate's lava lamp must go. In either case, you're going to have to eat. Setting up a kitchen you can work in may be a challenge, but in this chapter, I offer some solutions that should help.

Gearing Up

Cooking appliances can make cooking easier, and you have a range of cooking options available, from microwaves to slow cookers to hot plates. Whether you want to cook food quickly or start slow cooking while you're out all day, you'll find a cooking method to match your needs. And to go with those cooking appliances, in this section I also cover some other kitchen equipment you'll probably want to get your hands on.

Microwaves

If you have just one cooking appliance, it's likely a microwave. While many home cooks still use a microwave oven as a time-saving defroster, reheater, and popcorn popper, rest assured that microwaving is an excellent moist-cooking method. Cooking in the microwave is also convenient if you're watching your weight, as many microwave recipes eliminate the fat that would be used in more traditional stovetop and oven recipes.

Microwaves are available in varying wattages, which will affect cooking times (the lower the watts, the slower the cooking). The recipes in this cookbook were tested in a 1,000-watt oven, and the cooking times represented at the beginning of all cooking time ranges. If you have a lower wattage appliance, such as a 700-watt microwave oven (check your owner's manual), look to the end of the time range. You'll learn how your microwave works the more you cook in it.

Turntables make microwave cooking more hands-off. Microwaves can become concentrated, causing hot spots in your appliance. To ensure even cooking, foods should be stirred and rotated. If your microwave isn't equipped with a turntable, remember to rotate the dish manually once or twice during most cooking times. You can purchase turntablelike gadgets if your microwave didn't come with one.

Microwave-safe cookware is required for microwave cooking; check the bottom of your dishes and containers to see if they're marked as such. You can test any dishes you're uncertain of by placing the dish in the microwave along with a microwave-safe glass half-filled with water inside or touching the dish. Cook on high power for 1 minute. While the water should be warm, the dish shouldn't be. If the dish is warm, it's not microwave-safe.

The recipes included in this book call for microwave-safe glass or Pyrex dishes. Many times, you'll need to watch what's happening in the microwave, and the clear cookware lets you see when the water's boiling or when the batter's rising.

> **Lecture Hall**
>
> Even though the microwaves heat the food and not the containers, the food will transfer heat, making the containers hot. Be sure to use oven mitts and potholders for microwave cooking.

Slow Cookers

Slow cookers are great appliances for convenience cooking. You can assemble the ingredients in your slow cooker in the morning, set it to cook while you're at class or work, and come home to a prepared meal.

Learning Curve

While you know never to leave a kitchen appliance on unattended, the slow cooker is the exception that proves the rule. Still, precaution is always recommended in the kitchen: pull the slow cooker away from the wall, clear a space around the appliance, and be certain the cord and plug are undamaged. Follow all your appliance manufacturer's instructions, and you can safely leave your slow cooker on overnight or while you're gone.

Slow cookers are available in a number of sizes ranging from 1 quart to 6½ quarts. The recipes in this book call for a 3½- to 4-quart slow cooker, as these are standard sizes for preparing main dishes.

Once you have assembled the recipe in your slow cooker, covered it, and turned on the called-for heat level, it's imperative that you do … nothing. Don't lift the lid—not to stir, not to check the recipe's progress, not just to peek. The lifting of the lid causes significant heat loss in an appliance that takes time to regain that heat, and the cooking time will have to be increased. A recipe may instruct you to remove the cover near the end of cooking time to add pasta or herbs that can't be incorporated at the start, and that's fine. These recipes are taking the slow cooker's capabilities into consideration and should be followed as directed.

Electric Skillets

These deep-sided square cook surfaces set on legs allow stovetop-type cooking when you don't have access to a stove. Home cooks value electric skillets for their larger size with greater volume and high-domed lids. A prong that connects the skillet to an electrical outlet has a temperature dial that allows you to choose your cooking heat. The recipes in this book call for a moderate 11-inch nonstick electric skillet with temperatures from simmer to 425°F.

If you have access to a stove, you can translate the recipes for stovetop preparation. Use a skillet with enough volume to hold the ingredients comfortably. Use the simmer-to-425°F suggested dial settings to determine the typical low-to-high stovetop dial setting, using the cooking directives, such as bring to a boil, as your best guide.

Of Higher Learning

If you have a larger electric skillet, you might have to try harder to hold smaller amounts of ingredients in a more confined area. More fluid ingredients will spread thinner across the surface, and you might have to decrease the temperature, using the cooking directives, such as simmer, as your guide.

Electric Woks

The wok, that clever piece of Chinese cookware, has gently sloping sides down to a rounded or flat bottom—perfect for tossing foods quickly and keeping them in the pan. Electric woks can be used free of the stovetop, requiring only an electrical outlet.

The recipes in this book call for a typical 6-quart nonstick electric wok with the heat set from low to high. You can use a stovetop wok for these recipes if you prefer. Electric cooktops need flat-bottomed woks while rounded-bottom woks equipped with a metal ring for stability are intended for gas stoves.

Indoor Electric Grills

If you want the high-heat-produced crusty surface that results from grilling but don't have access to a charcoal or gas grill, an electric indoor grill that sits on the counter-top is an option. The recipes in this cookbook use a nonstick dual-contact-type indoor electric grill, the most recognizable brand being the George Foreman Grill. Dual-contact grills, with their hinged, corrugated plates, hold the food while cooking on both sides at once. For easy cleanup, be sure to set the drippings-catching dish under the gently sloping appliance whenever you cook fat-rendering foods.

Lecture Hall

Residence halls and student apartments might have regulations on what types of cooking appliances may and may not be used. Safety concerns are the primary focus, so always follow such rules.

Hot Plates

Hot plates are portable electric or gas burners. They allow you to use standard pots and pans as you would for stovetop cooking when you don't have a large stove. You can choose a compact single burner or a double-burner version, or even a 4- or 6-burner gas model, for preparing multiple dishes.

Blenders

Standing blenders are handy for mixing drinks, puréeing soups, whipping up dips, and liquefying sauces. The recipes in this cookbook can be executed with the most basic of blenders. You may prefer a blender with a glass jar, as plastics take on odors from the blended foods.

Your blender jar should have a tight-fitting lid with a removable cap, which allows you to continue blending while adding ingredients. You'll also want low- and high-speed options. Blenders are available with any number of selections, such as purée, blend, chop, etc. You likely don't need 40 features; just choose a blender that can accomplish everything you need it to do.

Stovetop and Oven

Depending on your living arrangements, you may or may not have access to a stove. If you do, you likely are using a traditional gas or electric stove with front and back burners on the stovetop above a thermal oven.

Most likely, you aren't the owner. If you aren't familiar with the appliance, you might want to use an oven thermometer that hangs from the rack inside. You'd be surprised how many ovens don't hold the temperature set on the dial. In my experience, the oven probably runs hot if it's not correlating with the temperature dial, which can result in overcooked foods.

When you're using the stovetop, remember to keep all flammables away from the burners—oven mitts, potholders, dishcloths, this cookbook. (My mom's 1968 Betty Crocker cookbook still sports the scorch mark from the time I turned on the wrong burner.) Also, get into the habit of turning pot handles in to avoid accidents and burns.

Learning Curve

Because ovens may have hot spots and bakeware may block heat, especially when using two racks, you should rotate your foods. Switch the pans on the top and bottom racks if using both, and turn the pans 180 degrees, moving the food at the back of the oven to the front.

Basic Utensils

When you begin to stock your kitchen, no matter how large or small, you'll need some basic tools. Consider some of the following utensils based on your cooking habits.

Box grater This four-sided tool allows you to shred or grate foods, such as cheese or carrots, using surfaces of variously sized rasps.

Can opener Manual or electric, until all cans offer ring-pull lids, you'll need a can opener.

Colander This free-standing bowl perforated with small holes is used to drain foods, such as pasta and vegetables.

Corkscrew You'll need one of these pig-tailed devices if you cook with wine to pull the cork from the bottle.

Food processor You might want a motorized method of chopping, slicing, shredding, grating, julienning, mixing, blending, and puréeing.

Lecture Hall _____

As mentioned in Chapter 1, knife safety is a must. Know how to handle and work with knives. Your fingers—or someone else's—will thank you.

Knife You'll want to consider having at least a paring knife and a chef's knife.

Meat mallet Boneless cuts of meat and poultry cook more evenly and quickly when pounded with the smooth side of this tool. The spiked side is used to tenderize meats.

Mixing bowls To prepare a basic baking recipe, you'll need a medium and a large bowl for combining ingredients.

Rubber spatula When you need to scrape a bowl clean, reach for this flexible tool (perhaps made of silicone).

Spatula The flat, wide area of this tool is useful for turning pancakes, grilled cheese sandwiches, and hamburgers. If you're working with nonstick surfaces, opt for a plastic or silicone spatula.

Spoon Create your own assortment of plastic, metal, and wooden spoons, which may be solid or slotted.

Thermometer An instant-read thermometer will tell you when it's safe to eat meats and other foods.

Cookware

When you're short on storage space, you want to get the most versatile cookware to meet all your needs. My favorite set of dishes that go from oven or microwave to refrigerator or freezer to dishwasher are made of Pyrex. The set includes a 3-cup bowl, 6-cup (1½-quart) bowl, 8×8×2-inch (2-quart) dish, and 13×9×2-inch (3-quart) dish, each with a dishwasher-safe plastic lid.

Should you do a lot of stovetop cooking, you'll want a saucepan, a skillet, and a sauté pan with a lid. If you bake cookies, you'll need cookie sheets and wire racks for cooling. If you're a frozen pizza lover, you might want a pizza pan or a large baking sheet.

Know what type of cooking you do before you go buying cookware. If you haven't done much cooking before, you may not know yet what to buy or what you'll use. Ask cooks you know what their favorite cookware is. Do they most often use their cast-iron skillet? Could they not live without their broiler pan? (Look in the drawer under the oven; you just might find the one that came with the oven.) Do they never use the 9-quart Dutch oven they received as a wedding gift?

Try to borrow some of the cookware you think you'll need before committing to any. When you find yourself at the sink washing a borrowed pie plate every night, get your own. If the person you borrowed it from asks for the double boiler back so she can melt chocolate and you pull everything out of the cabinet to get to it, maybe you can just borrow it again if you need it.

Storage Containers

With cooking comes leftovers. You'll need some way to keep them fresh, so you'll need at least a small collection of storage containers. A number of inexpensive plastic storage containers are available. Stacking containers with interlocking lids are good when storage space is limited. Sets featuring various volumes and shapes provide you with the best size for every situation; you may need more space available to store such a collection.

Microwaving in plastic is not recommended, so you might want storage containers that can go from the fridge to the microwave. Look for small glass or Pyrex containers with plastic lids. You'll find them in various sizes and may want a variety. If you'll want to use them for freezing or wash them in the dishwasher, choose those that are labeled for these uses.

Learning Curve _____

When choosing storage containers that will also be used for microwave cooking or reheating, look for round dishes. Microwaves tend to concentrate in corners, leading to overcooking. If you need a square or rectangular dish, choose one with rounded corners to help with this problem.

If you don't require storage containers very often, a box of plastic bags is space-efficient. Buy special freezer-grade bags if you'll be putting the food in the freezer.

Keeping the Cupboards and Fridge Full

The food items you keep stocked in your kitchen quarters will likely be a compromise between necessity and cost. Some of the supermarket's choices may be suited to your needs, be it little refrigeration space, limited preparation area, or special health needs.

Canned Foods

The original convenience foods, canned items keep especially well. Check for a stamped best-by or use-by date on the packaging. Don't buy cans that are dented, and immediately discard cans that are bulging.

Some canned foods are high in sodium, as salt is often used in the processing. Many more canned items are available in no-salt-added versions lately. These foods contain the sodium that's found naturally in the foods, but no salt was used to process the foods. See the nutrition facts panel for sodium content.

Convenience Boxes

Any number of boxed convenience foods are available at your local supermarket—rice mixes, slow-cooker meals, heat-and-serve mac and cheese. These convenience foods often have a few drawbacks: high calories, fat, and sodium content and higher price tags than homemade versions.

Convenience foods also have some pluses. You can find more health-focused versions if you look—whole-grain rice mixes, reduced-fat varieties, low-sodium offerings. They often contain everything you need to prepare the dish. They keep well. They can be just more—well—convenient than gathering a number of ingredients, especially if you have a particularly space-limited kitchen.

Dried Pastas and Grains

Dried pastas have a long shelf life, are inexpensive, and are easy to cook. Plus, pastas are available in a wide array of shapes to keep you interested and well fed.

Some grains also have a long shelf life. Check the package for best-by or use-by dates. Whole grains can't be stored as long, as they can become rancid. Still, they'll keep for months, and they provide great nutritional benefits.

Keep your favorite pastas and grains on-hand. These ingredients can always be the base for a great, satisfying dish.

Learning Curve

If you buy a quantity of a whole grain you won't use in a short time, you can prolong its shelf life by storing it in an airtight container in the refrigerator for up to 6 months.

Dried Herbs and Spices

The baking aisle in your local supermarket is well stocked with dried herbs and spices. Often, you'll find them in small quantities. Sometimes, they'll even be offered in bulk. These are the most often called-for spices in this cookbook:

Of Higher Learning

For more information on choosing, storing, and using herbs and spices turn to Chapter 6.

- Garlic powder

- Pepper

- Salt

Other herbs and spices used in at least five recipes are:

- Basil

- Cinnamon, ground

- Crushed red pepper flakes

- Ginger, ground

- Onion powder

- Oregano

- Parsley flakes

- Vanilla extract

Here are some other herbs and spices to consider for your spice rack:

◆ Cayenne

◆ Chili powder

◆ Chives

◆ Cilantro

◆ Cloves, ground

◆ Cumin, ground

◆ Curry powder

◆ Dill weed

◆ Dry mustard

◆ Italian seasoning

◆ Nutmeg, ground

◆ Paprika

◆ Sesame seeds, toasted

◆ Thyme

Nonperishable Meats

If you haven't already, make a point to find the supermarket aisle with the packaged meats. There you'll discover a great variety of heat-and-eat and ready-to-serve meats beyond tuna fish and Spam. The seasoned tuna fillets, salmon fillets, and chicken breasts may cost more than your budget can afford, but watch for sales on these items. These single-serving-size, pantry-shelf items can be the cornerstone of a quick-fix meal for a student on the go.

When you look, you'll also find shrimp, clams, beef, chili, and more. If your kitchen quarters and shopping ability can't sustain much fresh meat, chicken, and fish, nonperishable meats may stretch your food choices.

Precooked Meats

Many supermarkets have a deli section and a nearby refrigerated case with precooked meat offerings. If you don't have access to an oven but have a hankering for roasted chicken, you can pick up a hot bird on your way home. The refrigerated case could offer precooked ham in slices, cubes, and diced. Take the time to find out just what can be had where you shop.

Precut Veggies and Fruits

If you're not one for preparing fruits and vegetables for snacking, take up the supermarket on their offer to do it for you. Precut veggies and fruits are also convenient for buying single servings. A cantaloupe may go to waste before you can eat it all, but a small plastic container of cantaloupe chunks requires no prep work and no waste. Look in the produce department for a section with small portions for sale in clear plastic containers marked by store labels.

The supermarket may also have a salad bar offering. You can then choose exactly what you want, be it a handful of sliced mushrooms or a bowlful of lettuce leaves.

If you'll use larger amounts of prepared fruits and vegetables, many manufacturers have discovered the boon of selling ready-made ingredients. You'll find packages of shredded carrots, celery sticks, coleslaw mix, green beans, sliced mushrooms, sliced apples, and much, much more.

Learning Curve

Prepared items might cost a bit more than do-it-yourself foods. Still, ready-to-use foods can be cost-effective if they save you time and get you cooking.

Ingredients Called for in This Book

You might need further information on some of the ingredients called for in the recipes included in this book. Here's a quick breakdown:

Drained minced garlic   You'll see this entry in several recipes. Find this minced garlic packed in water in jars; check your produce department. I like drained minced garlic for the time it saves. Just drain the water off the called-for amount. If you

Of Higher Learning

One small clove of garlic yields about ½ teaspoon minced garlic.

prefer to cook with fresh garlic, no problem. Mince fresh garlic to the given measurement in a recipe.

Fat-free, less-sodium chicken broth   More healthful with a generally accepted taste, several recipes call for a can or a portion of this broth. You can always substitute vegetable broth, if you prefer. Many of the recipes will be suitable for a vegetarian diet when this substitution is made.

Ground round   For recipes that include ground beef, I've called for ground round as the more healthful choice. Ground round is priced higher per pound than ground chuck or ground beef, yet ground round is 90 percent lean to 10 percent fat. If you're more concerned with your grocery budget, you can substitute other ground beef, be it 70/30, 80/20, or 85/15, if you prefer. Should you want to prepare the recipes with even less fat, substitute a leaner ground beef or ground turkey breast.

Light butter with canola oil   I like to use this type of butter because it has 60 percent less cholesterol and 50 percent less fat than regular butter. A 1 tablespoon serving has just 5 grams fat—rather than the 11 grams found in butter—which cuts the number of calories in half, from 100 to 50. Total cholesterol milligrams are also more healthful at 5 milligrams per serving of light butter with canola oil versus 30 milligrams in butter.

When you bake, for successful recipes, you'll need to use a butter or margarine with at least 60 percent fat. I've adapted the necessary recipes in this cookbook to work with the light butter with canola oil. As always, you can substitute the butter or margarine of your choice.

The Least You Need to Know

- Many cooking appliances are available to help you prepare any number of recipes, even if you don't have access to a stove.

- Even bare-minimum kitchen quarters need basic cookware, tools, and storage solutions.

- The supermarket is packed with foods that'll meet your dietary needs.

Part 2

Morning, Noon, or Night

A college schedule doesn't follow a typical 9-to-5 day that might have been the norm at your parents' house (or at least one you've seen on TV). Early morning classes, mandatory practices, and all-night study sessions can make routine next to impossible.

The great news about breakfast foods, sandwiches, soups, and salads is that, no matter the time of day, your stomach always welcomes the familiar flavors and textures. Plus, many of the recipes included in Part 2 are low cost, keeping your stomach full while doing the same for your wallet.

"I brought a hummus and roasted pepper wrap into an exam. What did you do?"

Chapter 4

Good Morning Meals

In This Chapter

- ◆ Selecting good eggs
- ◆ Proper care of eggs and egg products
- ◆ Great egg-y recipes to jump-start your day

As a student, your responsibility is to get your brain ready to learn. The good news is this may be one of the easiest and most enjoyable responsibilities you'll ever have. Are you ready? Get this: you need to eat.

You need to eat a healthful breakfast, yes, but it can be delicious, quick, and budget-friendly, too. If you choose eggs for breakfast—or any other time—you need to use the best-quality, safest eggs so you're not sidelined by a food-borne illness.

Egg-cellent Education

Buy eggs from a refrigerated case. Open the carton before loading it into your shopping cart. The eggshells should appear clean and uncracked. You might also want to wiggle each egg lightly; if the shells are cracked on the undersides, often the egg will leak into its cup and be "glued" down. Finally,

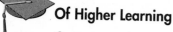

Of Higher Learning

Contrary to what many think, brown-shelled eggs are not more nutritious than white-shelled eggs. The color of the eggshell is just an indicator of the breed of the hen.

before taking the carton home, check its sell-by date to be sure the eggs are as fresh as possible. Do the same if you're buying a refrigerated egg product.

Store eggs in their carton in a cold place in the refrigerator—not in the door—as soon as you're home. Don't for any reason turn the eggs over; they're packed large side up to retain freshness. Eggs should keep for up to 5 weeks past the stamped sell-by date.

If the eggs need to be held longer, you can freeze them. Don't freeze them in their shells, though. Lightly beat the yolks and whites together and freeze in a small, hard-sided, freezer-safe container. You can separate the yolks from the whites and freeze just the whites, if you like. Frozen eggs will keep for nearly a year. Move the frozen eggs to the refrigerator the night before you want to use them. If a recipe calls for eggs at room temperature, set the thawed eggs on the counter for up to 30 minutes before using.

Lecture Hall

Never cook an egg in its shell in your microwave. When it explodes, the best possible outcome will be an incredible, inedible mess. You could also damage your microwave and possibly injure yourself or others.

Hard-cooking may also save eggs from being wasted. Hard-cooked eggs will keep for up to 1 week in the refrigerator. (See the variation paragraph on Chapter 5's Shortcut Egg Salad Sandwich recipe for hard-cooking instructions.)

If you're uncertain about the freshness of your eggs, you can easily test the eggs you wish to use. Fill a deep bowl with tap water and gently add the eggs. Eggs that sink are safe; those that float are foul and must be discarded. (Only test eggs you're ready to use, as eggs shouldn't be washed of their protective coating.)

Cooked eggs should have firm whites and yolks. Egg dishes should reach 160°F on a food thermometer. If your eggs will be runny or the recipe calls for eggs that will not be cooked or only partially cooked, you must use pasteurized eggs; the carton will be marked as pasteurized (and priced higher). Refrigerated egg product is labeled as fat-free and pasteurized.

Eating raw or undercooked regular eggs puts you at risk for salmonella, a food-borne illness. Especially vulnerable are people with chronic illnesses, senior citizens, young children, and pregnant women; these individuals and those cooking for them should be particularly vigilant in safe handling and food preparation.

Grab-n-Go Burrito 𝄢

To make this breakfast burrito a take-along sandwich, wrap it in foil just as you folded the tortilla, rolling the foil down as you eat.

2 large eggs

2 tsp. 50-percent-less-fat bacon pieces

1 soft-taco-size whole-wheat tortilla

2 TB. 2-percent-milk shredded cheddar and Monterey Jack cheese

2 TB. chunky-style salsa

1 TB. fat-free sour cream

Yield: 1 serving
Prep time: 5 minutes
Cook time: 3 to 6 minutes
Each serving has:
332 calories
162 calories from fat
18 g fat
5 g saturated fat
21 g protein
19 g carbohydrates

1. Spray a 12-ounce microwave-safe round glass dish with at least 2-inch sides with nonstick cooking spray. Crack eggs into the dish. Beat with a fork until mixed and lemon-colored. Add bacon pieces and stir. Cook on medium power (50 percent) for 1 or 2 minutes. Remove from the microwave and stir with a fork, breaking up egg. Cook on medium power (50 percent) for 1 or 2 minutes more. Stir again. Cook on medium power (50 percent) for ½ to 1½ minutes or just until egg is set but not dry. Stir.

2. Place tortilla on a large microwave-safe plate. Sprinkle cheese down the center of tortilla. Cook on high power for 20 to 60 seconds or until tortilla is warm and cheese begins to melt.

3. To assemble, scoop eggs down the center of tortilla over cheese. Spoon salsa and sour cream over top. Roll up, folding 1 side over filling, bringing the bottom up, and folding the other side over.

Learning Curve

To save on fat, calories, and cholesterol (not to mention fridge space), substitute a pasteurized refrigerated egg product such as Egg Beaters for the 2 eggs. Follow the microwave cooking instructions on the package, stirring in bacon when cooked.

Chocolate-Chip Pancakes $

Tender and light, sweet and addictive, these quick-mix pancakes don't even need syrup.

Yield: 1 serving
Prep time: 2 minutes
Cook time: 8 minutes
Each serving has:
493 calories
151 calories from fat
17 g fat
8.5 g saturated fat
12 g protein
77.5 g carbohydrates

½ cup reduced-fat baking mix (such as Bisquick Heart Smart baking mix)

¼ cup semi-sweet chocolate chips

2 TB. fat-free sour cream

1 TB. pasteurized refrigerated egg product, such as Egg Beaters

⅓ cup fat-free milk

1. Heat an 11-inch electric skillet to 350°F. Spray with nonstick cooking spray.

2. In a medium bowl, combine baking mix and chocolate chips, and stir until chocolate chips are coated.

3. Make a *well* in the center of dry ingredients. Add sour cream, egg product, and milk. Stir until dry ingredients are moistened.

4. Pour ¼ cup batter into the skillet for each pancake, cooking in batches. Cook for 2 minutes, or until the tops of pancakes are bubbly and the undersides are browned. Turn with a plastic spatula and cook on the other sides for 2 minutes or until the undersides are browned. Serve immediately.

Class Notes

When a recipe directs you to make a **well** in the dry ingredients, push the ingredients in the bowl to the side, making a depression in the center where you'll add the wet ingredients.

Classic French Toast 𝄢

French toast can be served with maple syrup, flavored syrups, fruit toppings, butter or margarine, confectioners' sugar, whipped cream, chopped nuts—the options are endless!

1 large egg

⅓ cup fat-free milk

½ TB. granulated sugar

4 slices whole-grain cinnamon raisin bread

Yield: 2 servings
Prep time: 5 minutes
Cook time: 4 to 6 minutes
Serving size: 2 slices
Each serving has:
281 calories
52 calories from fat
6 g fat
2 g saturated fat
10 g protein
48 g carbohydrates

1. Heat an 11-inch electric skillet to 350°F. Spray with nonstick cooking spray.

2. Meanwhile, crack egg into a wide, shallow dish. Beat with a fork to blend. Add milk and sugar, and stir with the fork. Add 1 bread slice to the dish, turning to coat both sides completely. Allow any excess egg mixture to drip back into the dish.

3. Place bread slice in the skillet. Repeat with 3 remaining bread slices. (Discard any remaining egg mixture.) Cook for 2 or 3 minutes, or until the undersides are browned as desired. Turn over using a plastic spatula. Cook for 2 or 3 minutes on the other sides, or until browned as desired. (Refrigerate any leftovers and reheat in a toaster, if necessary.)

Variation: You can use any bread you have on hand, coating as many slices as the egg mixture will coat completely. Cook dipped slices in batches if they all won't fit into the skillet at once.

Lecture Hall

Always wash your hands—as well as any utensils, dishes, and work surfaces—in warm, soapy water after handling raw eggs. They can carry salmonella bacteria that can cause illness and even death. If you have a compromised immune system, choose pasteurized eggs or substitute pasteurized refrigerated egg product for regular eggs.

Apple-n-Cheddar-Topped Toast $

With smooth cheddar cheese melting over spiced apple slices, this toast is as close as you can come to eating apple pie for breakfast!

Yield: 1 serving
Prep time: 1 minute
Cook time: 2 or 3 minutes
Each serving has:
357 calories
71 calories from fat
8 g fat
4.5 g saturated fat
10 g protein
61 g carbohydrates

1 slice whole-grain cinnamon raisin bread

⅓ cup ready-made apple pie filling

1 slice 2-percent-milk cheddar cheese

1. In a toaster, toast bread to desired doneness. Place toast on a microwave-safe plate. Spoon apple pie filling over toast. Place cheese on top.

2. Cook on high power for ½ to 1½ minutes or until cheese is melted as desired. Serve immediately.

Learning Curve

Transfer the remaining apple pie filling to a storage container with a lid and refrigerate. You can use the leftover filling for more Apple-n-Cheddar-Topped Toast, stir some into plain hot oatmeal, or top off a batch of Classic French Toast.

Start-Your-Day Parfaits ⨍

The oats will soften as they stand in the yogurt, making a creamy-textured oatmeal that's ready as soon as you wake up.

½ cup uncooked quick oats

1 (6-oz.) container low-fat lemon yogurt

1 (14.5-oz.) can pitted red tart cherries packed in water, drained

1. In a small bowl, stir oats into yogurt to coat.

2. Spoon ¼ cup cherries into each of 2 (1¼-cup or larger) cups with lids. Layer ¼ cup oat mixture over top of cherries. Repeat layering. Sprinkle few remaining cherries on top. Cover and refrigerate overnight.

Yield: 2 servings
Prep time: 5 minutes
Chill time: 6 to 8 hours
Serving size: 1 cup
Each serving has:
183 calories
13 calories from fat
1.5 g fat
0 g saturated fat
7 g protein
37 g carbohydrates

Learning Curve

Recipes can be adjusted to suit your tastes. From this recipe, you can mix and match your favorite yogurt flavors and fruits. Fresh fruits should be washed and chopped, if needed; canned fruits should be drained and chopped, if needed; and frozen fruits should be thawed, drained, and chopped, if needed.

Overnight Peaches and Cream Oatmeal $

This ready-when-you-wake oatmeal is sweet enough to serve straight from the pot, or you could add a splash of milk and a touch of sugar if you like.

Yield: 5 servings
Prep time: 2 minutes
Cook time: 6 to 8 hours
Serving size: 1 cup
Each serving has:
258 calories
42 calories from fat
5 g fat
2 g saturated fat
5 g protein
38 g carbohydrates

1 (15-oz.) can sliced yellow cling peaches in pear juice and water

Water

½ cup fat-free *sweetened condensed milk*

2 cups uncooked old-fashioned rolled oats

1. Spray a 3½- to 4-quart slow cooker with nonstick cooking spray.

2. Drain peaches into a liquid measuring cup. Add enough water to the measuring cup to measure 4 cups. Turn peaches into the bottom of the slow cooker. Slowly pour water over peaches. Pour in sweetened condensed milk. Evenly distribute oats in the slow cooker.

3. Cover the slow cooker and cook on low for 6 to 8 hours or until liquid is absorbed.

Class Notes

Sweetened condensed milk is evaporated milk with about a 40 percent sugar content. You cannot substitute regular evaporated milk for sweetened condensed milk in recipes. To store the remaining sweetened condensed milk from this recipe, pour it into a storage container with a lid and refrigerate for up to 2 weeks.

Fast-Fix Home Fries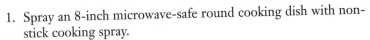

A great accompaniment to nearly any breakfast plate, these home fries aren't as crisp as fried potatoes, but you do eliminate the fat by microwaving.

1 large all-purpose potato

2 TB. diced yellow onions

⅛ tsp. salt

⅛ tsp. garlic powder

Pinch ground black pepper or to taste

Yield: 2 servings
Prep time: 5 minutes
Cook time: 7 to 9 minutes
Serving size: ½ potato
Each serving has:
76 calories
1 calorie from fat
0 g fat
0 g saturated fat
2 g protein
17 g carbohydrates

1. Spray an 8-inch microwave-safe round cooking dish with non-stick cooking spray.

2. Scrub potato. On a cutting board with a sharp knife, dice potato, and add to the prepared dish. Add onions, salt, garlic powder, and pepper, and stir to combine.

3. Cover the dish with plastic wrap, venting one side. Cook on high power (100 percent) for 4 or 5 minutes. Remove the dish from the microwave, and stir. Recover, venting, and rotate the dish, if needed. Cook on high power for 3 or 4 minutes or until tender. Stir before serving.

Learning Curve _____

To ensure even cooking, keep your diced potato and onion pieces of equal size.

Ham and Swiss Quiche $$$$

Delicious enough for company fare, this quiche is easy to cut into wedges with a sharp knife; a pie server or small spatula makes serving easy.

Yield: 6 servings
Prep time: 12 minutes
Cook time: 27 to 30 minutes
Serving size: 1 wedge
Each serving has:
176 calories
65 calories from fat
7 g fat
4 g saturated fat
18 g protein
10 g carbohydrates

⅓ cup plain breadcrumbs

1½ cups pasteurized refrigerated egg product (equal to 6 eggs)

1 cup refrigerated fully cooked lean diced ham

½ cup chopped broccoli

¼ cup chopped yellow onions

¼ cup thinly sliced carrots

⅓ cup fat-free milk

1 cup finely shredded Swiss cheese

½ tsp. ground black pepper

½ tsp. dried parsley flakes

¼ tsp. paprika

1. Spray an 8×2-inch microwave-safe round glass dish with non-stick cooking spray. Distribute breadcrumbs evenly over the bottom of the dish, shaking as needed.

2. In a large bowl, combine egg product, ham, broccoli, onions, carrots, milk, cheese, pepper, parsley flakes, and paprika. Stir. Slowly pour over breadcrumbs in the dish, using the back of a spoon to smooth out the top.

3. Cook on medium power (50 percent) for 27 to 30 minutes or until nearly set in center. Rotate dish, if needed, and carefully tip to redistribute unset egg product every 5 minutes during cooking time. Let stand for 2 or 3 minutes before serving.

Variation: You can use your favorite veggies in this quiche. Just keep the total measurement to 1 cup chopped or thinly sliced vegetables. You can also substitute your favorite cheese, including a lower-fat 2-percent-milk cheese.

Learning Curve

Be sure to use a 2-inch-deep dish and not a pie plate, as the egg will puff up during cooking.

5

Grand Sandwiches

In This Chapter

◆ Quick, filling sandwiches

◆ Matching your favorite fillings with the best breads

◆ Storing, freezing, and thawing breads

When you're short on time but big on hunger, a sandwich fits the bill. Not only are the sandwiches in this chapter fast to fix and filling, many of them are good take-alongs for a meal on the go. PB&J and lunchmeat sandwiches are easy enough to make—but so are a number of other great sandwiches you might not have thought of. You'll find plenty to choose from in these pages, along with tips for getting the most out of your bread purchases.

Bread Dissertation

Most breads are sold in family-size packages, leaving you looking for solutions if you can't eat that much bread before it goes bad. If you and your roommates share groceries, you might be able to eat your way through a loaf of bread or a package of buns before mold sets in. Or you might be fortunate enough to shop at a bakery or a supermarket that offers buns and breads for sale individually. Even if family-size servings are your only option, you can still make a plan. You can use your favorite bread for a number of different sandwiches, regardless of the bread type called for in the recipes.

Should you have a breadbox, store your breads in it. Otherwise, keep your bread in a dark place without temperature extremes, such as a pantry shelf not abutting a stove. If you have to leave your bread on the countertop, pick a spot that doesn't catch a sunray and isn't above the dishwasher. Breads may also be frozen to preserve freshness. Freeze fresh breads in serving-size portions in resealable plastic freezer bags to thaw as needed.

> **Learning Curve**
>
> To thaw frozen bread, bring the bread to room temperature while in its unopened packaging. It should only take a little while on the countertop. Don't try to thaw bread in the microwave; it'll leave the bread dried out.

When you still find yourself with stale bread on your hands, you can make Classic French Toast (recipe in Chapter 4) or Classic Italian Bread Salad (recipe in Chapter 13). The bread won't go to waste, and the results are quite tasty.

Tortilla Tutorial

Refrigerated whole-wheat tortillas keep well, plus they're versatile. The Ranchero BLT Wrap and Grilled Veggie Wrap call for tortillas. You could also use tortillas to enclose the fillings for the Golden-Toasted Rachel Sandwich, Grilled Stuffed-Pita Pizza, Vegetarian Italian Sausage Sandwich with Peppers and Onions, and Shortcut Egg Salad Sandwich. Think creatively and you may discover a new favorite sandwich combination while stretching your food budget by minimizing waste.

Tortillas and pita pockets should be refrigerated in their packaging, making these breads a good choice when a longer shelf life is needed.

Monterey Ranch Burgers $$

Top your burger with your favorite toppings—a slice of tomato, onion rings, pickles, lettuce, ketchup, mustard, whatever. You just won't need a slice of cheese—it's already in there!

1 lb. ground round

1 (0.4-oz.) pkg. ranch salad dressing mix

1 cup 2-percent-milk shredded cheddar and Monterey Jack cheese

4 whole-wheat hamburger buns

Yield: 4 servings
Prep time: 4 minutes
Cook time: 5 minutes
Serving size: 1 hamburger
Each serving has:
456 calories
179 calories from fat
20 g fat
9 g saturated fat
34 g protein
21 g carbohydrates

1. Heat a dual-contact indoor electric grill with the drippings-catching dish in place.

2. In a medium bowl, combine ground round, salad dressing mix, and cheese. Using your hands, thoroughly mix ground round mixture and shape into 4 (½-inch-thick) patties.

3. Grill patties for 5 minutes (cooking in batches depending on the size of your grill) or until done (160°F on a food thermometer). Serve hamburger patties on buns.

Variation: You can grill the prepared hamburger patties over a hot grill or on a broiler pan coated with nonstick cooking spray. Grill or broil for 5 to 7 minutes, turning once, or until done.

Lecture Hall

Always wash your hands with warm, soapy water after handling raw meats to keep from cross-contaminating with E. coli and other bacteria that may cause illness or even death. If you don't like to get your hands dirty, slip them into plastic bags that you can turn inside out when removing and toss when you're done.

Ranchero BLT Wrap $$

As easy to prepare as a traditional BLT, this sandwich is even tastier with a Tex-Mex twist.

Yield: 1 serving
Prep time: 2 minutes
Cook time: 2 to 2½ minutes
Each serving has:
279 calories
134 calories from fat
15 g fat
5 g saturated fat
12 g protein
20 g carbohydrates

1 soft-taco-size whole-wheat tortilla

4 slices turkey bacon

2 tsp. low-fat ranch salad dressing

2 tsp. tomato salsa

¼ cup chopped or shredded lettuce

¼ cup diced tomatoes

1. Place tortilla on a microwave-safe plate. Cook on high power for 20 to 30 seconds or until warmed.

2. Line another microwave-safe plate with a double layer of white paper towels. Arrange bacon slices on the paper towels, and cook on high power for 1 or 2 minutes. Rearrange bacon by turning slices over and moving inside slices to the outside. Cook on high power for 1 or 2 minutes more or until done as desired. Remove bacon to another paper towel and blot dry.

3. Meanwhile, spread salad dressing and salsa over tortilla, leaving a 1-inch margin around the edge. Scatter lettuce and tomatoes over top. Lay bacon over veggies. Roll up tortilla, folding over 1 side, pulling up the bottom, and folding over the other side. Serve immediately.

Variation: You can cook the turkey bacon in a skillet on a stovetop according to the package directions, if desired.

Lecture Hall _____

Be sure to use only plain white paper towels when microwaving. The inks used to print designs on paper towels could leach into your foods. If you only have design-printed paper towels, be sure to place the white back facing your foods.

Golden-Toasted Rachel Sandwich 💲💲

This version of the popular Reuben sandwich is just as delicious—but with a lot less fat and calories.

2 slices rye bread

Fat-free buttery spray

2 TB. fat-free Thousand Island salad dressing

¼ lb. reduced-fat deli-style chopped turkey

6 TB. well-drained sauerkraut

1 slice low-fat Swiss cheese

Yield: 1 serving
Prep time: 2 minutes
Cook time: 6 minutes
Each serving has:
394 calories
71 calories from fat
8 g fat
3 g saturated fat
29 g protein
48 g carbohydrates

1. Heat an 11-inch nonstick electric skillet to 325°F.

2. Spray 1 side of each bread slice with buttery spray to coat; place butter side down on a plate. Spread the other sides of bread with 1 tablespoon salad dressing each. Layer turkey, sauerkraut, and cheese on 1 bread slice. Place other bread slice on top, dressing side down.

3. With a spatula, transfer sandwich to the electric skillet. Cook for 3 minutes or until the underside is browned as desired. Turn sandwich with the spatula, and cook the other side for 3 minutes or until browned as desired. Remove sandwich with the spatula to the plate, cutting in half to serve.

Learning Curve

The term *spatula* covers many types of cooking utensils. An icing spatula resembles an oversize butter knife. A rubber spatula is perfect for scraping batters when baking. The spatula you should use with a nonstick skillet is a wide, plastic "pancake turner" that won't scratch the surface.

Grilled Stuffed-Pita Pizza $$

This quick-fix pocket pizza is sure to satisfy your craving for an ooey, gooey pizza pie in just a few minutes.

Yield: 1 serving
Prep time: 3 minutes
Cook time: 2 or 3 minutes
Each serving has:
305 calories
46 calories from fat
5 g fat
1 g saturated fat
25 g protein
41 g carbohydrates

1 (7- or 8-in.) whole-wheat pocket pita bread	¼ cup fat-free mozzarella cheese
¼ cup prepared pizza sauce	8 slices turkey pepperoni

1. Heat a dual-contact indoor electric grill.

2. On a cutting board with a sharp knife, cut an X in the top only of pita bread, being careful not to cut through the bottom of the pocket. Gently pull back the flaps of pita bread, and evenly spoon pizza sauce over the bottom of pita bread. Sprinkle cheese over pizza sauce. Arrange pepperoni slices over cheese. Lay the flaps back in place to close pita bread.

3. Transfer stuffed pita bread to the electric grill, flap side up. Cook for 2 or 3 minutes or until heated through and cheese is melted. Carefully slide onto a serving plate. Cut into wedges along X marks to serve.

Learning Curve

Turkey pepperoni has only about a third of the fat and saturated fat of regular beef and pork pepperoni. Plus, you won't have that oil slick sliding around on your pizza.

Grilled Veggie Wrap $$

If you love vegetables, you'll relish the intense grilled flavor of this sandwich. Use your favorite veggies to personalize your wrap.

½ **very small zucchini squash, trimmed**

½ **very small yellow summer squash, trimmed**

1 thin slice large yellow onion

⅛ **medium red bell pepper**

1 medium button mushroom, trimmed

Pinch salt and ground black pepper

2 TB. diced tomatoes

1 thin slice Provolone cheese

1 soft-taco-size whole-wheat tortilla

1 TB. low-fat ranch salad dressing

Yield: 1 serving
Prep time: 6 minutes
Chill time: 6 or 7 minutes
Each serving has:
330 calories
130 calories from fat
14.5 g fat
5.5 g saturated fat
15 g protein
37 g carbohydrates

1. Heat an 11-inch electric skillet to 350°F. Coat with nonstick cooking spray.

2. On a cutting board with a sharp knife, cut zucchini squash and summer squash into thin slices lengthwise. Cut onion in half and separate into half rings. Cut red bell pepper into thin strips (about 5). Cut mushroom into thin slices. Add zucchini squash, summer squash, onion, red bell pepper, and mushroom to the skillet. Sprinkle on salt and pepper. Cook and stir for 5 minutes or until vegetables are tender.

3. Add tomatoes to the skillet, and stir vegetables into a pile. Turn off heat, and lay cheese slice over vegetables. Cover the skillet with the lid, and let stand for 1 or 2 minutes or until cheese is melted.

4. While cheese melts, place tortilla on a microwave-safe plate. Cook on high power for 20 to 30 seconds or until warmed. Turn tortilla over, and spread salad dressing over tortilla, leaving a 1-inch margin around edge. Using a large, slotted spatula, transfer vegetable mixture to tortilla. Roll up, folding 1 side over, pulling up the bottom, and folding over the remaining side. Wrap in foil, if desired, leaving a small opening in the bottom to allow for draining to keep tortilla from becoming soggy. Serve immediately.

Learning Curve

Red bell peppers are often pricey, so pick them up on sale. You can clean and prepare them as they'll be called for in recipes, freezing them in resealable freezer bags for several months.

Vegetarian Italian Sausage Sandwich with Peppers and Onions $$

When you're craving this street-fair favorite but can't afford the fat and calories, try this vegetarian version for a low-fat, great-tasting sandwich.

Yield: 1 serving
Prep time: 2 minutes
Cook time: 5 to 8 minutes
Each serving has:
378 calories
60 calories from fat
7 g fat
1 g saturated fat
18 g protein
61 g carbohydrates

½ **medium green bell pepper and/or red bell pepper**

¼ **medium yellow onion**

1 TB. ketchup

1 frozen meatless Italian-style soy protein sausage

1 whole-wheat sausage-style split roll

1. With a sharp knife on a cutting board, cut green bell pepper into thin strips. Thinly slice onion and then cut in half. Place bell pepper and onion in a small (about 2-cup) microwave-safe glass dish with rounded corners. Cover tightly with plastic wrap. (Do not vent.) Cook on high power for 3 or 4 minutes or until nearly tender.

2. Carefully pull back plastic wrap from the side farthest away from you. Stir ketchup into bell peppers and onions until all are coated. Re-cover, venting plastic wrap. Cook on high power for 1 to 2 minutes or until tender and heated through.

3. On a microwave-safe plate, cook sausage in the microwave according to package directions, placing roll on the plate during the last 15 to 20 seconds to warm, if desired. Place sausage on roll and spoon bell pepper mixture over top. Serve immediately.

Variation: For stovetop preparation of the bell pepper and onion mixture, heat 2 teaspoons olive oil in a 10-inch nonstick skillet over medium heat. Add bell pepper and onion to the skillet. Sauté for 7 to 9 minutes, or until tender. Stir in ketchup; cook just until heated through.

Learning Curve

To clean a bell pepper, use a sharp knife to cut out the stem, remove the seeds, and cut off ribs (white membranes). If you're not using the bell pepper whole, you can cut the pepper in half after removing the stem and it'll be easier to clean.

Shortcut Egg Salad Sandwich *

You can make this creamy sandwich spread taste eggier if you add the mayonnaise and mustard just to taste.

2 large eggs

2 TB. reduced-fat mayonnaise

1 tsp. prepared yellow mustard

1 or 2 TB. minced red or green bell pepper or celery

Pinch salt and ground black pepper

2 slices whole-wheat or multigrain bread

Yield: 1 serving
Prep time: 4 minutes
Cook time: 5 or 6 minutes
Each serving has:
376 calories
157 calories from fat
17 g fat
4 g saturated fat
18 g protein
35 g carbohydrates

1. Crack eggs into a 12-ounce microwave-safe round glass dish. With the tines of a fork, make an X in each egg yolk. Cook on high power for 5 or 6 minutes or until nearly set, tilting to redistribute uncooked egg and rotating, if needed, halfway through cooking time. Remove the dish from the microwave and let stand for 2 minutes or until set. Chop eggs.

2. Meanwhile, combine mayonnaise, mustard, bell pepper, salt, and black pepper in a small bowl. Stir until blended and then stir in chopped eggs until well coated. (Chill egg salad, if desired.) Spread egg salad over 1 slice of bread, closing sandwich with remaining bread slice.

Variation: To hard-cook eggs on the stovetop, place eggs in a single layer in a saucepan and cover eggs with cold water. Cover the saucepan and bring the water to a boil over high heat. When boiling, remove the saucepan from the heat. Leaving the saucepan covered, allow the eggs to stand for 20 minutes. Then rinse the eggs immediately in cold water, letting the others stand in cold water as you peel each egg.

Learning Curve _____

Hard-cooked eggs should have lovely yellow yolks, especially if you use older eggs instead of fresh ones. If you happen to find a green-tinted yolk, don't worry. It's okay to eat.

Chapter 6

Super Soups

In This Chapter

- ◆ Cooking with flavor: spices and herbs
- ◆ Choosing and storing fresh and dried herbs
- ◆ Stocking your spice rack

You *could* cook without herbs and spices … but why would you want to? If you'll be cooking, do yourself a favor and get a selection of seasonings. How much you'll be cooking, what type of kitchen quarters you have available, and what kinds of recipes you prefer dictate how extensive or specific that collection is.

Learning how to buy, store, and cook with herbs and spices helps you make decisions that make cooking a pleasure and fit your needs. What do you need beyond salt and pepper? You get to decide.

Helping Herbs

The recipes in this cookbook call for dried herbs with their fresh herb measurement equivalents as alternatives. Dried herbs are readily available and easy to store. Keep them in their original plastic or glass jars.

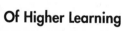

Learning Curve _____

If you buy dried herbs from bulk bins, invest in small glass jars. You can refill empty, cleaned plastic containers with the same herb as the original. Plastic takes on the odors of the contents, so you'll want to keep the same herbs to avoid mixing tastes and labeling confusion.

The newer a dried herb is, the stronger the flavor. Buy only the amount of herbs you'll use in a short time—up to 6 months. You might be able to keep a dried herb for up to a year by adding a little more of the herb than called for in a recipe. The best test is to sniff the jar when you open it. A weak aroma means a weak flavor—and that you should replace the herb.

Fresh herbs are available in bunches, plastic containers, or even squeeze tubes. The herbs should appear fresh, not wilted, yellowed, spotted, moldy, or slimy. Follow the directions for storing prepackaged herbs. Fresh herb bunches can be stored in a plastic bag in the refrigerator. Wrap the stem ends in a moist, not soggy, paper towel before putting them in an airtight plastic bag, but don't wash fresh herbs until you're ready to use them. Gently pat dry the herbs you've washed with paper towels. When you cook with fresh herbs, you'll want to add them near the end of the cooking time, as they are more delicate.

You'll need more of a fresh herb because its dried counterparts are more concentrated. A good rule of thumb is a 3:1 ratio, with 1 tablespoon fresh herb being equal to 1 teaspoon dried herb. Whichever form you're using, always adjust seasonings to taste.

Spice Seminar

Spice purists insist on buying whole spices and grating them personally. For those of us who are too busy, ground spices are perfectly convenient. As with dried herbs, buy only the amount you'll use within 6 months and store them in their original containers or small glass jars with tight-fitting lids.

Of Higher Learning _____

Herbs are the leaves of plants. Spices are many other parts of plants and even trees—bark, seeds, stems, buds, and rhizomes.

Set up your spice rack—be it a drawer, a lazy Susan, or an alphabetized cabinet—in a cool, dark place (that means away from the stove) with the dried herbs and spices you use in your cooking. Note the date the container is opened to help you track your usage and to spot those seasonings that might need to be replaced.

Pizza Parlor Tomato Soup ⚡

Top a bowl of pizza-flavored soup with any of your favorite toppings—diced turkey pepperoni, chopped black olives, chopped green onions, diced green bell peppers, or others.

1 (10.75-oz.) can tomato soup

1 soup can water

¼ tsp. garlic powder

¼ tsp. dried oregano

⅓ cup uncooked pastina or other tiny pasta

½ cup low-fat finely shredded mozzarella cheese

¼ cup french-fried onions

Yield: 2 servings
Prep time: 2 minutes
Cook time: 7 to 10 minutes
Serving size: 1 cup soup
Each serving has:
259 calories
68 calories from fat
7.5 g fat
4 g saturated fat
9 g protein
37 g carbohydrates

1. In a 1-quart microwave-safe round glass dish, stir together soup and water. Stir in garlic powder and oregano. Cook on high power for 3 or 4 minutes or until *simmering*. Stir in pastina. Cook on high power for 4 to 6 minutes or until pastina is tender, stirring and rotating, if needed, halfway through the cooking time.

2. Remove soup mixture from the microwave and stir. Stir in cheese until melted. Sprinkle 2 tablespoons french-fried onions over each serving, and serve immediately.

Variation: To prepare this soup on the stovetop, stir together soup, water, garlic powder, and oregano in a saucepan. Cook over medium-high heat until simmering. Stir in pastina. Reduce heat slightly and continue simmering for 4 to 6 minutes, or until pastina is tender, stirring occasionally. Remove the saucepan from heat. Stir in cheese until melted. Serve as directed.

Class Notes _____

Simmering is a term that describes gentle bubbling of a liquid that happens at a lower temperature than boiling.

Summer Gazpacho $$

This quick, fat-free version of the classic cold soup is refreshing when the sun is scorching.

Yield: 2 servings
Prep time: 5 minutes
Chill time: 1 hour
Serving size: ¼ cup
Each serving has:
30 calories
3 calories from fat
0 g fat
0 g saturated fat
1 g protein
7 g carbohydrates

1 medium tomato

¼ large cucumber

1 thin slice medium yellow onion

⅛ medium green bell pepper

¼ cup vegetable juice cocktail

¼ tsp. drained minced garlic

¼ tsp. dried parsley flakes

¼ tsp. chili powder

1. On a cutting board with a sharp knife, peel and coarsely chop tomato. Peel and coarsely chop cucumber. Quarter onion slice. Coarsely chop green bell pepper.

2. In a blender, combine tomato, cucumber, onion, green bell pepper, vegetable juice cocktail, garlic, parsley flakes, and chili powder. Cover and purée on high speed for 10 seconds or until desired consistency is reached.

3. Pour soup into a container with a lid. Cover and chill for at least 1 hour. Stir before serving.

Variation: If you prefer a chunkier texture to your gazpacho, reserve a portion of the vegetables before puréeing for a few seconds. Then, add the reserved vegetables and purée for a few seconds more, or until desired consistency is achieved.

Learning Curve

To easily peel a tomato, submerge it in boiling water for about 10 seconds. Remove it with tongs or carefully use two spoons. When the tomato is just cool enough to handle, use a sharp knife and/or your fingers to remove the peel.

Lentil and Tomato Soup $

Pair a cup of this mildly spicy soup with Hummus in Minutes (recipe in Chapter 15) and a hearty pita pocket for a delicious Middle Eastern–flavored lunch.

1 tsp. extra-virgin olive oil

2 tsp. drained minced garlic

2 tsp. dried cilantro leaves

½ tsp. crushed red pepper flakes

1 (14.5-oz.) can stewed tomatoes, undrained

½ tsp. ground cumin

⅓ cup lentils

3 cups water

Yield: 3 servings
Prep time: 3 minutes
Cook time: 50 minutes
Serving size: 1 cup
Each serving has:
212 calories
51 calories from fat
6 g fat
1 g saturated fat
9 g protein
33 g carbohydrates

1. Add olive oil to a 6-quart nonstick electric wok set to medium-low heat. Heat oil for 1 minute. Add garlic, cilantro leaves, and crushed red pepper flakes, and sauté for 2 minutes or until aromatic. Add stewed tomatoes and stir. When simmering, add cumin, lentils, and water. Stir.

2. Increase heat to high and bring to a boil. Reduce heat to low. Cover and simmer for 40 minutes or until lentils are plump and tender, stirring occasionally and breaking up tomatoes as desired.

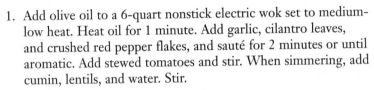 **Variation:** For stovetop preparation, follow directions as given, using a large saucepan with a lid.

Learning Curve _____

Lentils are great soup beans because they don't require soaking as most other dried beans do. You should still sort through and rinse the lentils before using. Look for small pebbles or shriveled beans that are sometimes overlooked in processing and toss those.

Veggie Beef Noodle Soup $$

This satisfying soup is perfect for dorm-room cooking, as you can keep the ingredients on hand for a while and then pop them in the microwave whenever you're hungry.

Yield: 5 servings	
Prep time: 3 minutes	
Cook time: 17 or 18 minutes	
Serving size: 1 cup	

Each serving has:
221 calories
26 calories from fat
3 g fat
1.5 g saturated fat
11 g protein
37 g carbohydrates

1 (2.25-oz.) pkg. sliced dried beef

2 cups water

1 (3-oz.) pkg. beef-flavored ramen noodle soup

1 (14.5-oz) can zucchini with Italian-style tomato sauce

2 cups frozen vegetable soup mix vegetables

1. On a cutting board with a sharp knife, cut the stack of beef slices into ½-inch strips. Place in a small container, cover with warm water, and let stand.

2. Pour 2 cups water into a 1½-quart microwave-safe glass bowl. Cook on high power for 4 or 5 minutes, or until boiling. Add ramen noodles, breaking up to fit in the bowl. Cook on high power for 3 minutes or until tender, stirring and rotating, if needed, halfway through cooking time. Stir in noodle soup seasoning packet.

3. Drain beef. Add to noodle mixture with zucchini and vegetables, and cook on high power for 10 minutes or until vegetables are tender, stirring and rotating, if needed, halfway through the cooking time.

 Variation: Prepare beef strips as directed. Prepare ramen noodle soup in a large saucepan according to package directions for stovetop preparation. Stir in drained beef strips, zucchini, and vegetables. Bring to a boil. Reduce heat, cover, and simmer for 10 minutes or until vegetables are tender, stirring once or twice.

Lecture Hall _____

If your microwave doesn't have a turntable, don't walk away and forget to rotate the dish you're cooking. Every microwave behaves differently, and yours may have a "hot spot." Rotating ensures even heating throughout.

Instant Rice Soup $

Quick and easy, you can stir up this pantry-shelf soup anytime hunger strikes.

1 tsp. chicken bouillon granules	2 TB. diced carrots
Pinch garlic powder	2 TB. diced yellow onions
1 cup water	1 tsp. dried parsley flakes or 1 TB. chopped fresh parsley
¼ cup instant brown rice	

Yield: 1 serving
Prep time: 3 minutes
Cook time: 10 minutes
Each serving has:
117 calories
7 calories from fat
1 g fat
0 g saturated fat
2 g protein
25 g carbohydrates

1. Stir bouillon granules and garlic powder into water in a 3-cup microwave-safe glass bowl. Add rice, carrots, and onions, and stir to mix. Cover with plastic wrap, venting, and cook on high power for 5 minutes, rotating if needed.

2. Remove the bowl from the microwave. Quickly stir in parsley flakes. Cover tightly with plastic wrap and let stand for 5 minutes. Stir before serving.

Learning Curve _____

If you're chopping fresh herbs, first air-dry or dry the herbs with a paper towel after washing. Wet herbs stick to your knife.

Home-Style Beef Stew $$$

When you're craving something rib-sticking and belly-warming, fill your bowl with this stew.

Yield: 4 servings
Prep time: 12 minutes
Cook time: 6 to 8 hours
Serving size: 1 cup
Each serving has:
288 calories
74 calories from fat
8 g fat
3 g saturated fat
28 g protein
25 g carbohydrates

1 large all-purpose potato

1 small yellow onion

1 rib celery

16 baby carrots

1 lb. cubed stew beef

1 (14-oz.) can fat-free, less-sodium beef broth

¼ cup quick-cooking tapioca

1 bay leaf

¼ tsp. ground cloves

¼ tsp. each salt and ground black pepper

1. On a cutting board with a sharp knife, coarsely chop potato, onion, and celery. In the bottom of a 3½- to 4-quart slow cooker coated with nonstick cooking spray, combine potato, onion, celery, and carrots.

2. On a cutting board with a sharp knife, trim fat off beef, and add beef to the slow cooker.

3. In a small bowl, combine broth, tapioca, bay leaf, cloves, salt, and pepper. Pour into the slow cooker, and stir to mix. Cover and cook on low heat for 6 to 8 hours or until vegetables are tender and beef is done (170°F on a food thermometer).

Learning Curve

Remove the bay leaf before serving this stew and any other dish that calls for the seasoning. The brittle leaf isn't pleasant to bite down on unexpectedly and might have sharp edges that can cause injury.

Turkey and White Bean Chili $$

Fill your bowl and add a sprinkling of shredded cheddar cheese
and a dollop of sour cream. Or ladle this chili over a serving of
whole-wheat spaghetti and top with chopped onions and shredded
cheddar cheese for a Cincinnati chili–style dish.

1 medium yellow onion	**1 (8-oz.) can tomato sauce**
½ medium green bell pepper	**1 tsp. chili powder**
½ lb. ground turkey	**¼ tsp. salt**
1 (14.5-oz.) can diced toma-toes, undrained	**⅛ tsp. paprika**
1 (15.5-oz.) can *cannellini* beans, rinsed and drained	**⅛ tsp. ground ginger**

1 Clove Garlic diced
1- 2 C WATER

Yield: 5 servings
Prep time: 3 minutes
Cook time: 50 to 55 minutes
Serving size: 1 cup
Each serving has:
226 calories
65 calories from fat
7 g fat
2 g saturated fat
19 g protein
22 g carbohydrates

1. On a cutting board with a sharp knife, chop onion and green
   bell pepper into ½-inch squares.

2. In a 6-quart nonstick electric wok set to medium heat, cook
   and stir ground turkey, onion, and green bell pepper *GARLIC* for 4 to 6
   minutes or until meat is browned. Unplug the wok and drain.

3. Add tomatoes, beans, tomato sauce, chili powder, salt, paprika,
   and ginger to the wok, and stir to combine. Plug in the wok
   again, set over high heat, and bring mixture to a boil. Reduce
   heat to low, cover, and simmer for 45 minutes, stirring occasionally. *add water to thin.*

Variation: For stovetop preparation, follow the directions
given, using a large saucepan with a lid.

Class Notes

Cannellini beans are a type of white bean of an ivory
coloring with a velvety texture. White beans—cannellini,
great northern, navy, and white kidney beans—can be used
interchangeably in most recipes.

Chapter 7

Big Salads

In This Chapter

- ◆ Selecting leafy greens
- ◆ Washing and storing greens
- ◆ Great salads that will fill you up

Whether you're preparing a big salad or lining a plate for appearances, your lettuce options extend beyond iceberg. Knowing what flavors to expect and how to handle leafy greens will make you more comfortable choosing lettuces and serving salads.

A simple rule is that the heartier, more savory greens can be paired with big-flavored fixings and dressings; the mild, delicate greens may need only a drizzling of vinaigrette. If it tastes right, however, then it is right. Isn't it great to be the cook?

Lettuce Begin

A trip to the produce department to choose lettuce might prove overwhelming. You'll find any number of lettuce heads and prepackaged salad mixes. You should see crisp, fresh leaves that aren't brown, wilted, or slimy. If you're buying a cellophane package, inspect it carefully, turning it upside down, too.

Whether you're picking a packaged mix or selecting heads of lettuce, it's helpful to know how certain lettuces taste. A few of the most popular salad greens follow:

Arugula leaves are dark green and highly flavored, often used to add a peppery taste. Heads are loose with irregularly notched leaves, but you'll usually find arugula, or rocket, in bunches.

Bibb lettuce has very delicate, sweet, light green leaves. A head is small and loosely round.

Butter lettuce leaves are tender and light green with a velvety or buttery feel. A head is loosely round, a bit bigger than Bibb lettuce.

Curly endive leaves are pale green and bitter with yellow centers that are a bit milder tasting. Heads are loose and frilly looking.

Escarole is bitter tasting. The loose heads have big, ruffled green leaves.

Frisée is a young head of curly endive. Leaves are still tender and pale, but with a bitter taste. Heads are loose and lacy, or "frizzy."

Green-leaf lettuce is mild tasting and generally pleasing to all. A head is loose with broad, delicate, ruffled leaves.

Of Higher Learning

Prepackaged salad mixes are convenient. The leaves are already torn, you can get a tasty combination of leafy greens without having to buy four or five heads of lettuce, plus the combinations are chosen for you.

Iceberg lettuce is a popular offering at salad bars due to its inexpensive cost. Light-colored leaves are watery, thick, and crisp. Heads are tight and round, resembling cabbages.

Oakleaf lettuce is delicate and mild. The leaves remind you of oak leaves, as you would expect, colorfully tinged and lobed. Heads are loose.

Radicchio leaves are deep red in color, bitter in flavor, and crisp in texture. Heads are tighter, either round or elongated.

Red-leaf lettuce is like green-leaf lettuce, but with purplish-red coloring on the leaves' ruffles.

Romaine leaves are the traditional greens making up a Caesar salad. They're crisp and sweet, and the heads are elongated. You can also buy the hearts of the paler, crunchy leaves.

Spinach leaves are dark green and hearty. Sold in mature and baby forms, you might want to trim the coarse stems from more mature leaves. Unpackaged spinach is available in bunches.

Learning Curve

Bunches of fresh spinach may be particularly sandy because of their growing conditions. If the leaves need more than a good rinse, fill a large bowl or pot with warm water and gently shake the spinach while it's immersed in the water. Any sand should sink to the bottom of the bowl or pot. Repeat the process until agitating the spinach doesn't deposit sand on the bottom of the bowl or pot.

Lettuces are best left unwashed until you're ready to use them. Store cellophane packages unopened in the crisper drawer. If you've opened the packages, force out as much air as possible without damaging the leaves and close tightly. Heads of lettuce can be stored in the crisper in plastic bags. Check prepackaged salads for best-by or use-by dates. More delicate greens will only keep for 3 or 4 days usually. Heartier lettuces may be good for up to 10 days.

Prepackaged mixes are prewashed, but you should wash what you'll be using before serving. You can place the torn leaves into a colander and gently rinse them in cold water. Set them aside to dry or gently pat in paper towels before tossing the salad. Heads of lettuce can be dirtier. Wash their leaves in a clean sink or a large bowl full of cold water, gently agitating them. Change the water until it's clean. Gently blot the leaves dry with paper towels. Washed lettuces can be held in the refrigerator while you prepare the meal until you are ready to use them.

Learning Curve

Salad greens should be dressed just before serving, as the dressing will cause the leaves to wilt.

Always use a light hand when washing and drying lettuces, as they'll bruise easily. Drying them helps the dressing cling better, keeping its flavor full and not watered down. You'll use less dressing, and thereby less calories, for a sensational taste.

Big Buffalo Salad $$

A mild buffalo sauce adds a nice tang to the chicken served with traditional wings fixings on a bed of greens—of course you can toss in any of your favorite salad fixings.

Yield: 1 serving
Prep time: 3 minutes
Cook time: 5 minutes
Each serving has:
225 calories
112 calories from fat
12 g fat
2 g saturated fat
21 g protein
14 g carbohydrates

1½ TB. light butter with canola oil

1½ TB. hot pepper sauce

1 (3-oz.) boneless, skinless chicken breast

2 ribs celery

8 baby carrots

1½ cups mixed salad greens

2 TB. low-fat blue cheese or ranch salad dressing

1. Heat a dual-contact electric grill with drippings-catching dish in place.

2. In a small bowl large enough to hold chicken breast, combine 1 tablespoon light butter and 1 tablespoon hot pepper sauce, and stir until well blended.

3. Trim fat from chicken breast, place chicken breast in butter mixture, and coat thoroughly. (Discard any unused butter mixture.) Grill chicken breast for 5 minutes or until done (170°F on a food thermometer).

4. Meanwhile, on a cutting board with a sharp knife, coarsely chop celery and carrots. Toss on a serving plate with salad greens.

5. In another small bowl, combine remaining ½ tablespoon light butter and remaining ½ tablespoon hot pepper sauce, and stir until well blended.

6. On a cutting board with a sharp knife, cut chicken breast into bite-size pieces. Turn chicken pieces into butter mixture, and toss to coat. Add to the serving plate with salad greens, and drizzle salad dressing over all.

Lecture Hall

Do not reuse the same small bowl you used for mixing the buffalo sauce, and always discard any uncooked sauce or marinade that came in contact with raw meat. A marinade can be used after holding raw meat only if it's brought to a full boil for 5 minutes.

Baby Spinach and Salmon Salad $$$

Fast and filling, this salad's spinach leaves compliment the bold flavor of the salmon.

1 small tomato

¼ medium cucumber

1 green onion

1 cup packed baby spinach

1 (3-oz.) pouch ready-to-use boneless, skinless pink salmon

1 TB. minced green bell pepper

1 TB. lemon juice

2 tsp. extra-virgin olive oil

¼ tsp. dried dill weed or ¾ tsp. chopped fresh dill

Pinch ground black pepper

Yield: 1 serving
Prep time: 5 minutes
Each serving has:
206 calories
96 calories from fat
11 g fat
2 g saturated fat
18 g protein
13 g carbohydrates

1. On a cutting board with a sharp knife, cut tomato into wedges. Peel and coarsely chop cucumber. Trim the roots and the ends of the green tops of green onion, and finely chop.

2. Line a serving plate with baby spinach. Scatter tomato and cucumber over spinach.

3. In a small bowl, combine salmon, green onion, green bell pepper, lemon juice, olive oil, dill weed, and black pepper. Stir until well blended. Spoon over spinach to serve.

Learning Curve _____

Cucumbers don't have to be peeled to be eaten; if you prefer, you can leave the peel intact. Many cucumbers sold in supermarkets are waxed for a glossy appearance and should probably be washed with a commercial fruit-and-vegetable wash to remove the wax and any chemicals.

Crab Salad in Avocado Halves $$$

A fresh ocean taste, this crab salad is perfectly complimented by the smooth mouthfeel of the avocado.

Yield: 2 servings
Prep time: 5 minutes
Chill time: 30 minutes
Serving size: 1 avocado half
Each serving has:
245 calories
134 calories from fat
15 g fat
2 g saturated fat
9 g protein
21 g carbohydrates

1 green onion

½ (8-oz.) pkg. fat-free fully cooked crab-flavored seafood made with surimi (imitation crabmeat)

½ TB. drained diced pimiento

¼ cup reduced-fat tartar sauce

Pinch ground black pepper

1 ripe avocado

1 tsp. lemon juice

1. Trim root end and green top edges from green onion. On a cutting board with a sharp knife, chop green onion.

2. Turn out crab-flavored seafood onto a cutting board, and chop into bite-size pieces with a sharp knife.

3. In a small bowl with a lid, combine green onion, crab-flavored seafood, pimiento, tartar sauce, and pepper. Stir until blended. Cover and chill for at least 30 minutes, or until chilled and flavors are blended.

4. On a cutting board with a sharp knife, cut avocado in half lengthwise around the pit, and carefully twist halves to separate. Push a knife blade near the handle into the pit, gently twist, and pull up the pit to remove. Carefully use a spoon to separate avocado pulp from the peel. Rub lemon juice over avocado halves to prevent discoloration.

5. Scoop crab-flavored seafood mixture into hollows of avocado halves to serve.

Learning Curve

If you need to keep a peeled avocado for a while, coat all exposed surfaces with lemon juice and cover the avocado directly with plastic wrap, making sure it touches and conforms to the avocado pulp.

Simple Sweet and Crunchy Chicken Salad $$

Serve this easy-mix salad scooped on a lettuce-lined plate with a variety of in-season fruits or spread it on hearty whole-grain bread for a sumptuous sandwich.

1 (7-oz.) pouch ready-to-use chicken breast

3 TB. reduced-fat mayonnaise

½ tsp. lemon juice

¼ cup dried cranberries

¼ cup unsalted chopped walnuts

Pinch ground black pepper

Yield: 3 servings
Prep time: 3 minutes
Chill time: 30 minutes (if desired)
Serving size: ½ cup
Each serving has:
224 calories
91 calories from fat
10 g fat
1 g saturated fat
20 g protein
12 g carbohydrates

1. In a small bowl with a lid, combine chicken, mayonnaise, and lemon juice, and stir until chicken is coated. Add dried cranberries, walnuts, and pepper, and stir until evenly distributed.

2. Cover and chill for at least 30 minutes before serving, if desired.

Learning Curve

You can substitute an equal amount of white ground pepper for black ground pepper in a recipe if the appearance of dark pepper flakes bothers you.

Olive and Pimiento Tuna Salad $

Scoop this creamy tuna salad onto a lunch platter with lightly steamed or raw vegetables—baby carrots, cauliflower florets, cucumber rounds, or your favorites—and crackers. Or spread on hearty whole-grain bread for a filling sandwich.

Yield: 1 serving
Prep time: 2 minutes
Each serving has:
216 calories
100 calories from fat
11 g fat
2 g saturated fat
21 g protein
7 g carbohydrates

1 (3-oz.) pouch ready-to-use light tuna in water

3 TB. drained sliced green olives with pimientos

½ tsp. lemon juice

3 TB. reduced-fat mayonnaise

1. In a small bowl, combine tuna, green olives with pimientos, and lemon juice, and stir to mix. Add mayonnaise, and stir until well blended.

2. Serve immediately, or cover and chill, if desired.

Learning Curve _____

Lemon juice brightens the flavor of many foods and is good to keep on hand in the kitchen. Fresh lemon juice is the most flavorful, but if you can't make it to the supermarket often or if you find fresh lemons too expensive, bottled lemon juice from concentrate is a convenient, inexpensive alternative.

Chive-Sprinkled Cottage Cheese Tomato Wedges $$

You're not going to find anything easier for a quick-fix lunch or pick-me-up than this. It's satisfying served alongside your favorite multigrain crackers, too.

1 medium tomato

½ cup fat-free or low-fat small-curd cottage cheese

1 tsp. dried chives or 1 TB. chopped fresh chives

⅛ tsp. ground black pepper

Pinch salt (optional)

Yield: 1 serving		
Prep time: 2 minutes		
Each serving has:		
109 calories		
14 calories from fat		
2 g fat		
1 g saturated fat		
15 g protein		
9 g carbohydrates		

1. On a cutting board with a sharp knife, core tomato by cutting around the stem end at an angle toward the center and removing the core. Cut tomato into wedges by cutting an X into tomato without cutting through the bottom, turn tomato ¼ turn, and repeat. Transfer tomato to a serving plate, allowing wedges to fall open.

2. In a small bowl, stir together cottage cheese, chives, and pepper until blended.

3. Sprinkle salt (if using) over inside of tomato. Spoon cottage cheese mixture into hollow of tomato, and serve immediately.

Variation: Stuff a tomato with your favorite fillings, such as Olive and Pimiento Tuna Salad, Simple Sweet and Crunchy Chicken Salad, or the crab salad from Crab Salad in Avocado Halves (recipes in this chapter). You might also want to try potato salad, macaroni salad, turkey salad, ham salad, or any of your other favorite cold salads. Leftovers of Veggie-Packed Rice Salad and Too-Good Two-Bean Salad (recipes in Chapter 16) are other options.

Learning Curve _____

You can seed the tomato for this and other recipes if you prefer. After cutting the first X in the tomato, turn the tomato upside down over the sink and gently squeeze the tomato in your palm to release the seeds.

Make-Ahead Veggie Lover's Pasta Salad $$

Packed with a variety of your favorite veggies, this pasta salad makes a good lunch, or you could serve it as a ready-to-go side salad.

Yield: 2 servings
Prep time: 2 minutes
Cook time: 20 to 23 minutes
Chill time: 6 to 8 hours
Serving size: 1¼ cups
Each serving has:
206 calories
47 calories from fat
5 g fat
0.5 g saturated fat
6 g protein
34 g carbohydrates

1 cup uncooked whole-wheat rotini pasta

1 cup raw chopped or thinly sliced vegetables (tomatoes, cucumbers, bell peppers, olives, broccoli, carrots, zucchini, mushrooms, frozen or canned peas, etc.)

¼ cup low-fat Italian salad dressing

1. Pour 3 cups hot water into a 1-quart microwave-safe round glass dish. Cook on high power for 7 or 8 minutes or until boiling. Add pasta, and cook on high power for 13 to 15 minutes or until done. Drain and rinse in cold water.

2. In a medium bowl with a lid, combine pasta, vegetables, and salad dressing. Stir to coat well, cover, and chill overnight or for 6 to 8 hours. Stir again before serving.

Variation: You can add some protein to this salad if you like. Replace a portion of the vegetable measurement with fully cooked diced meats—lean ham, chicken breast, turkey breast—or flaked tuna or salmon. Drained canned beans—kidney, garbanzo, black—are also a nice addition.

Learning Curve

Rinsing the pasta in cold water helps stop the cooking process and starts the chilling process for cold pasta dishes.

Part 3

Main Courses

If you're new to cooking for yourself, maybe the most dreaded question of each day is: "What's for dinner?" The recipes in Part 3 help answer this question and ease the anxiety. Whether you need a fast-fix dish, a single-serve entrée, or a budget-friendly meal, you'll find a recipe to whip up and enjoy in the following pages.

Recipes here for beef, pork, chicken, turkey, fish, seafood, and meatless meals offer variety for palate-pleasing options. Take advantage of the diversity to get all the nutrients and health benefits your body needs for high-performance brain power.

"Dude. Freshmen take a girl out for pizza. You've got to poach a salmon for her."

Chapter 8

Meaty Meals

In This Chapter

- Selecting fresh beef and pork
- Storing meats properly
- Meat cooking and handling safety

If you were the kid who asked "Mom, what's for dinner?" and expected to hear "pork chops" or "hamburgers" in reply, you'll need to learn how to handle and cook meats now. From purchasing to preparing, a little know-how will keep you safe from food-borne illnesses—and well fed.

Meat Curriculum

If you shop for your meats at a supermarket, you'll want to know you're getting the freshest quality possible. Look for beef with a consistent red coloring with any fat on the meat white in color. Beef shouldn't appear gray or brown where exposed to air, which can indicate deterioration. You can also feel the meat through the plastic packaging to ensure firmness and avoid any mushy offerings.

Pork cuts should be a deep pink color with the fat white and the texture firm. You can also bring any packaged meats up to your nose to sniff for smells that may tip you off to the meat's quality.

Learning Curve _____

Safe handling starts in the supermarket. One trick is to slip your hand into a plastic bag provided by the store (in the produce department if nowhere else), turning it inside out. Pick up your desired package of meat and pull the bag right side out around it. This should catch any leaks, keeping raw meat juices from seeping onto other items in your shopping cart and then your bagged purchases.

When you get home to your apartment or dorm, you can keep your meats in their original packaging inside the plastic bags. Store them on the lowest shelf at the back of the refrigerator. This should be the coldest part of your refrigerator and keeps any raw juices from leaking onto and contaminating foods on lower shelves. Beef cuts can be held for up to 4 days; pork cuts can keep for up to 3 days; and ground meats shouldn't be left for more than 2 days.

When you don't have plans to use the meat right away, prepare it for freezing. Divide larger packages into serving sizes; for you, that may mean a single pork chop or ¼ pound ground beef. Write on the freezer bag or container what the meat is and its weight, if needed. Note the date, too. Use beef cuts within 10 months. Small cuts of pork should be used within 3 months. Ground meats will only retain their quality for 2 or 3 months.

Thawing is easy. Move a package from the freezer to the refrigerator. Never thaw meats on the counter at room temperature. If you're in a hurry, thaw meats in the microwave. You'll have to keep a watchful eye on the package—turning, rotating, and rearranging as necessary for even thawing without cooking the edges. Use the meat immediately if you've defrosted it in the microwave.

When preparing a meat recipe, your most important ingredient is hot, soapy water. Wash everything that comes in contact with the raw meat—your hands, work surfaces and cutting boards, plates, and utensils. When you think your recipe's done, use a thermometer to know for sure.

Drunken Beef and Mushroom Spaghetti $$$$

This deep, rich sauce makes the beef look great while allowing you to skip the usual step of browning the meat before slow cooking.

1 lb. lean beef stew meat

1 (1.35-oz.) pkg. 50-percent-less-sodium onion soup mix

1 (1.5-oz.) pkg. spaghetti sauce mix

1 (8-oz.) can no-salt-added tomato sauce

1 cup low-sodium vegetable juice cocktail

¼ cup red wine

1 cup sliced button mushrooms

4 cups hot water

8 oz. multigrain spaghetti

Yield: *4 servings*
Prep time: 12 minutes
Cook time: 6 to 8 hours
Serving size: ½ cup spaghetti with 1 cup beef sauce
Each serving has:
495 calories
80 calories from fat
9 g fat
3 g saturated fat
36 g protein
64 g carbohydrates

1. On a cutting board with a sharp knife, trim fat from stew meat. Add meat to a 3½- to 4-quart slow cooker coated with nonstick cooking spray. Sprinkle in onion soup mix and spaghetti sauce mix. Pour tomato sauce, vegetable juice cocktail, and wine over all. Add mushrooms, and stir to mix. Cover and cook on low heat for 6 to 8 hours or until meat is done (170°F on a food thermometer for well done).

2. Pour water into a 1½-quart microwave-safe glass bowl, and cook on high power for 8 or 9 minutes or until boiling. Add spaghetti to boiling water, breaking as needed to fit into the bowl. Cook on high power for 9 or 10 minutes or until done. Drain. Serve beef mixture over spaghetti.

Learning Curve

Regular canned tomato products and seasoning mixes are high in sodium. With several of these products called for in this recipe, using as many low-sodium versions as possible keeps the finished sauce from tasting too salty.

Mac-n-Cheeseburger Pies $$

You'll feel like you're creating an elaborate meal with this recipe, but it's ever so easy to prepare this hamburger shell filled with ready-made macaroni and cheese.

Yield: 2 servings
Prep time: 5 minutes
Cook time: 9 to 11 minutes
Serving size: 1 casserole
Each serving has:
400 calories
97 calories from fat
11 g fat
5 g saturated fat
36 g protein
40 g carbohydrates

1 (8-oz.) pkg. frozen reduced-fat macaroni and cheese

¼ cup frozen peas

¼ tsp. garlic powder

⅛ tsp. hot pepper sauce

½ lb. ground round

2 TB. ketchup

2 TB. plain breadcrumbs

⅛ tsp. onion powder (optional)

⅛ tsp. paprika (optional)

1. Loosen the box around the frozen macaroni and cheese and turn into a 6-cup microwave-safe glass bowl. (If the frozen block doesn't fit the bowl nicely, hit it squarely on a clean, hard surface to break it in half.) Add peas, garlic powder, and hot pepper sauce to bowl. Cover with plastic wrap, venting. Cook on high power for 5 or 6 minutes or until bubbly, stirring and rotating, if needed, halfway through cooking time. Set aside, covered.

2. Meanwhile, combine ground round, ketchup, breadcrumbs, and onion powder (if using) in a medium bowl. Mix thoroughly with your hands. Divide mixture in half, and shape each half into a thin patty and press into each of 2 (12-ounce) microwave-safe glass casseroles or similar dishes. Shape mixture to bottom and up sides of casseroles.

3. Cook casseroles, uncovered, on high power for 2½ to 3 minutes or just until browned, rotating halfway through the cooking time if needed. Drain well and pat dry with paper towels.

4. Spoon ½ macaroni and cheese mixture into each hamburger shell. Cook, uncovered, on high power for 1 or 2 minutes or until macaroni and cheese mixture is heated through and hamburger shells are done (160°F on a food thermometer). Sprinkle paprika (if using) over casseroles to color.

Learning Curve

Choose the macaroni and cheese dish—as well as any frozen foods—carefully, as the nutritional values vary from package to package. Macaroni and cheese offerings can range from 4½ grams fat up to 12 grams or more per serving.

Easy Chili Mac $$

Garnish each hearty serving to taste with a little low-fat shredded cheddar cheese, a dollop of fat-free sour cream, and/or chopped green onions, if you like.

4 cups hot water

1½ cups uncooked multi-grain rotini pasta

½ small yellow onion

½ small green bell pepper

½ lb. ground round

¼ tsp. salt

½ tsp. Italian seasoning

1 (8-oz.) can tomato sauce

1 cup water

½ cup frozen whole-kernel corn

¼ cup sliced black olives (optional)

Yield: 2 servings
Prep time: 1 minute
Cook time: 19 to 22 minutes
Serving size: 2 cups
Each serving has:
450 calories
64 calories from fat
7 g fat
3 g saturated fat
35 g protein
63 g carbohydrates

1. Pour hot water into a 1½-quart microwave-safe glass bowl, and cook on high power for 8 or 9 minutes or until boiling. Add pasta, and cook on high power for 10 or 11 minutes or until done, rotating if needed. Drain.

2. Meanwhile, on a cutting board with a sharp knife, chop onion and green bell pepper into ½-inch squares.

3. In an 11-inch nonstick electric skillet, combine ground round, onion, green bell pepper, salt, and Italian seasoning. Heat the skillet to 325°F. Cook and stir, breaking up meat, for 5 or 6 minutes or until meat is browned. Unplug the skillet, drain, and replug in.

4. Stir tomato sauce, 1 cup water, corn, and black olives (if using) into the skillet. Bring to a boil, reduce heat to 200°F, cover, and simmer for 5 to 7 minutes or until corn is tender, stirring once or twice. Stir in pasta. Cook, uncovered, for 1 or 2 minutes, or until heated through and liquid is *reduced* as desired.

Class Notes

Reduce refers to boiling or simmering a broth or sauce to remove some of the water content, resulting in a more concentrated flavor and color.

Like Mom's Spaghetti and Meatballs $$

Don't be surprised if your roommates request this home-style favorite.

Yield: 2 servings
Prep time: 8 minutes
Cook time: 20 to 24 minutes
Serving size: 1 cup spaghetti with 5 meatballs and ½ cup sauce
Each serving has:
548 calories
105 calories from fat
12 g fat
4 g saturated fat
44 g protein
68 g carbohydrates

½ lb. ground round

¼ cup plain breadcrumbs

2 TB. minced yellow onions

2 eggs, at room temperature, or equivalent fat-free pasteurized refrigerated egg product

2 TB. fat-free milk

1 tsp. Worcestershire sauce

¼ tsp. each salt and ground black pepper

4 cups hot water

4 oz. whole-wheat thin spaghetti

1 cup prepared spaghetti sauce

1. In a large bowl, combine ground round, breadcrumbs, onions, eggs, milk, Worcestershire sauce, salt, and pepper. Using your hands, thoroughly mix until well blended, and shape into 1½-inch meatballs.

2. Arrange meatballs in a circle with 1 meatball in the center of an 8-inch microwave-safe pie plate or other round dish. Cook on high power for 4½ to 5½ minutes, turning meatballs over and exchanging center meatball with most browned meatball from circle halfway through cooking time, rotating if needed. Transfer to a paper towel–lined microwave-safe plate. Cover and blot with additional paper towels. Verify meatballs are done (160°F on a food thermometer) before serving.

3. Pour water into a 1½-quart microwave-safe glass bowl. Cook on high power for 8 or 9 minutes or until boiling. Add spaghetti, breaking as necessary to fit the bowl. Cook on high power for 5 or 6 minutes or until done. Drain.

4. Pour spaghetti sauce into a 3-cup microwave-safe glass bowl, and cover with plastic wrap, venting. Cook on high power for 2 or 3 minutes, stirring halfway through cooking time, rotating if needed.

5. Serve spaghetti sauce over spaghetti and meatballs, reheating meatballs for 20 to 30 seconds on high power, if necessary.

Crowd-Pleasing Mac and Dogs $

Easy and inexpensive, this tomato-sauce dish can be zipped up with a sprinkling of grated Parmesan cheese.

3½ cups water

1½ cups uncooked multi-grain elbow macaroni

6 reduced-fat hot dogs

1 tsp. extra-virgin olive oil

¼ cup chopped yellow onions

1 tsp. drained minced garlic

1 (10.75-oz.) can tomato soup

½ soup can water

1 tsp. dried oregano or Italian seasoning

Pinch salt and ground black pepper

Yield: 6 servings
Prep time: 2 minutes
Cook time: 17 to 19 minutes
Serving size: 1 cup
Each serving has:
319 calories
38 calories from fat
4 g fat
1 g saturated fat
18 g protein
53 g carbohydrates

1. Pour 3½ cups water into a 1-quart microwave-safe glass bowl, and cook on high power for 8 or 9 minutes or until boiling. Add macaroni and cook on high power for 7 or 8 minutes or until done. Drain.

2. Meanwhile, on a cutting board with a sharp knife, slice hot dogs into bite-size pieces.

3. Heat an 11-inch nonstick electric skillet to 325°F. Add olive oil and heat for 1 minute. Add hot dogs, onions, and garlic. Cook and stir for 3 to 5 minutes or until hot dogs are browned and onions are translucent. Add tomato soup, ½ soup can water, oregano, salt, and pepper, and stir to combine. Reduce heat and simmer while macaroni cooks, stirring occasionally.

4. Add macaroni when done. Stir to coat, and cook for 2 minutes or until heated through.

 **Variation:** For stovetop preparation, cook macaroni in a saucepan according to the package directions. Heat olive oil in a large nonstick skillet over medium-low to medium heat. Proceed with the recipe as directed.

Learning Curve _____

Watch for the word *meanwhile* in recipes. You can save time by preparing one portion of the dish as another preparation continues without your hands-on attention.

Smothered Pork Steaks over Noodles $

Don't let the longer cooking time scare you from trying this recipe. The bulk of that time is hands-off, and longer cooking tenderizes inexpensive cuts of meat.

Yield: 2 servings
Prep time: 12 minutes
Cook time: 65 minutes
Serving size: 1½ cups noodles with ½ of pork mixture
Each serving has:
640 calories
140 calories from fat
16 g fat
5 g saturated fat
47 g protein
76 g carbohydrates

½ **large tomato**

½ **medium green bell pepper**

½ **small yellow onion**

1 lb. pork shoulder blade steak

1 (8-oz.) can tomato sauce

¼ **tsp. each salt and ground black pepper**

4 cups hot water

3 cups uncooked yolk-free extra-wide whole-wheat egg noodles

1. On a cutting board with a sharp knife, cut tomato into wedges. Cut green bell pepper into strips. Cut onion into thin wedges.

2. On another cutting board with another sharp knife, trim fat strips and bone from pork steak, cutting steak into serving pieces.

3. Heat an 11-inch nonstick electric skillet to 400°F. Spray with nonstick cooking spray, if desired. Add pork steak pieces, and quickly brown for 1 minute on each side or until each side is just browned. Turn off heat.

4. Spoon tomato sauce over pork steak, lifting pieces to allow tomato sauce under pieces to prevent sticking during cooking. Scatter tomato wedges, green bell pepper strips, and onion wedges over pork steak pieces. Evenly sprinkle salt and pepper over all. Return heat to 400°F, cover, and bring to a boil. Reduce heat to simmer and cook, covered, for 1 hour or until meat is done (170°F on a food thermometer for well done).

5. Meanwhile, pour 4 cups hot water into a 1½-quart microwave-safe glass bowl. Cook on high power for 8 or 9 minutes or until boiling. Stir in noodles, and cook on high power for 6 or 7 minutes or until done. Drain. Serve pork steak mixture over noodles.

Variation: For stovetop preparation, follow the directions given for pork steak, using a large skillet with a lid. Cook noodles in a saucepan according to the package directions.

Lecture Hall

Prevent cross-contamination by keeping the work surfaces and utensils used for meat preparation separate from those used for other preparations, such as vegetable cutting. Also, remember to wash everything in hot, soapy water—including your hands.

Saucy Slow-Cooker Chops $$$

Five ingredients, a 10-minute prep time, and dinner is ready when you are. Add a tossed salad, and serve the pork chops over rice for a delicious meal.

1 medium yellow onion

½ medium green bell pepper

4 (¾-in.-thick) boneless center-cut pork chops

¼ cup firmly packed light brown sugar

½ cup ketchup

Yield: *4 servings*
Prep time: 10 minutes
Cook time: 6 to 8 hours
Serving size: 1 pork chop with ¼ of sauce
Each serving has:
233 calories
46 calories from fat
5 g fat
2 g saturated fat
22.5 g protein
24 g carbohydrates

1. On a cutting board with a sharp knife, slice onion and cut green bell pepper into strips. Place in a 4-quart slow cooker coated with nonstick cooking spray, separating onion into rings.

2. On a cutting board with a sharp knife (different board and knife or thoroughly cleaned), trim fat from pork chops. Add pork chops to the slow cooker over vegetables.

3. In a small bowl, stir brown sugar into ketchup until mixed. Pour into the slow cooker over pork chops. Cover and cook on low heat for 6 to 8 hours or until meat is done (170°F on a food thermometer for well done).

Learning Curve

If you have less time available when slow cooking, a recipe giving the cooking time for low heat can usually be cooked on high heat for about half the time.

Grilled Pork Chops with Sweet-Tart Apple Salsa *$$$*

Pork pairs up perfectly with fruit, but you can grill these chops to serve with the salsa or chutney of your choice.

Yield: 4 servings
Prep time: 5 minutes
Chill time: 30 minutes
Cook time: 10 minutes
Serving size: 1 pork chop with ⅓ cup salsa

Each serving has:
195 calories
46 calories from fat
5 g fat
2 g saturated fat
22 g protein
15 g carbohydrates

¼ cup apple juice

1 medium tart eating apple (Granny Smith, Golden Delicious, etc.)

¼ cup diced sweet onions

¼ cup golden or dark raisins

¼ tsp. ground cinnamon

Pinch ground nutmeg

4 (¾-in.-thick) boneless center-cut pork chops

¼ tsp. each salt and ground black pepper

1. Pour apple juice into a medium bowl with a lid.

2. On a cutting board with a sharp knife, dice apple, discarding core. Add apple to apple juice as you cut to prevent discoloration. Stir in sweet onions and raisins. Add cinnamon and nutmeg, and stir until evenly coated. Cover and chill for at least 30 minutes.

3. Meanwhile, coat the grill rack or a broiler pan with nonstick cooking spray. Heat grill or broiler to high.

4. On a cutting board with a sharp knife (different board and knife or thoroughly cleaned), trim excess fat from pork chops. Place pork chops on a plate or on the prepared broiler pan. Evenly sprinkle salt and pepper over pork chops on both sides.

5. Transfer pork chops to the grill rack or place the broiler pan 4 to 6 inches from the heat. Grill or broil for 10 minutes, turning and rearranging halfway through cooking time. Let stand for 1 or 2 minutes. Check for doneness (170°F on a food thermometer) before serving alongside salsa.

Learning Curve

It's safe to serve cuts of pork (not ground pork) at medium doneness—160°F on a food thermometer—if you prefer.

Chapter 9

Poultry Plates

In This Chapter

- ◆ Choosing chicken and turkey
- ◆ Freezing poultry for future use
- ◆ Preparing poultry with safety in mind

Tender and juicy, poultry is the perfect palette for many cooks. Its mild flavor allows success with any number of seasonings, other meats, vegetables, and/or fruits. With such taste variations, its low cost, and lean protein choices, you can serve poultry regularly.

Poultry Tutorial

When shopping, make the meat department your last stop before the checkout to ensure safety. At the meat department, check out the offerings. Poultry packaged in clear plastic should have a consistent coloring without bruising or other discolorations. Fat may appear white to pale yellow. Yellow-colored chickens aren't of a better quality than those whose skin looks creamy white; the difference in coloring only indicates the diet the chicken ate. Test the firmness of the poultry's flesh, if possible. And it never hurts to give a package a good whiff to check for any foul odors.

Look for a sell-by or use-by date, and prepare the poultry within 1 week of a sell-by date and before the use-by date. Fresh poultry can be held for 2 days if quickly stored in the coldest part of the refrigerator. If you won't be cooking the poultry soon, freeze it, stopping the clock ticking on any stamped dates.

Of Higher Learning

While hormones aren't used in chickens, antibiotics can be administered for disease prevention. Requirements mandate an antibiotic-free period before slaughter to clear any traces from the chicken's system.

To freeze, place serving-size portions in resealable plastic freezer bags. Chicken parts, turkey cuts, and ground poultry can be frozen for 4 to 6 months. Label the freezer bags carefully to ensure safety. If you want fast from fridge preparation, trim the poultry of excess fat before freezing. Some cooks prefer to remove the fat while the flesh is still partially frozen, as it may be easier.

If you've purchased skin-on poultry—oftentimes it's less expensive—you can remove the skin before freezing, before cooking, or after cooking. The skin on a fresh, uncooked chicken is easier to remove while the bone is in. Some cooks like to prepare chicken with the skin on to retain moisture. As long as you remove the skin before serving, you won't be adding any fat or calories to the chicken.

Poultry Safety

When working with poultry for freezing or cooking, guard against cross-contamination. Wash your hands before and after. Wash the work surfaces, cutting board, utensils, and everything else that comes in contact with the raw poultry, too.

Safety continues when thawing frozen poultry. Remember, do not thaw food on the countertop. Move your freezer bag from the freezer to the refrigerator for easy thawing. The microwave can make quick work of defrosting. Follow the manufacturer's directions, turning, rotating, and redistributing the poultry as necessary. Poultry parts should be arranged with the meatiest portions to the outside of a circle. Immediately cook any poultry thawed in the microwave. Meats cannot be partially cooked and then held to finish cooking later, as harmful bacteria will not have been destroyed.

Two-Ingredient Dude Ranch Chicken Breast *$*

Serve this tender chicken breast as a main course, or cut it into strips to serve over mixed greens with salad fixings.

1 (3-oz.) boneless, skinless chicken breast half	**¼ cup fat-free ranch salad dressing**

1. Trim fat from chicken breast and place in a quart-size resealable plastic bag. Pour salad dressing into the bag. Close the bag, forcing out air and coating chicken with salad dressing. Chill for at least 30 minutes or up to 8 hours.

2. Heat a dual-contact indoor electric grill. When heated, remove chicken from salad dressing, allowing any extra salad dressing to drip off and blotting excess salad dressing with a paper towel, if necessary, as any thick salad dressing will char. Discard plastic bag and extra dressing.

3. Grill chicken for 5 minutes, or until done (170°F on a food thermometer).

Yield: 1 serving
Prep time: 3 minutes
Chill time: 30 minutes to 8 hours
Cook time: 5 minutes
Each serving has:
118 calories
26 calories from fat
3 g fat
1 g saturated fat
18 g protein
4 g carbohydrates

Lecture Hall

Be sure to use only fat-free salad dressing to keep the chicken from burning on the surface under the direct heat contact.

Crunchy Dijon Chicken Breasts $$

While you're making dinner and cooking chicken already, bake two additional chicken breast halves to have on hand for later.

Yield: 2 servings	

Prep time: 6 minutes

Cook time: 20 to 25 minutes

Serving size: 1 chicken breast half

Each serving has:

240 calories

29 calories from fat

3 g fat

1 g saturated fat

42 g protein

5 g carbohydrates

3 TB. plain breadcrumbs

1½ TB. grated Parmesan cheese

¼ tsp. *Italian seasoning*

⅛ tsp. garlic powder

⅛ tsp. ground black pepper

4 (3-oz.) boneless, skinless chicken breast halves

2 TB. Dijon mustard

1. Preheat the oven to 425°F. Coat a medium or large baking sheet with nonstick cooking spray.

2. In an 8-inch pie plate or other shallow dish, combine breadcrumbs, cheese, Italian seasoning, garlic powder, and pepper. Stir to mix, and set aside.

3. On a cutting board with a sharp knife, trim excess fat from chicken breast halves. Spread 1 tablespoon Dijon mustard over each of 2 chicken breast halves. Dredge mustard-coated chicken breast halves in breadcrumb mixture to coat.

4. Arrange all 4 chicken breast halves on the baking sheet, and bake in the center of the oven for 20 to 25 minutes or until done (170°F on a food thermometer). Serve coated chicken breast halves, and cool and refrigerate plain chicken breast halves for use in another recipe.

Variation: If you don't have Italian seasoning, you can substitute ⅛ teaspoon dried basil plus ⅛ teaspoon dried oregano.

Class Notes

Italian seasoning is a blend of dried herbs, usually basil, oregano, rosemary, and thyme.

Hot Grilled Thighs

Brace yourself for an extra-spicy kick when you bite into these thighs—and then be prepared to enjoy them thoroughly.

2 lb. chicken thighs

1 TB. crushed red pepper flakes

1 TB. ground ginger

1 tsp. anise seeds

1 tsp. ground black pepper

¾ tsp. ground cloves

½ tsp. ground white pepper (optional)

1 TB. honey

Yield: 4 servings
Prep time: 15 minutes
Chill time: 30 minutes
Cook time: 10 to 12 minutes
Serving size: 1 thigh
Each serving has:
295 calories
82 calories from fat
9 g fat
2 g saturated fat
45 g protein
6 g carbohydrates

1. Remove skin from chicken thighs, and pull meat from the bones. Rinse skinned and boned chicken thighs under running water, and pat dry with paper towels.

2. In an 8-inch pie plate or other shallow dish, combine crushed red pepper flakes, ginger, anise seeds, black pepper, ground cloves, and white pepper (if using), and stir to blend. Stir in honey until well blended.

3. Pull chicken thighs through honey mixture to coat lightly on both sides. Place coated chicken thighs on a baking sheet, and chill for at least 30 minutes.

4. Meanwhile, coat the grill rack with nonstick spray and heat the grill to high. Transfer chicken thighs to the grill, cover, and grill for 10 to 12 minutes or until done (180°F on a food thermometer), turning and rearranging halfway through the cooking time.

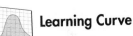

Learning Curve

If you prefer your food a bit less spicy, you can adjust the spices in this and any other recipe.

Down-Home Chicken and Stuffing $$

Serve this hearty stuffing alongside mashed potatoes with gravy.

Yield: 4 servings
Prep time: 2 minutes
Cook time: 4 to 6 hours
Serving size: 1 heaping cup
Each serving has:
289 calories
38 calories from fat
4 g fat
1 g saturated fat
20.5 g protein
40.5 g carbohydrates

1 (10-oz.) can chunk chicken breast, drained

1 (6-oz.) pkg. stuffing mix for chicken

1½ cups fat-free milk

1 cup fat-free, less-sodium chicken broth

¼ cup pasteurized refrigerated egg product or 2 large eggs

1. Coat a 3½- to 4-quart slow cooker with nonstick cooking spray. Add chicken and stuffing mix to the slow cooker and stir.

2. In a small bowl, combine milk, broth, and egg product until mixed. (If using eggs, stir until eggs are blended.) Pour into the slow cooker over chicken and stuffing mix, and gently stir to mix.

3. Cover and cook on low heat for 4 to 6 hours or until heated through and liquid is absorbed.

Learning Curve

If you're a careful measurer, you can pour all the liquid ingredients into a liquid measuring cup together to save on a little cleanup. If you pour in a little too much, though, you can't correct the measurement, and instead of saving on cleanup, you might waste ingredients.

Lemony Chicken and Rice Casserole $$$

This easy-mix one-dish meal is complimented by a tossed green salad.

½ **medium zucchini squash**

¼ **medium red bell pepper**

1½ **tsp. cornstarch**

¼ **tsp. garlic powder**

¾ **cup fat-free, less-sodium chicken broth**

2 **TB. lemon juice**

¾ **cup uncooked instant brown rice**

1 **(7-oz.) pouch ready-to-use chunk chicken breast**

Yield: 2 servings		
Prep time: 3 minutes		
Cook time: 15 to 17 minutes		
Serving size: 1 cup		
Each serving has:		
325 calories		
38 calories from fat		
4 g fat		
1 g saturated fat		
31 g protein		
39 g carbohydrates		

1. On a cutting board with a sharp knife, *dice* zucchini and red bell pepper. Place in a 3-cup microwave-safe glass bowl, cover tightly with plastic wrap (do not vent), and cook on high power for 3 or 4 minutes or until vegetables are crisp-tender.

2. Meanwhile, combine cornstarch, garlic powder, broth, and lemon juice in a small bowl, and stir just until smooth.

3. When vegetables are done, carefully pull back the plastic wrap. Briefly stir broth mixture to mix and pour onto vegetables. Stir in rice to moisten. Re-cover with plastic wrap, venting, and cook on high power for 6 or 7 minutes or until rice is tender. Remove the bowl from the microwave, covering with plastic wrap tightly. Let stand for 5 minutes.

4. Stir chicken into rice mixture. Re-cover with plastic wrap, venting. Cook on high power for 30 to 60 seconds, or until heated through.

Class Notes

Dice is a cooking directive that indicates you should cut the ingredient into small squares of about ¼ inch.

Creamy Turkey and Veggie Pasta $$

This hearty, satisfying casserole dish prepared in the microwave makes for good dorm-room eating.

Yield: 2 servings

Prep time: 5 minutes

Cook time: 25 to 30 minutes

Serving size: 1¼ cups

Each serving has:

347 calories

80 calories from fat

9 g fat

2 g saturated fat

32 g protein

37 g carbohydrates

3 cups hot water

¾ cup uncooked whole-wheat rotini pasta

1 cup frozen mixed vegetables

1 TB. all-purpose flour

½ cup fat-free milk

½ tsp. instant chicken bouillon granules

Pinch ground black pepper

Pinch garlic powder

½ lb. 93-percent-lean ground turkey

1. Pour water into a 1-quart microwave-safe round glass dish, and cook on high power for 6 or 7 minutes or until boiling. Add pasta, and cook on high power for 13 to 15 minutes or until done.

2. Meanwhile, measure frozen vegetables into a colander and run under warm tap water to defrost. Drain pasta into the colander over vegetables, and set aside.

3. Combine flour and about ⅓ of milk in a small container with a tight-fitting lid, and shake well until smooth. Pour into the dish used to cook the pasta. Add remaining milk, bouillon granules, pepper, and garlic powder, and stir to blend. Set aside.

4. Place ground turkey into a 3-cup microwave-safe glass bowl, and cook on high power for 1 to 1½ minutes. Stir to break up meat and redistribute. Cook on high power for 1 to 1½ minutes, or until nearly all of meat is browned. Drain well and blot ground turkey with paper towels. (All meat should be browned now.)

5. Stir milk mixture again to blend, cook on high power for 1 to 1½ minutes, and stir and rotate if needed. Cook on high power for 1 to 1½ minutes or until thickened. Stir. Add ground turkey, pasta, and vegetables, and stir until evenly coated. Cook on high power for 2 minutes or until heated through and vegetables are tender, stirring halfway through the cooking time and rotating if needed.

Lecture Hall

Note the milk is divided in this recipe, so don't just dump it all in at the first mention. Add part to the cornstarch and later pour in the remainder.

Turkey-Topped Tater

A fluffy potato topped with crisp-tender onions and peppers and cheesy turkey is perfect with a dollop of sour cream.

1 large all-purpose potato

¼ lb. 93-percent-lean ground turkey

2 TB. diced yellow onions

2 TB. diced green bell pepper

⅛ tsp. dried thyme

Pinch ground black pepper

¼ tsp. Worcestershire sauce

2 tsp. light butter with canola oil

3 TB. 2-percent-milk shredded sharp cheddar cheese

Yield: 1 serving
Prep time: 3 minutes
Cook time: 7 or 8 minutes
Each serving has:
393 calories
129 calories from fat
14 g fat
5 g saturated fat
30 g protein
36 g carbohydrates

1. Scrub potato and poke all over with the tines of a fork. Place on a microwave-safe plate, and cook on high power for 3 or 4 minutes. Turn potato over and cook on high power for 2 minutes more or until fork-tender. Remove from the microwave and let stand while you prepare turkey mixture.

2. While potato cooks, crumble ground turkey on a microwave-safe plate lined with a triple layer of white paper towels. Scatter onions and green bell pepper over turkey. Sprinkle on thyme and pepper. Add Worcestershire sauce, being careful to keep on turkey without dripping onto toweling. Cook on high power for 1½ to 2 minutes or just until turkey appears browned. Remove from the microwave, break up turkey with a fork, and transfer to a double layer of paper towels, blotting turkey dry. Let stand.

3. Split potato and fluff pulp with a fork. Work butter into pulp. Spoon turkey mixture over potato, and sprinkle cheese over top. Cook on high power for 30 to 60 seconds or until cheese starts to melt and turkey is done (165°F on a food thermometer).

Variation: If you prefer the onions and bell peppers to be tender, place them in a small microwave-safe bowl first and cover them tightly with plastic wrap. (Do not vent.) Cook on high power for 1 or 2 minutes or until nearly tender. Proceed with recipe as directed.

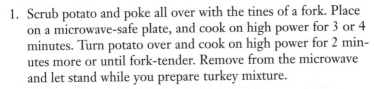

Learning Curve

If you purchase ground turkey in a 1- to 1¼-pound package, simply divide it into ¼-pound servings to freeze. Resealable plastic freezer bags are great for this. They take up little space, and you can write the contents and date right on the bag.

Pizza-Topped Pasta $$$

Yield: 1 serving
Prep time: 2 minutes
Cook time: 21 to 24 minutes
Each serving has:
407 calories
101 calories from fat
11 g fat
3 g saturated fat
20 g protein
57 g carbohydrates

All the best pizza-pie toppings spooned over rotini create a delicious single-serve dish.

4 cups hot water

¾ cup uncooked whole-wheat rotini pasta

2 tsp. extra-virgin olive oil

1 small tomato

½ small yellow onion

½ small green bell pepper

2 TB. sliced black olives (optional)

12 slices turkey pepperoni

⅛ tsp. each salt and ground black pepper

2 or 3 TB. finely shredded low-fat mozzarella cheese

1. Pour water into a 6-cup microwave-safe glass bowl, and cook on high power for 8 or 9 minutes or until boiling. Add pasta, and cook on high power for 13 to 15 minutes or until done. Drain pasta, drizzle on 1 teaspoon olive oil, and toss to coat.

2. Meanwhile, on a cutting board with a sharp knife, chop tomato into ½-inch squares. Chop onion into ½-inch squares. Remove stem, seeds, and ribs (white membranes) from green bell pepper, and chop pepper into ½-inch squares.

3. Heat an 11-inch nonstick electric skillet to 350°F. Heat remaining 1 teaspoon olive oil for 1 minute and then add onion, green bell pepper, and black olives (if using) and sauté for 3 to 5 minutes or until onion is *translucent*. Add turkey pepperoni slices, stir, and cook for 1 or 2 minutes. Stir in tomato, salt, and pepper, and cook and stir for 1 or 2 minutes. Reduce heat and simmer for 3 to 5 minutes or until heated through.

4. Spoon tomato mixture over pasta, and sprinkle cheese over top to serve.

Learning Curve

Translucent is a cooking visual that requires the ingredient to be clear-looking or partially transparent.

Chapter 10

Fish Dishes

In This Chapter

- Buying and keeping fish fresh
- Cooking a quick and nutritious fish dish
- Safe fish consumption guidelines

Fish is healthful, fast to fix, and great-tasting. With a few of the recipes in this chapter, you might soon find yourself easily meeting the current dietary guidelines of eating fish three times a week.

Even if you don't have easy access to fresh fish, you'll find great varieties of individually frozen fish. Store the package in your freezer and then move a single fillet to the refrigerator to thaw when you need it. You'll have a meal in minutes—perfect for your busy lifestyle!

Gone Fishing

When you're in the market for fresh fish, trust your senses. If a cut fish is tinged around the edges or shows any discoloration, pass it up. The flesh should look translucent and shiny. Press the flesh, or ask the fish monger to; the indentation should spring back. Pass up soft or mushy fish. Fresh fish should have a mild, clean smell.

Immediately refrigerate or prepare your purchase for freezing when you get home. If the fish was marked as previously frozen—an identification that must be made by the vendor—you should cook it that day or the next day at the latest. Previously frozen fish cannot be refrozen.

Frozen fish is often a good value. Watch for ice crystals that may indicate partial thawing and refreezing. To thaw fish you've frozen or purchased frozen, place it in the refrigerator for several hours or overnight.

Fish Cooking School

Cooking fish requires the same safe handling as for other meats. Wash your hands, cutting board, utensils, and dishes with hot, soapy water. Don't place cooked fish back on a plate that held the raw fish.

When cooking, you can check fish for doneness by sight. The flesh will have an opaque appearance, and finfish will flake easily with a fork. As a general rule, you'll need to bake or broil fish for about 10 minutes per each inch of thickness at the thickest point. Don't become overly cautious and cook it just a bit longer. The fish will be overdone, rubbery, and chewy. A fillet that is flaking on its own is overcooked. If a fillet thins dramatically at the ends, you can tuck the ends under while cooking to even out the thickness.

Fish and Health

Fish can provide lean protein, and the fat in oily fish, such as salmon, tuna, and sardines, offers omega-3 essential fatty acids that help heart health. Some fish may adversely affect your health with its high mercury content. Healthy adults should limit shark, swordfish, king mackerel, and tilefish to one serving each month.

Much has been debated over salmon, wild versus farmed. Wild salmon is more costly but does go on sale occasionally. Processed wild salmon is an affordable solution—and a convenient fix in ready-to-use, drain-free pouches—if you're shying away from farmed salmon. Advisories are always changing, so you'll need to keep yourself updated.

Flounder in a Flash $$

A mildly seasoned coating for a mildly flavored fish allows you to pair this entrée with the bold-tasting side dishes you like.

1½ TB. plain breadcrumbs	Pinch ground black pepper
½ tsp. grated Parmesan cheese	1 tsp. extra-virgin olive oil
¼ tsp. dried basil or ¾ tsp. chopped fresh basil	2 (3-oz.) *fillets* flounder

Yield: 2 servings
Prep time: 5 minutes
Cook time: 2 or 3 minutes
Serving size: 1 fillet
Each serving has:
146 calories
73 calories from fat
8 g fat
2 g saturated fat
15 g protein
2.5 g carbohydrates

1. On a sheet of waxed paper or a plate, combine breadcrumbs, Parmesan cheese, basil, and pepper. Stir to mix (you can use your fingers).

2. Rub ½ teaspoon olive oil over both sides of each fillet. *Dredge* each side of each fillet in breadcrumb mixture to coat lightly. Place each fillet on a white paper towel, fold over paper towel to enclose, and place seam side down on a microwave-safe plate.

3. Cook on high power for 2 or 3 minutes. Let stand, covered, for 2 minutes. Check doneness by flaking with a fork. Serve immediately.

Class Notes

Fillet refers to a flat, boneless slice of fish. Most often, *filet* refers to a piece of meat, like filet mignon.

Dredge is the action of covering a piece of food with a dry ingredient or mixture of ingredients such as seasoned flour or cornmeal. To coat these fish fillets, pull them through the breadcrumb mixture, allowing it to adhere to the moist fillets.

Barbecue Salmon $$$

The familiar flavor of salmon is complimented tastefully and effortlessly with your favorite barbecue sauce.

Yield: 2 servings
Prep time: 2 minutes
Cook time: 11 to 16 minutes
Serving size: 4 ounces
Each serving has:
219 calories
113 calories from fat
13 g fat
2.5 g saturated fat
23 g protein
2 g carbohydrates

½ **lb. skin-on salmon fillet**

3 TB. prepared barbecue sauce

1. Heat broiler. Coat a broiler pan with nonstick cooking spray.

2. Place salmon skin side down on the broiler pan, and broil about 4 to 6 inches from heat for 10 minutes per each inch of thickness or until fish flakes easily with a fork.

3. Spread barbecue sauce over top of salmon and broil for 1 minute or until bubbly. Immediately remove from broiler. To serve, cut salmon in half widthwise without cutting through skin. Carefully slide a flat spatula between salmon and skin to remove.

Chive and Garlic Tilapia $$

Add a squeeze of lemon juice, if you like, to this fast and healthful main course.

Yield: 1 serving
Prep time: 2 minutes
Cook time: 3 or 4 minutes
Each serving has:
69 calories
11 calories from fat
1 g fat
0 g saturated fat
14 g protein
0 g carbohydrates

1 (2.5-oz.) fillet tilapia

1 tsp. water

Pinch salt and ground black pepper

¼ **tsp. dried chives or ¾ tsp. chopped fresh chives**

¼ **tsp. drained minced garlic**

1. Place tilapia fillet in a small microwave-safe glass dish just large enough to hold it. Add water to the dish, and sprinkle salt and pepper over tilapia. Sprinkle chives and garlic over tilapia. Cover with plastic wrap, venting.

2. Cook on high power for 45 to 90 seconds or until tilapia just appears opaque. Let stand, covered, for 2 minutes. Check for doneness by flaking with a fork. Return the dish to the microwave for very short time intervals, 10 or 15 seconds, if necessary. Serve immediately.

Lemon-Butter Tilapia $$

Lemon juice and light butter coat this mild fillet deliciously.

1 tsp. light butter with canola oil	Salt and ground black pepper
1 tsp. lemon juice	Pinch dried parsley flakes or chopped fresh parsley
1 (2.5-oz.) fillet tilapia	

Yield: 1 serving
Prep time: 3 minutes
Cook time: 3 minutes
Each serving has:
87 calories
26 calories from fat
3 g fat
1 g saturated fat
14 g protein
1 g carbohydrates

1. Preheat the broiler. Coat a broiler pan with nonstick cooking spray.

2. In a very small bowl, combine light butter and lemon juice, and stir to blend. Place tilapia on the broiler pan. Spread ½ of butter mixture over tilapia, turn tilapia over, and spread remaining butter mixture over the other side. Broil 4 to 6 inches from heat for 3 minutes or just until fish flakes easily with a fork.

3. Lightly season with salt and pepper, and sprinkle on parsley flakes to color. Serve immediately.

Variation: To prepare this dish in the microwave, prepare the tilapia for cooking as directed, placing it in a small microwave-safe glass dish just large enough to hold it. Cover with plastic wrap, venting. Cook on high power for 45 to 90 seconds or until tilapia just appears opaque. Let stand, covered, for 2 minutes. Check for doneness by flaking with a fork.

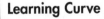

Learning Curve _____

Purchase a package of individually frozen tilapia fillets to have on hand. Thaw a single fillet to enjoy this flavorful and fast fish dish. You can assemble the ingredients while the broiler preheats.

Au Gratin Potatoes with Tuna and Green Beans ✄

This pantry-shelf dinner saves the day when there's nothing in the fridge.

Yield: 4 servings	
Prep time: 5 minutes	
Cook time: 25 minutes	
Serving size: 1 cup	
Each serving has:	
78 calories	
15 calories from fat	
2 g fat	
1 g saturated fat	
7 g protein	
9 g carbohydrates	

1 (4.9-oz.) pkg. au gratin potato mix or other flavored potato mix

1 (14.5-oz.) can *no-salt-added* green beans, drained

1 (3-oz.) pouch ready-to-use light tuna in water

1. Preheat the oven according to the potato mix package directions. Coat a 1½-quart casserole dish with nonstick cooking spray.

2. Turn potatoes and sauce mix from the package into the dish. Add boiling water, milk, and light butter with canola oil as directed on the package.

3. Stir green beans and tuna into potato mixture. Bake according to the package directions, and let stand to thicken sauce. Serve hot.

Variation: To prepare in the microwave or on the stovetop, follow the package directions for the appropriate method, stirring in green beans and tuna before cooking.

Class Notes

No-salt-added is a term used to label a food made without the salt that's normally used in processing, but still contains the sodium that's a natural part of the food itself. Packaged potato mixes and tunas are both high in sodium, so if you can use no-salt-added green beans, which are easy to find, the finished dish won't taste too salty.

Creamy-Salmon-Stuffed Peppers $$$

Enjoy this fresh-tasting filling for tender bell peppers.

2 medium green bell peppers

¼ cup plain breadcrumbs

⅛ tsp. cayenne

1 (7.1-oz.) pouch ready-to-use boneless, skinless pink salmon

2 TB. *minced* onions

1 TB. minced celery

2 TB. reduced-fat mayonnaise

2 TB. fat-free pasteurized refrigerated egg product

1 tsp. Worcestershire sauce

Yield: 2 servings
Prep time: 5 minutes
Cook time: 12 to 14 minutes
Serving size: 1 bell pepper
Each serving has:
233 calories
58 calories from fat
6.5 g fat
2 g saturated fat
22 g protein
19 g carbohydrates

1. With a sharp knife, cut off tops of green bell peppers. Remove seeds and cut out ribs (white membranes). Place green bell peppers in a deep 1½-quart microwave-safe glass dish. Add enough water to the dish to measure halfway up green bell peppers. (Pour a little water into bell peppers to keep them from floating, if necessary.) Cover with plastic wrap, venting, and cook on high power for 5 or 6 minutes or until softened. Drain.

2. Meanwhile, in a medium bowl, stir breadcrumbs and cayenne together. Add salmon, onions, celery, mayonnaise, egg product, and Worcestershire sauce. Stir until mixed, and lightly spoon mixture evenly into green bell peppers. Re-cover with plastic wrap, venting. Cook on high power for 5 or 6 minutes or until heated through and green bell peppers are tender, rotating halfway through the cooking time, if needed. Let stand, covered, for 2 minutes before serving.

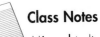

Class Notes

Minced indicates that the ingredient should be cut into very small pieces, only ⅛ inch or even smaller.

Basil Shrimp over Linguine $$$

Tossing the no-cook sauce with freshly cooked linguine makes for an easy, warm dinner dish you can garnish with shredded Parmesan cheese, if you like.

Yield: 2 servings
Prep time: 2 minutes
Cook time: 16 to 19 minutes
Serving size: 1½ cups
Each serving has:
343 calories
70 calories from fat
8 g fat
1 g saturated fat
18 g protein
48 g carbohydrates

3 cups hot water

4 oz. whole-wheat linguine

1 (3.53-oz.) pouch ready-to-serve premium shrimp

½ tsp. dried basil or ½ TB. chopped fresh basil

⅓ cup well-seasoned low-fat Italian salad dressing

1 *Roma* (plum) *tomato*

1. Pour water into a 1-quart microwave-safe round glass dish, and cook on high power for 6 or 7 minutes or until boiling. Add linguine, breaking as needed to fit into the dish. Cook on high power for 10 to 12 minutes or until done, rotating if needed.

2. Meanwhile, drain shrimp and turn into a medium serving bowl. Sprinkle basil over shrimp, and pour salad dressing over shrimp. Let stand while linguine cooks.

3. On a cutting board with a sharp knife, dice tomato into ¼-inch pieces.

4. Drain linguine and turn into shrimp mixture. Add tomato and toss until evenly coated. Serve immediately.

Class Notes _____

Roma tomatoes are small, elongated tomatoes often used for Italian dishes. Sometimes they're labeled *plum tomatoes*.

Linguine in Clam Sauce $$$

A flavorful pasta, the green bell pepper and onion highly season this dish, and the clams serve as a secondary depth of taste.

4 cups hot water

4 oz. uncooked whole-wheat linguine

1 small green bell pepper

1 small yellow onion

1½ to 2 TB. extra-virgin olive oil

1 tsp. drained minced garlic

⅓ cup clam juice

½ tsp. dried basil

⅛ tsp. crushed red pepper flakes

Pinch salt and ground black pepper

1 (6.5-oz.) can minced clams in clam juice, drained

Yield: 4 servings
Prep time: 1 minute
Cook time: 19 to 22 minutes
Serving size: 1 cup
Each serving has:
175 calories
29 calories from fat
3 g fat
0 g saturated fat
7 g protein
29 g carbohydrates

1. Pour hot water into a 1½-quart microwave-safe glass bowl, and cook on high power for 8 or 9 minutes or until boiling. Add linguine to boiling water, breaking up linguine as needed to fit into the bowl. Cook on high power for 10 to 12 minutes or until done. Drain.

2. Meanwhile, on a cutting board with a sharp knife, remove stem, seeds, and ribs (white membranes) from green bell pepper, and chop into ½-inch squares. Chop onion into ½-inch squares.

3. Heat an 11-inch nonstick electric skillet to 325°F. Add olive oil, and sauté green bell pepper, onion, and garlic for 3 or 4 minutes or until onion is translucent. Add clam juice, basil, crushed red pepper flakes, salt, and pepper, and stir. Bring to a boil. Reduce heat and simmer, uncovered, for 5 or 6 minutes or until vegetables are tender. Add clams and stir. Cook for 1 or 2 minutes more or just until heated through.

4. Turn linguine into clam sauce. Toss until evenly coated. Turn off heat. Serve immediately.

 Learning Curve

You'll find bottled clam juice and canned minced clams in the supermarket aisle near the canned tuna and other meats.

11

Vegetable Victuals

In This Chapter

- ◆ Choosing and caring for cutting boards
- ◆ Yummy vegetarian pasta dishes
- ◆ Filling veggie dishes

Cooking without cutting is nearly impossible. Cutting is the simple method cooks use for preparing ingredients for even cooking, allocating serving sizes, removing unwanted portions, releasing flavor, and more.

All the delicious vegetables you'll need for budget-friendly meatless meals benefit from proper preparation. So sharpen your knives, set out your cutting boards, and gather your ingredients. Magnificent meatless meals await you!

A Cut Above

You may be tempted to forego a cutting board for the kitchen counter. Don't. You'll only end up ruining the counter or your knife, and probably both. Hard surfaces such as the kitchen counter dull your knife blade. A cutting board protects the counter from scratches and gouge marks and keeps your knife sharp for as long as possible.

Cutting boards are essential tools in any kitchen. You'll find them available in any number of sizes, styles, and materials. Wood and plastic are your common choices.

Learning Curve

To make a mild bleach cleaning solution, carefully mix 1 quart water with 1 teaspoon regular bleach. Use paper towels for cleaning, and rinse the cutting board well with hot water afterward. (Never mix bleach with another cleaner, especially an ammonia-based one. Find a chemistry major to explain the production and dangers of chlorine gas.)

I suggest a plastic cutting board. Wooden cutting boards are more high maintenance if cared for properly. They should be seasoned with mineral oil before using and frequently thereafter. The wood shouldn't be soaked or run through the dishwasher, and it needs to dry completely before you put the cutting board away. Your busy lifestyle right now may be better suited to plastic cutting boards. You can soak these cutting boards, if needed, and wash them in the dishwasher, if they are dishwasher-safe (check before you buy). Should you not have access to a dishwasher, you might want to clean your cutting boards occasionally with a mild bleach solution.

What style of cutting board and how many cutting boards depends on your cooking habits. If you cook meats or fish, you probably need at least two cutting boards to prevent the possibility of cross-contamination. One cutting board should be designated for preparing meat and fish, and another can be used for vegetables, fruits, and other foods. Buy as large a size as you can comfortably wash and store. Choose two different colors if it helps you remember which cutting board is assigned to which task. Or you could buy one sturdy type for cutting meats and fish along with a flexible style for chopping veggies, fruits, and other foods so they can be easily funneled into your recipes.

Cutting boards absorb flavors and odors even with regular cleaning. If you chop a lot of onions and start noticing a vague flavor contamination in your apple slices, you might need a separate cutting board for fruits and other less-pungent foods. Maybe you can only eek out enough space to store one cutting board. Look for a style that allows you to cut on both sides, and then mark them—nontoxicly—so you can quickly identify the proper side for the job.

When you've finished using the cutting board, rinse it off in cool water. Clean it in the dishwasher if possible. Otherwise, wash it well in hot, soapy water, drying completely before storing. When your cutting board starts to look too cut up and shabby, it's time for a new one.

Quick-Blend Spinach Pesto $$

Spoon this bright green, fresh-tasting pesto over a cup of your favorite pasta, and add fresh Italian bread and a tossed salad for a filling meal.

¾ cup packed fresh spinach

¼ cup grated Parmesan cheese

½ tsp. dried basil or ½ TB. chopped fresh basil

¼ tsp. drained minced garlic or 1 small clove fresh garlic

Pinch salt

2 TB. extra-virgin olive oil

Yield: 2 servings
Prep time: 8 minutes
Serving size: 3 table-spoons
Each serving has:
153 calories
136 calories from fat
15 g fat
3.5 g saturated fat
4 g protein
1 g carbohydrates

1. Rinse spinach in running water. Spread on paper towels, and blot dry.

2. Add spinach, Parmesan cheese, basil, garlic, and salt to a blender. Cover and blend on high speed for 1 or 2 minutes or until thick and finely chopped. Stop blender and scrape down sides as necessary.

3. Remove the cap from the blender lid. Slowly add olive oil while pulsing on low speed, stopping to scrape down sides as necessary. Serve immediately.

Learning Curve

If you need to hold the pesto or have leftovers, refrigerate the pesto directly covered with plastic wrap, pressing the plastic wrap onto the surface of the pesto to help it retain its color.

Zippy Broccoli and Pasta $

Broccoli lovers will enjoy this simple-to-prepare pasta dish with the added zing of crushed red pepper flakes.

Yield: 1 serving
Prep time: 5 minutes
Cook time: 13 to 15 minutes
Each serving has:
296 calories
107 calories from fat
12 g fat
2 g saturated fat
11 g protein
39 g carbohydrates

1 stalk broccoli

½ tsp. drained minced garlic

¼ tsp. crushed red pepper flakes

½ cup uncooked whole-wheat rotini pasta

2½ cups water

2 tsp. extra-virgin olive oil

1 TB. grated *Parmesan cheese*

1. On a cutting board with a sharp knife, cut broccoli into small florets. (Reserve stalk for another recipe or discard.) Place broccoli florets in a round 1½-quart microwave-safe glass bowl. Add garlic, crushed red pepper flakes, and pasta. Pour in water. Cook on high power for 13 to 15 minutes or until broccoli and pasta are tender. Drain, reserving as much garlic and red pepper flakes as possible.

2. Drizzle olive oil over broccoli mixture, and toss to coat. Scatter Parmesan cheese over top to serve.

Class Notes

Parmesan cheese is a hard, dry, flavorful cheese commonly grated or shredded to season dishes, often Italian-style recipes. It keeps well when purchased as a chunk and can also be bought prepared for convenience. Try to fit a natural style of this cheese into your budget, as some of the canister-type Parmesans are not very flavorful.

Busy-Day Bean and Pasta Toss $$

The ingredients in this recipe combine to create a warm dinner dish that's nice with a sprinkling of grated Parmesan cheese.

4 cups hot water

1½ cups uncooked whole-wheat rotini pasta

1 (15.5-oz.) can cannellini beans, rinsed and drained

1 medium tomato

1 rib celery

½ small yellow onion or sweet onion

1½ TB. extra-virgin olive oil

1 TB. dried parsley flakes

⅛ tsp. each salt and ground black pepper

Yield: 4 servings
Prep time: 3 minutes
Cook time: 21 to 25 minutes
Serving size: 1¼ cups
Each serving has:
253 calories
57 calories from fat
6 g fat
1 g saturated fat
10 g protein
40 g carbohydrates

1. Pour water into a 1½-quart microwave-safe round glass dish. Cook on high power for 8 or 9 minutes or until boiling. Add pasta and cook on high power for 12 to 14 minutes or until nearly tender. Add beans and cook on high power for 1 or 2 minutes or until beans are heated through and pasta is done. Drain and return to the dish.

2. Meanwhile, on a cutting board with a sharp knife, chop tomato into ½-inch squares. Thinly slice celery. Dice onion.

3. Stir olive oil into pasta mixture. Add tomato, celery, onion, parsley, salt, and pepper, and stir until evenly distributed. Serve immediately.

Of Higher Learning

Rotini translates from Italian as "twists." These short, screw-like lengths of pasta may be affectionately known as "springs" from your childhood.

Shortcut Fettuccini Alfredo $$

This reduced-fat version of an indulgent favorite is still creamy and delicious—just without the guilt.

Yield: 2 servings
Prep time: 1 minute
Cook time: 19 to 22 minutes
Serving size: 1½ cups
Each serving has:
391 calories
78 calories from fat
9 g fat
3 g saturated fat
21 g protein
57 g carbohydrates

Learning Curve

If you prefer long strands of fettuccine and have access to a stovetop, be sure to use a large pot. As the fettuccine softens, it will become flexible enough to slip entirely into the boiling water.

4 cups hot water

4 oz. uncooked fettuccine

2 stalks broccoli

2 oz. fat-free cream cheese

½ cup fat-free milk

2 TB. light butter with canola oil

⅓ cup grated Parmesan cheese

⅛ tsp. ground black pepper or ground white pepper

Pinch ground nutmeg

1. Pour water into a 1½-quart microwave-safe glass dish, and cook on high power for 8 or 9 minutes or until boiling. Add fettuccine, breaking as needed to fit in the dish. Cook on high power for 5 minutes.

2. Meanwhile, on a cutting board with a sharp knife, cut broccoli into bite-size florets. (Discard stalks or reserve for another recipe.) Stir fettuccine, and add broccoli. Cook on high power for 5 to 7 minutes or until fettuccine is tender and broccoli is tender-crisp. Drain loosely.

3. Meanwhile, on a cutting board with a sharp knife, cut cream cheese into cubes. Set aside.

4. Coat an 11-inch nonstick electric skillet with nonstick cooking spray, and pour milk into the skillet. Set heat to 200°F. Add light butter and cook, stirring frequently, for 2 minutes or until melted. Add cream cheese and cook, stirring frequently, for 2 or 3 minutes or until melted.

5. Reduce heat to warm. Stir in Parmesan cheese, pepper, and nutmeg until smooth. Add fettuccine and broccoli, and stir until coated and heated through. Serve immediately.

Variation: Cut up about 1½ cups asparagus, green beans, bell peppers, cauliflower, or other vegetables to use in place of the broccoli. Add canned quartered artichoke hearts, whole or sliced mushrooms, or other canned items to the cooking fettuccine for the last 1 or 2 minutes.

Onion-Smothered Potato and Cheddar Pierogis $$

A Polish favorite, pierogis found in the freezer case make it easy to enjoy these potato-stuffed pasta turnovers anytime.

1 (16.9-oz.) pkg. frozen potato-and-cheddar pierogis	2 medium yellow onions
	2 TB. extra-virgin olive oil

Yield: 4 servings
Prep time: 5 minutes
Cook time: 10 to 12 minutes
Serving size: 3 pierogis with ¼ of onions
Each serving has:
250 calories
62 calories from fat
7 g fat
2 g saturated fat
6.5 g protein
40.5 g carbohydrates

1. In an 8×2-inch round microwave-safe glass dish, place frozen pierogis. Fill with water to within ½ inch of the top of the dish, and cook on high power for 5 minutes to defrost. Drain.

2. Meanwhile, on a cutting board with a sharp knife, slice onions and halve. Pour 1 tablespoon olive oil into an 11-inch electric skillet and heat to 300°F for 1 minute. Add onions, breaking into ring halves, and stir to coat onions with oil. Cook for 6 minutes, stirring frequently, or until onions are softened and lightly browned.

3. Push onions into a corner of the electric skillet. Add pierogis to skillet, shaking off any remaining water before adding, as it will cause splattering. Cook for 2 or 3 minutes or until the under-sides are browned as desired. *Drizzle* remaining 1 tablespoon olive oil over top of pierogis. Turn and cook the other sides for 2 or 3 minutes or until browned as desired. Serve pierogis topped with onions.

Class Notes

Drizzle refers to sprinkling drops of a liquid lightly over a food. In this dish, the small amount of olive oil needs to cover all the pierogis for even browning and easy release from the skillet.

Rice Medley Stuffed Peppers $$$$

Complete your meal by serving these hearty bell peppers with creamy mashed potatoes, spooning the extra rice mixture over the top.

Yield: 6 servings
Prep time: 8 minutes
Cook time: 6 to 8 hours
Serving size: 1 bell pepper half
Each serving has:
273 calories
34 calories from fat
4 g fat
2 g saturated fat
13 g protein
49 g carbohydrates

1 (28-oz.) can crushed tomatoes

2 cups cooked brown rice

1 (15-oz.) can dark red kidney beans, rinsed and drained

1 (10-oz.) pkg. frozen whole-kernel corn

1 cup 2-percent-milk sharp cheddar cheese

¼ cup diced yellow onions

2 tsp. Worcestershire sauce (optional)

⅛ tsp. hot pepper sauce or ground black pepper

3 medium to large green bell peppers

1. In a large bowl, combine crushed tomatoes, brown rice, kidney beans, corn, cheese, onions, Worcestershire sauce (if using), and hot pepper sauce. Stir until well mixed.

2. On a cutting board with a sharp knife, remove stems, seeds, and ribs (white membranes) from green bell peppers. Cut each bell pepper in half. Spoon rice mixture into bell pepper halves, arranging in a 3½- to 4-quart slow cooker coated with nonstick cooking spray. Spoon any remaining rice mixture into the slow cooker over stuffed peppers. Cover and cook on low heat for 6 to 8 hours or until bell peppers are tender.

Variation: For a pretty presentation, use 4 or 5 small bell peppers, leaving them whole instead of cutting them in half but still cutting off the tops, of course.

Learning Curve

Green bell peppers freeze nicely. If you've planned ahead, you can pull cleaned bell pepper halves from your freezer for quick assembly of this recipe. Just defrost the bell pepper halves under warm running water before stuffing.

Cayenne-Crusted Tofu Stir-Fry $$

Have a bed of hot cooked brown rice ready to receive this fast stir-fry filled with your favorite vegetables—or at least what needs to be used up from the fridge.

3 oz. extra-firm tofu

⅛ tsp. cayenne

2 TB. lemon juice

2 TB. reduced-sodium soy sauce

½ tsp. ground ginger

1 TB. extra-virgin olive oil

½ tsp. drained minced garlic

1 cup chopped or sliced vegetables (bell peppers, asparagus, broccoli, onions, carrots, celery, snow peas, bamboo shoots, etc.)

¼ tsp. sesame seeds (optional)

Yield: 1 serving	
Prep time: 3 minutes	
Cook time: 6 minutes	
Each serving has:	
217 calories	
105 calories from fat	
12 g fat	
2 g saturated fat	
13 g protein	
16.5 g carbohydrates	

1. On a cutting board, lay the block of tofu on it side. Gently sprinkle cayenne over exposed side of tofu, turning to coat all sides lightly. With a sharp knife, cut tofu into ¼-inch-thick slices. Set aside.

2. In a small bowl, stir together lemon juice, soy sauce, and ginger until blended. Set aside.

3. Add olive oil to a 6-quart nonstick electric wok. Set the wok to medium-high heat. Add garlic and sauté for 10 seconds. Add vegetables and *stir-fry* for 2 minutes or until vegetables are crisp-tender. Push vegetables aside.

4. Pour in lemon juice mixture and bring to a boil. Add tofu slices, and stir-fry for 1 minute. Sprinkle in sesame seeds (if using), and stir-fry for 1 minute. Turn off heat and serve immediately.

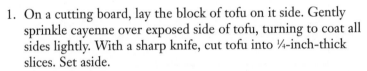

Class Notes _____

Stir-fry is a cooking instruction that directs you to move and turn small pieces of food as they cook in a wok or skillet over high heat. Preparation is essential to the success of a stir-fry dish. All the ingredients must be ready and nearby before you begin cooking, as you have to stir continually once you start.

Part 4

Studying Abroad

When you get bored with burgers and know you'll turn green if you have to munch on one more salad, broaden your horizons. Ethnic cuisines are popular in America because of their innovative flavors and novel tastes.

I've chosen four of the most requested foreign cuisines to highlight in Part 4—Mexican, Italian, Asian, and Mediterranean. Each region boasts a unique melding of flavors that can keep your taste buds tingling.

"Not quite honor roll yet, Dad, but I just made my first bouillabaisse."

12

Mexican Flourish

In This Chapter

- ◆ Serving up Mexican and Tex-Mex dishes with flair
- ◆ Using low-fat and fat-free dairy in your cooking
- ◆ Storing dairy products for flavor and quality

Mexican cuisine, along with its sister fare Tex-Mex, has firmly established itself in American cookery. You must take care, though, that its traditional fat content doesn't take hold as well. One source of fat in any number of popular Mexican dishes is dairy.

Regular dairy products are high in saturated fat. Saturated fat increases the amount of cholesterol in your blood that can clog your arteries and lead to heart disease. While the results of a fatty diet seem far into the future, changes you make now can make it easy to enjoy your life now and for many years to come. Substituting reduced-fat dairy products is one of the easiest dietary changes you can make.

Dairy Wisdom

Milk, many cheeses, yogurt, sour cream, and butter are all available in reduced-fat versions. The recipes in this cookbook call for reduced-fat or fat-free dairy products whenever possible, but you can substitute higher-fat products if you like. If the dairy product is served as is and not cooked, you can substitute a lower-fat or fat-free version, if you prefer.

Milk is commonly found in whole, 2-percent reduced-fat, 1-percent low-fat, and fat-free skim. Use the lowest-fat milk you can. You may find that fat-free milk is acceptable in cooking even if you don't prefer it for drinking. You can also choose reduced-fat or fat-free milk powder, evaporated milk, and sweetened condensed milk. Light is milk's enemy, destroying the effectiveness of added vitamin A, so buy milk in light-blocking cartons when possible. Don't keep the milk carton on the counter or table any longer than necessary.

> **Learning Curve**
>
> Baked goods need a certain amount of fat to be successful, so you'll need to use dairy products that contain some fat in those recipes.

You can find many varieties of cheeses in 2-percent-milk, low-fat, and fat-free versions. A number of the recipes included here call for 2-percent-milk cheeses. They're a good compromise when it comes to mouthfeel, texture, and melting qualities. For some recipes, a fat-free version won't be detected so you may as well save on the fat and calories. Cheeses will keep best if stored closed airtight in the crisper drawer of the fridge.

A number of recipe developers won't use fat-free dairy products, preferring the taste and performance of full-fat or just reduced-fat ingredients, especially sour cream and yogurt. I find that in many recipes, the trade-offs are worth the least amount of fat and calories. To keep sour cream, yogurt, and cottage cheese fresh, store them—securely closed—upside down in a cold part of the refrigerator for the most airtight barrier.

> **Learning Curve**
>
> Dairy is perishable, so buy the freshest products you can find, checking the sell-by or use-by dates on the packaging.

Baking recipes require a butter with at least 60 percent fat. All other recipes in this cookbook call for light butter with canola oil. Canola oil has a mild taste and is high in heart-healthful monounsaturated fat that makes the butter lower in total fat, cholesterol, and calories—as well as spreadable straight from the refrigerator. Keep butter covered and cold to preserve flavor and avoid picking up other refrigerator odors.

Sandwich-Style Chili Rellenos $$

The mild chilies lend a great taste to this melted cheese sandwich that's delicious served with salsa.

1 (4.5-oz.) can chopped green chilies, drained

4 slices whole-wheat bread

2 slices Colby Jack or Monterey Jack cheese

½ cup fat-free milk

¼ cup fat-free pasteurized refrigerated egg product or 1 large egg

Yield: 2 servings
Prep time: 5 minutes
Cook time: 8 to 10 minutes
Serving size: 1 sandwich
Each serving has:
285 calories
96 calories from fat
11 g fat
5 g saturated fat
13 g protein
32 g carbohydrates

1. Evenly divide green chilies between 2 slices bread, evenly covering the surface. Cover each with 1 cheese slice, and close sandwiches with remaining bread slices.

2. In a shallow 8-inch pie plate or other shallow dish, combine milk and egg product. Stir with a fork until well blended.

3. Heat an 11-inch nonstick electric skillet to 325°F, and coat with nonstick cooking spray. Dip sandwiches into milk mixture on both sides as for French toast, allowing excess liquid to drip back into the pie plate. (Discard any remaining milk mixture.)

4. Add sandwiches to the skillet, and cook on each side for 4 or 5 minutes or until browned as desired. (Coat the skillet with nonstick cooking spray again when turning sandwiches, if needed.) Serve immediately.

Learning Curve

You can drain canned ingredients easily without dirtying a colander or strainer. Using a can opener, cut around the top of the can almost all the way around, stopping before the lid is completely removed. Then, holding the lid against the ingredients, turn the can upside down over the sink to drain the liquid. You may need to jiggle the can a little to allow all the liquid to drain.

Quick-Mix Black Bean and Salsa Quesadillas $

Hot and cheesy, these Mexican-style tortilla sandwiches are quick and easy to mix up.

Yield: 3 servings
Prep time: 5 minutes
Cook time: 12 minutes
Serving size: 1 quesadilla
Each serving has:
375 calories
84 calories from fat
9 g fat
4 g saturated fat
17 g protein
55 g carbohydrates

1 (15-oz.) can black beans, rinsed and drained

3 TB. chunky-style salsa

¼ tsp. garlic powder

¼ tsp. onion powder

¼ tsp. dried oregano

⅛ tsp. hot pepper sauce

6 soft-taco-size whole-wheat tortillas

¾ cup 2-percent-milk Mexican blend cheese or sharp cheddar cheese

1. In a medium bowl, mash black beans with a fork until pasty. Add salsa, garlic powder, onion powder, oregano, and hot-pepper sauce. Stir until well blended.

2. To assemble quesadillas, spread about ½ cup black bean mixture over 3 tortillas, leaving a ½-inch margin around edges. Sprinkle ¼ cup cheese over black bean mixture on each tortilla. Top with remaining tortillas.

3. Heat an 11-inch electric skillet to 350°F, and coat with non-stick cooking spray. Add 1 quesadilla and cook for 2 minutes or until the underside is browned as desired. Turn over with a wide spatula and cook the other side for 2 minutes or until browned as desired. Repeat with remaining quesadillas. To serve, cut into wedges with a *pizza cutter* or a sharp knife.

Class Notes _____

A **pizza cutter** is a sharp round blade at the end of a handle that cuts as it rolls, making quick work of cutting a pizza into slices. A pizza cutter is also useful for cutting quesadillas and other flat foods.

Brown Rice, Bean, and Cheese Burritos $$

The hearty filling for these burritos reheats well, so you can pre-pare individual burritos as needed. The rice mixture can also stand alone as a tasty side dish.

½ **green bell pepper**

1 (14.5-oz.) can petite-diced tomatoes, undrained

3 TB. chunky-style salsa

⅓ **cup water**

¼ **tsp. dried thyme**

¾ **cup uncooked instant brown rice**

1 (15-oz.) can black beans, rinsed and drained

8 soft-taco-size whole-wheat tortillas

1 cup 2-percent-milk sharp cheddar cheese

½ **cup fat-free sour cream (optional)**

Yield: 8 servings
Prep time: 5 minutes
Cook time: 25 minutes
Serving size: 1 burrito
Each serving has:
214 calories
43 calories from fat
5 g fat
2 g saturated fat
8.5 g protein
34 g carbohydrates

1. On a cutting board with a sharp knife, dice green bell pepper.

2. In an 11-inch nonstick electric skillet, combine tomatoes, salsa, water, green bell pepper, thyme, and rice. Heat the electric skillet on the highest setting, bringing the mixture to a boil. Cover, reduce heat, and simmer for 15 minutes or until most of liquid is absorbed.

3. Stir black beans into rice mixture. Cook, covered, on the sim-mer setting for 10 minutes or until heated through and rice is tender.

4. Meanwhile, heat tortillas in the microwave according to pack-age directions. Sprinkle 2 tablespoons cheese down the center of each tortilla. Spoon ½ cup rice mixture over cheese. Spoon 1 tablespoon sour cream (if using) over top. Roll up, folding 1 side over, pulling up the bottom, and folding over the other side.

Variation: For stovetop preparation, follow the electric skil-let directions as given, using a large nonstick skillet with a lid.

Learning Curve

Take care when draining canned black beans, as the packing liquid is dark and can stain. Rinse off any plastic colan-ders or strainers you use to drain and any work surfaces where you may leave can rings.

Crunchy Chicken Tacos $

Stuff your favorite toppings into these spicy tacos—diced tomatoes, shredded lettuce, diced onions, sliced olives, low-fat shredded cheese, salsa, and fat-free sour cream.

Yield: 6 servings
Prep time: 1 minute
Cook time: 5 minutes
Serving size: 2 tacos
Each serving has:
216 calories
73 calories from fat
8 g fat
2 g saturated fat
15 g protein
21 g carbohydrates

1 (12.5-oz.) can ready-to-use chunk chicken breast, drained

1 (1.25-oz.) pkg. taco seasoning mix

¾ cup water

12 taco shells

1. In an 11-inch nonstick electric skillet, combine chicken, taco seasoning mix, and water, and stir until mixed. Heat at 400°F and bring mixture to a boil. Reduce heat to 250°F, and simmer for 3 minutes or until most liquid is absorbed, stirring occasionally. Turn off heat.

2. Meanwhile, arrange needed taco shells on a *microwave-safe* plate. Cook on high power for 30 to 60 seconds or until warmed. Fill each taco shell with 2 ounces chicken mixture and toppings as desired.

Class Notes

Microwave-safe is a label given to dishes, bowls, and other cookware that can safely be used for cooking in the microwave. For information on testing for microwave-safeness, see Chapter 3.

Beefy Taco Springs $$

This spicy skillet casserole makes a lot, but it reheats well when you sprinkle the cheese on individual servings when you're ready to eat.

4 cups hot water

3 cups uncooked multi-grain rotini pasta

1 large yellow onion

1 lb. ground round

1 (1.25-oz.) pkg. taco seasoning mix

¾ cup water

1 (4.5-oz.) can diced green chilies, drained

1 (2.25-oz.) can sliced black olives, drained

¾ cup 2-percent-milk shredded sharp cheddar cheese or Mexican blend cheese

Yield: 6 servings
Prep time: 3 minutes
Cook time: 20 to 22 minutes
Serving size: 1½ cups
Each serving has:
310 calories
66 calories from fat
7 g fat
3 g saturated fat
24 g protein
35 g carbohydrates

1. Pour hot water into a 1½-quart microwave-safe round glass dish, and cook on high power for 8 or 9 minutes or until boiling. Add pasta, and cook on high power for 10 or 11 minutes or until done. Drain.

2. Meanwhile, on a cutting board with a sharp knife, chop onion into ½-inch squares. Heat an 11-inch nonstick electric skillet to 350°F. Add ground round and onion, and cook and stir for 5 to 7 minutes or until meat is browned and onions are translucent. Unplug the skillet and drain.

3. Replug in the skillet and heat to 350°F. Add taco seasoning mix and ¾ cup water, stirring until blended. Bring to a boil. Reduce heat and simmer for 7 or 8 minutes or until liquid is absorbed, stirring occasionally. Stir in green chilies, black olives, and pasta to mix. Cook for 2 minutes or until heated through. Sprinkle 2 tablespoons cheese over each serving.

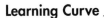 **Learning Curve** _____

Try to start with hot water when you want to boil water; you'll reach the boiling point a bit more quickly. Also, if you're salting your cooking water (which isn't necessary), do so only after it has come to a boil. Salted water has a higher boiling point, and therefore will take longer to boil.

Spicy Pinto Taco Toss $$

Try a dressing mix of salsa stirred into ranch salad dressing or serve with dollops of sour cream, salsa, and guacamole.

Yield: 5 servings
Prep time: 7 minutes
Cook time: 5 minutes
Serving size: 1 salad
Each serving has:
270 calories
47 calories from fat
5 g fat
2 g saturated fat
11 g protein
48 g carbohydrates

1 large tomato

2 green onions

1 (10-oz.) pkg. mixed salad greens

5 doz. baked tortilla chips

1 (2.25-oz.) can sliced black olives, drained

1 (15.5-oz.) can pinto beans, rinsed and drained

½ cup frozen whole-kernel corn

1 (1.25-oz.) pkg. taco seasoning mix

¾ cup water

10 TB. 2-percent-milk shredded Mexican blend cheese

1. On a cutting board with a sharp knife, coarsely chop tomato. Slice green onions. Line 5 serving plates with salad greens and tortilla chips. Scatter tomatoes, green onions, and black olives over top.

2. In an 11-inch nonstick electric skillet, combine pinto beans, corn, taco seasoning mix, and water. Stir to mix. Heat the skillet to 400°F and bring mixture to a boil. Reduce heat to 250°F and simmer for 3 or 4 minutes or until liquid is reduced. Turn off heat.

3. Spoon ⅓ cup mixture over each salad and sprinkle 2 tablespoons cheese on each. Serve immediately.

Learning Curve

Commercial taco seasoning mixes tend to be high in sodium and may taste salty. Low-sodium versions are available, if you prefer.

Fiesta Dip Platter $$

You'll be an instant hit if you layer this Mexican-flavored dip the night before and then carry it into a party with a bag of baked tortilla chips.

1 (16-oz.) can fat-free refried beans

1 (1.25-oz.) pkg. taco seasoning mix

1 (8-oz.) pkg. fat-free cream cheese, at room temperature

1 (8-oz.) pkg. shredded lettuce

1 (8-oz.) pkg. 2-percent-milk Mexican blend cheese

¾ cup diced tomatoes

¼ cup diced black olives

3 green onions

Yield: 15 servings
Prep time: 15 minutes
Chill time: 2 hours
Serving size: 2½×3-inch section
Each serving has:
94 calories
29 calories from fat
3 g fat
2 g saturated fat
7 g protein
8 g carbohydrates

1. Spread refried beans evenly over the bottom of a 13×9×2-inch dish or similar container.

2. In a small bowl, stir taco seasoning mix into cream cheese until well blended. Carefully spread cream cheese mixture over refried beans.

3. Cover cream cheese mixture with shredded lettuce, cheese, diced tomatoes, and black olives, in that order.

4. On a cutting board with a sharp knife, finely chop green onions. Scatter over top of black olives.

5. Cover and chill for at least 2 hours or overnight.

Learning Curve

Open the cream cheese package first when you're assembling the ingredients for this recipe. Fat-free cream cheese is a bit softer than regular cream cheese. Still, taking the chill off it helps you blend in the taco seasoning mix, which should be stirred in until no white streaks remain.

Fast and Fresh Guacamole $$

Scoop up this fresh dip with baked tortilla chips, or use it as a condiment for the Crunchy Chicken Tacos, Quick-Fix Black Bean and Salsa Quesadillas, or Spicy Pinto Taco Toss (recipes in this chapter).

Yield: 4 servings
Prep time: 5 minutes
Chill time: 1 hour
Serving size: 2 tablespoons
Each serving has:
73 calories
59 calories from fat
7 g fat
1 g saturated fat
1 g protein
4 g carbohydrates

1 large ripe avocado	½ tsp. chili powder
1 TB. minced yellow onions	¼ tsp. salt
1 tsp. lemon juice	Pinch garlic powder

1. On a cutting board with a sharp knife, cut avocado in half lengthwise around pit and gently twist to separate halves. Carefully push the knife blade into pit and slowly turn the knife a quarter turn to loosen and remove pit. With a spoon, scoop out pulp from avocado halves into a blender.

2. Add onions, lemon juice, chili powder, salt, and garlic powder to the blender. Blend or purée on high speed for 30 to 60 seconds or until desired consistency is reached, stopping to scrape down sides as necessary.

3. Spoon guacamole into a small container and cover with plastic wrap, pressing directly onto the surface of the guacamole to prevent discoloration. (Cover with lid as well, if available.) Chill for at least 1 hour before serving.

Learning Curve

To ripen a hard avocado more quickly, place it in a paper bag with an apple. Ethylene gas given off by the apple speeds up the avocado's ripening. You can also try a banana or tomato if you don't have an apple. A ripe avocado should yield slightly when light pressure is applied.

Chapter 13

Tastes of Italy

In This Chapter

- Shopping for pasta
- Cooking pasta to perfection
- Pairing pastas and sauces

Italian cooking immediately conjures up images of platters piled high with spaghetti, rigatoni, ravioli, linguine, and the like. Pasta takes center stage in many great Italian dishes, as well as in several of the recipes included in this cookbook.

Pasta's popularity might be based in its simplicity. A long shelf life, easy to cook, and a versatile blank canvas to flavor as you will—all these attributes, plus the fact that it's cholesterol-free and sodium-free, make the flour-and-water combination a great boon for cooks. Just a few pointers will make you a pasta pro.

Pasta Primer

Because fresh pastas tend to cost more and should be used soon after buying, I've called for dried pastas here. (If you prefer the texture and speed of fresh pastas, simply follow the package directions to use them in the recipes in this book.) Dried pastas are widely available, inexpensive, and long-lasting. Keep them in their original packaging for regular use, or an airtight container enables you to store them for 1 or 2 years.

With the new dietary guidelines calling for half of your grain consumption to be whole grains, the majority of recipes in this book call for whole-wheat or multigrain pastas when the pasta varieties are readily available in those cuts. Plus, more and more pasta shapes are being offered in whole-grain versions. While the whole-grain pastas are sometimes pricier than traditional pastas, they're often on sale. Opt to use a whole grain whenever possible for optimal health.

If you have access to a stovetop, you can prepare the pasta according to package directions, using plenty of water in a roomy pot. You can salt the cooking water if you prefer, but it's not necessary. Adding oil to the cooking water isn't necessary at all—just stir the pasta a couple minutes after you start cooking and occasionally as you can. The directions for the pasta recipes in this cookbook are for microwave cooking, should that be your only option. Preparing pasta in your microwave won't save you time; it'll take just as long as stovetop preparation.

Class Notes _____

Al dente is an Italian term meaning "to the tooth." Pasta should be cooked until it's still slightly firm to the bite and not until it's soft.

At the earliest given cooking time, you can test the pasta for doneness. Remove a strand or piece, cool, and taste. Pasta should be cooked just until *al dente*—not too chewy and not too gummy. Drain immediately. Don't rinse pasta you're serving hot; it'll stay warmer and the sauce will cling better.

Not all pasta sauces can be served with all pasta types. Several shapes are interchangeable, though, and may be prepared to your liking or as available. A simple rule is that light sauces are best paired with small or thin pastas while heavy, chunky sauces work well with large or thick shapes. Try smooth, creamy sauces with vermicelli, thin spaghetti, or linguine. Pasta cuts such as rigatoni, rotini, farfalle (bow ties), and penne can hold meat sauces, vegetable sauces, and thick cream sauces. Some pastas, such as penne, can be purchased in smooth and ridged styles. The ridges help pastas hold up to a thicker, chunkier sauce. Some of the smallest pastas—acini di pepe, orzo, and pastina—are found in soups. The largest pasta cuts—manicotti, cannelloni, and large shells—are perfect for stuffing.

Don't feel constrained to use only the pasta shape called for in a recipe. An appropriate substitution is easily, perhaps deliciously, made. Follow the cooking times on the package directions, whether using stovetop or microwave preparation.

Basta. Get cooking.

Grilled Pizza Margarita $$

A tossed green salad compliments the flavors of these slices nicely and makes for a filling meal.

1 Roma (plum) tomato

1 (8-in.) ready-to-use pizza crust

½ tsp. dried basil or ½ TB. chopped fresh basil

¼ tsp. drained minced garlic

⅛ tsp. dried oregano or ¼ tsp. chopped fresh oregano

Pinch crushed red pepper flakes

Pinch salt

½ tsp. extra-virgin olive oil

⅓ cup shredded low-fat mozzarella cheese

2 TB. shredded Parmesan cheese

Yield: 2 servings
Prep time: 5 minutes
Cook time: 2 or 3 minutes
Serving size: ½ pizza
Each serving has:
442 calories
96 calories from fat
11 g fat
3 g saturated fat
18 g protein
72 g carbohydrates

1. Heat the grill or the broiler to high heat.

2. Meanwhile, on a cutting board with a sharp knife, thinly slice tomato, and evenly arrange over pizza crust. Evenly sprinkle basil, garlic, oregano, crushed red pepper flakes, and salt over top. Drizzle on olive oil. Top with mozzarella cheese and Parmesan cheese.

3. Place pizza crust directly on the grill rack or a broiler pan 4 to 6 inches from the heat. Cook for 2 or 3 minutes or until crust is browned as desired and cheese is melted. Cut into wedges to serve.

Learning Curve _____

A serrated knife is best for cutting ripe tomatoes. The saw-like teeth cut through the peel and into the soft flesh without smashing it to a pulp.

Authentic Lasagna Micro-Quick $$$

Don't let the seemingly long directions scare you. Once you get the layering order straight in your mind, you'll soon be enjoying this classic Italian entrée.

Yield: 6 servings
Prep time: 15 minutes
Cook time: 28 to 34 minutes
Serving size: 2½×4-inch rectangle

Each serving has:
326 calories
52 calories from fat
6 g fat
3 g saturated fat
34 g protein
33 g carbohydrates

¾ lb. ground round

1½ cups spaghetti sauce

1 (8-oz.) pkg. fat-free shredded mozzarella cheese

9 oven-ready no-boil lasagna noodles

½ (15-oz.) container low-fat ricotta cheese

2 TB. shredded Parmesan cheese

½ cup water

1. Place ground round in a 6-cup microwave-safe glass bowl, and cook on high power for 1½ to 2 minutes. Stir to break up meat and redistribute, and cook on high power for 1½ to 2 minutes more or just until most of meat is browned. Stir well to break up meat, drain well, and blot with paper towels. (All meat should be browned now.) Stir spaghetti sauce into ground round.

2. Spread a very thin layer of meat mixture over the bottom of an 8×8×2-inch microwave-safe glass dish with rounded corners. Sprinkle a very thin layer of mozzarella cheese over top. Arrange 3 lasagna noodles, breaking as needed to fit, over mozzarella cheese. Spread ⅓ of ricotta cheese over noodles. Spread ⅓ of remaining meat mixture over ricotta cheese. Sprinkle ⅓ of remaining mozzarella cheese over meat mixture. Arrange 3 more lasagna noodles, breaking as needed to fit, in the opposite direction of previous noodles.

3. Spread ½ of remaining ricotta cheese over noodles. Spread ½ of remaining meat mixture over ricotta cheese. Spread ½ of remaining mozzarella cheese over meat mixture. Arrange remaining 3 lasagna noodles, breaking as needed to fit, again in the opposite direction of previous noodles.

4. Spread on remaining ricotta cheese, remaining meat mixture, and remaining mozzarella cheese in that order. Sprinkle Parmesan cheese over top.

5. Carefully pour water around the edges of the dish, and cover
    with plastic wrap, venting. Cook on high power for 20 to 25
    minutes or until bubbly and noodles are nearly tender, rotating
    every 5 minutes if needed. Let stand, covered, for 5 minutes
    before serving.

Learning Curve

To drain the ground round very well for this and other recipes, pour off the grease and then blot the meat with layers of
white paper towels until dry. You can turn out the meat onto a
plate lined with several layers of paper towels and blot it dry
with more paper towels if you find this method easier.

Gnocchi with Wilted Greens and Walnuts $$$

A delightful way to get your healthful, dark leafy greens, this chunky side dish could have more greens added with an extra drizzle of olive oil, if you like.

Yield: 4 servings	

Prep time: 2 minutes

Cook time: 15 to 17 minutes

Serving size: 1 cup

Each serving has:

432 calories

180 calories from fat

20 g fat

3 g saturated fat

15 g protein

50 g carbohydrates

5 cups hot water

1 (16-oz.) pkg. potato *gnocchi*

1½ cups packed torn mixed greens (spinach, kale, chard, etc.)

2 TB. extra-virgin olive oil

¾ cup unsalted walnut pieces

½ TB. drained minced garlic

Pinch each salt and ground black pepper

¼ cup shredded Parmesan cheese

1. Pour water into a 1½-quart microwave-safe bowl, and cook on high power for 10 or 11 minutes or until boiling. Add gnocchi, and cook on high power for 3 or 4 minutes or until tender. Drain.

2. Meanwhile, rinse and drain greens. Dry well on paper towels.

3. Add olive oil to an 11-inch nonstick electric skillet, set on 300°F, and heat olive oil for 1 minute. Add walnuts and garlic, and cook and stir for 2 minutes or until garlic is golden brown. Stir in greens. Season with salt and pepper. Sauté for 3 minutes or until greens are wilted.

4. Decrease heat to 200°F, add gnocchi, and stir until evenly coated. Cook for 2 minutes or until heated through. Sprinkle 1 tablespoon Parmesan cheese over each serving.

Class Notes

Gnocchi (pronounced *KNOCK-ee*) are small dumplings made of potatoes, ricotta cheese, or semolina flour and may have eggs or other ingredients added. They are prepared and served similarly to pastas.

Spring Asparagus with Penne Pasta $$

The crushed red pepper flakes add a kick to this terrific asparagus and pasta mix. It's just as delicious with only a pinch of the red pepper flakes, and you can even omit them, if you prefer.

4 cups hot water

1½ cups uncooked whole-wheat penne pasta

½ lb. asparagus

2 TB. extra-virgin olive oil

½ TB. lemon juice

Pinch each salt and ground black pepper

½ tsp. drained minced garlic

¼ tsp. crushed red pepper flakes or to taste

½ tsp. dried basil or ½ TB. chopped fresh basil

½ cup shredded Parmesan cheese

Yield: 4 servings
Prep time: 2 minutes
Cook time: 19 to 23 minutes
Serving size: 1 cup
Each serving has:
190 calories
62 calories from fat
7 g fat
2 g saturated fat
9 g protein
24 g carbohydrates

1. Pour water into a 1½-quart microwave-safe glass bowl, and cook on high power for 8 or 9 minutes or until boiling. Add pasta, and cook on high power for 10 to 12 minutes or until done. Drain.

2. Meanwhile, trim asparagus by snapping off bottom portions of spears. Cut spears into 1½-inch pieces. Toss asparagus with 1 tablespoon olive oil in an 11-inch nonstick electric skillet. Heat the skillet to 350°F, and *sauté* asparagus for 5 or 6 minutes or until tender-crisp and lightly charred. Drizzle lemon juice over asparagus, and season with salt and pepper, stirring to coat.

3. Reduce heat to 250°F, push asparagus to 1 corner of the skillet, and pour remaining 1 tablespoon olive oil into the opposite corner. Add garlic and sauté for 2 minutes or until golden. Add crushed red pepper flakes and sauté for 2 minutes.

4. Stir asparagus mixture and garlic mixture together and then stir in pasta and basil until evenly coated. Cook for 1 or 2 minutes or until heated through. Sprinkle 2 tablespoons Parmesan cheese over each serving.

Class Notes

Sauté is a cooking directive that instructs you to pan-cook a food over a lower heat than would be used for frying. You should stay nearby to stir the dish frequently.

Classic Italian Bread Salad $$

A flavorful salad, this needs to be served the same day it's made—but you should have no trouble tracking down a few other people willing to eat good food.

Yield: 4 servings
Prep time: 5 minutes
Standing time: 20 minutes
Serving size: 1 cup
Each serving has:
136 calories
21 calories from fat
2 g fat
0.5 g saturated fat
4 g protein
27 g carbohydrates

3 Roma (plum) tomatoes

½ small red onion

5 (1-in.-thick) slices day-old Italian bread

½ tsp. dried basil or ½ TB. chopped fresh basil

½ tsp. dried oregano or ½ TB. chopped fresh oregano

3 TB. low-fat balsamic vinaigrette salad dressing

1. On a cutting board with a sharp knife, chop tomatoes into ½-inch squares. Chop red onion into ½-inch squares. Chop bread into 1-inch pieces.

2. In a medium serving bowl, combine tomatoes, red onion, bread, basil, and oregano. Drizzle salad dressing over salad, and gently toss until mixed and coated. Let stand for 20 minutes and then gently toss again before serving.

Learning Curve

If your bread hasn't gone stale as soon as you had expected, you can still enjoy this great salad. Lay out the bread slices on a white paper towel and place them in the microwave. Cook on high power for about 30 seconds. Let the bread stand while you chop the tomatoes and red onion.

Italian Zucchini with Sweet Onions $

Tender and cheesy, these zucchini slices are a quick, tasty side dish.

1 medium zucchini squash
(about 8 in. long)

¼ medium sweet onion

2 tsp. light butter with canola
oil

Pinch salt and ground black
pepper

2 or 3 TB. grated Parmesan
cheese

Yield: 2 servings
Prep time: 4 minutes
Cook time: 6 or 7 minutes
Serving size: ¼ cup
Each serving has:
56 calories
26 calories from fat
3 g fat
1 g saturated fat
3 g protein
5 g carbohydrates

1. On a cutting board with a sharp knife, slice zucchini squash.
   Slice and halve sweet onion. Combine zucchini squash and
   sweet onion in an 8×2-inch microwave-safe round glass dish,
   and cover with plastic wrap, venting. Cook on high power for
   5 or 6 minutes or until tender-crisp, stirring and rotating, if
   needed, halfway through cooking time.

2. Lightly drain zucchini mixture if desired. Stir in light butter,
   salt, and pepper. Sprinkle Parmesan cheese across top of zucchini mixture, and re-cover with plastic wrap, venting. Cook
   on high power for 30 to 60 seconds or until heated through.
   Serve immediately.

Learning Curve _____

A zucchini squash should have smooth, unblemished skin.
To prepare a zucchini squash and other summer squashes for
slicing, first trim the stem end and the blossom end, discarding
them.

Chilled Flat Beans 💲

Serve this addictive, make-ahead side dish when the weather swelters.

Yield: 3 servings
Prep time: 3 minutes
Chill time: 4 hours
Serving size: ½ cup
Each serving has:
103 calories
64 calories from fat
7 g fat
1 g saturated fat
2 g protein
10 g carbohydrates

1 (14.5-oz.) can cut Italian green beans, rinsed and drained

2 TB. diced yellow onion

2 TB. extra-virgin olive oil

2 TB. *cider vinegar*

2 tsp. granulated sugar

¼ tsp. salt

1. In a wide, shallow bowl with a lid, combine beans, onion, olive oil, cider vinegar, sugar, and salt. Stir to mix thoroughly.

2. Cover and chill for at least 4 hours before serving.

 Class Notes _____

Cider vinegar is a red-tinged vinegar made from apple cider. It has a milder taste than white vinegar.

14

Asian-Inspired Favorites

In This Chapter

- ◆ Serving foods sensibly
- ◆ Storing and reheating leftovers safely
- ◆ Great-tasting stir-fries and other easy Asian dishes

The foods of the Far East have long influenced the cuisines of the world. In modern America, we've embraced the quick work of stir-frying along with the great flavors of soy sauce, teriyaki, sweet-and-sour sauce, and spicy curries.

One of our most enjoyed pleasures from Asian cuisine is Chinese carry-out and those immediately recognizable paper cartons. Whether your left-overs come from a Chinese restaurant or your own kitchen (where you can prepare the food more healthfully), the prepared foods need to be treated with the same respect you give raw foods if they're to remain safe to eat.

Leftover Course

The safe handling of cooked dishes begins with serving. The dishes and utensils you serve foods with need to be clean, not the ones used to prepare the raw ingredients. Becoming a clock-watcher is a good idea, too. Foods shouldn't be left unrefrigerated for more than 2 hours; if you're outside and it's above 90°F, you only have 1 hour. Leftovers should be placed in small, airtight containers in a refrigerator kept at a temperature below 40°F. You may need to use a refrigerator thermometer to know for sure.

Learning Curve

Some foods with molds can still be used. You can often cut out the moldy area in hard cheeses and firm fruits and vegetables. Carefully inspect the remaining food before using, and always remember the adage: when in doubt, throw it out.

Labeling leftover packages with the date will help you know what is and isn't safe to eat. Bad odors and visual molds are sure signs that foods have gone bad, but foods can be dangerous to eat before it comes to that. Refrigerated leftovers only have a number of days. Some foods only a have 1 or 2 days. Plan on repeating pizza, green salads (undressed), seafood, pasta and rice dishes, and fresh veggies soon. In 2 or 3 days, you should use up pasta and potato salads as well as dishes with ground meats. Most other leftovers such as meats, casseroles, soups and stews, and potatoes and other cooked vegetables are best eaten within 3 or 4 days.

Leftovers need to be reheated as carefully as they were originally cooked. Bring soups, as well as any sauces or gravies, to a full boil. Other dishes must be heated thoroughly and not just warmed up. That means a 165°F reading on a food thermometer. If you're using a microwave to reheat leftovers (the most popular method), cover and vent your dishes for best results. And don't forget to rotate the food during cooking if your microwave doesn't have a turntable.

Beef and Broccoli Stir-Fry $$$

Serve this simple stir-fry over brown rice with additional soy sauce or a drizzling of toasted sesame oil.

4 tsp. cornstarch

1 tsp. granulated sugar

½ tsp. drained minced garlic

4 tsp. reduced-sodium soy sauce

½ lb. stir-fry beef strips

1 TB. extra-virgin olive oil

2 cups broccoli florets

½ cup coarsely chopped sweet onions or yellow onions

⅓ cup fat-free, less-sodium beef broth

Yield: 2 servings
Prep time: 3 minutes
Cook time: 10 minutes
Serving size: 1¼ cups
Each serving has:
256 calories
90 calories from fat
10 g fat
3 g saturated fat
29 g protein
11.5 g carbohydrates

1. In a medium bowl, combine cornstarch, sugar, garlic, and soy sauce, and stir until blended. Add beef strips and stir to coat evenly. Set aside.

2. Heat a 6-quart nonstick electric wok to medium-high heat. Add olive oil and heat for 1 minute. Add prepared beef strips and stir-fry for 3 minutes or until browned. Quickly remove to a clean bowl and set aside.

3. Add broccoli and onions to the wok. Pour in broth. Stir-fry for 4 minutes or until broccoli is crisp-tender. Return beef strips to the wok, and stir-fry for 2 minutes or until heated through. Turn off heat and serve immediately.

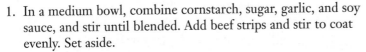

Learning Curve

Beef prepared for stir-frying can be pricey, but if you do the prep work yourself, you can save some money. It's pretty easy: trim the fat from beef tenderloin or another favorite beef cut and slice into strips.

Napa Cabbage and Chicken Chow Mein $$$$

When you're craving authentic Asian flavor, invest in a few "specialty" ingredients for this stir-fry dish.

Yield: 2 servings
Prep time: 5 minutes
Cook time: 16 to 19 minutes
Serving size: 2 cups
Each serving has:
379 calories
102 calories from fat
11 g fat
2 g saturated fat
28 g protein
41 g carbohydrates

1 medium head *Napa cabbage*

2 green onions

3 cups hot water

½ (6-oz.) pkg. uncooked chow mein noodles

2 (3-oz.) boneless, skinless chicken breast halves

1 TB. sesame oil

1 TB. sodium-free rice wine vinegar

2 tsp. drained minced garlic

⅛ tsp. crushed red pepper flakes or to taste

2 TB. extra-virgin olive oil

2 tsp. reduced-sodium soy sauce

½ tsp. toasted sesame seeds (optional)

1. On a cutting board with a sharp knife, coarsely chop Napa cabbage, discarding core and thickest stems. Trim root ends and edges of green tops from green onions and finely chop.

2. Pour hot water into a 1-quart microwave-safe glass bowl. Cook on high power for 6 or 7 minutes or until boiling. Add chow mein noodles, breaking as needed to fit in the bowl. Cook on high power for 3 minutes or until done. Drain.

3. Meanwhile, on a cutting board with a sharp knife, trim excess fat from chicken breast halves and cut into ½×3-inch strips. Place in a medium bowl, and add sesame oil, rice wine vinegar, garlic, and crushed red pepper flakes. Stir to coat evenly.

4. Heat 1 tablespoon olive oil in a 6-quart nonstick electric wok to medium-high heat for 1 minute. Add chicken mixture, and stir-fry for 2 or 3 minutes or until all of chicken is white. Remove to a clean small bowl and set aside.

5. Add remaining 1 tablespoon olive oil to the wok. Add Napa cabbage and stir-fry for 2 minutes or until wilted. Stir in chow mein noodles and stir-fry for 1 minute or until heated through. Stir in soy sauce, chicken mixture, and green onions, and stir-fry for 1 or 2 minutes or until heated through. Turn off heat.

6. Sprinkle ¼ teaspoon sesame seeds (if using) over each serving.

Variation: For an economical chow mein noodle substitute, cook and drain a package of ramen noodles without the seasoning packet.

Class Notes

Napa cabbage, also referred to as *Chinese cabbage,* is a member of the cabbage family with thick stems, crisp texture, and fresh, mild flavor. The tight heads are elongated with crinkly edged, pale green leaves.

Simple Sweet-and-Sour Chicken $$$

Easy to make and so versatile, this chicken can be served whole over a bed of Chinese noodles or cut up on a bed of rice.

4 (3-oz.) boneless, skinless chicken breast halves

⅔ cup apricot preserves

1 (8-oz.) bottle low-fat Catalina salad dressing

Yield: 4 servings
Prep time: 5 minutes
Cook time: 4½ to 5½ hours
Serving size: 1 chicken breast half with sauce
Each serving has:
173 calories
36 calories from fat
4 g fat
0.5 g saturated fat
20 g protein
14 g carbohydrates

1. Trim fat from chicken breast halves. Arrange chicken in a 3½- to 4-quart slow cooker coated with nonstick cooking spray.

2. In a small bowl, stir apricot preserves into salad dressing to blend. Pour over chicken breast halves.

3. Cover slow cooker and cook on low heat for 4½ to 5½ hours or until done (170°F on a food thermometer).

Lecture Hall

Resist the urge to peek! Lifting the cover off a slow cooker while cooking will cause a significant heat loss that the slow cooker cannot quickly regain. Unless a recipe directs you to add ingredients or stir at a given time, leave the lid on.

Teriyaki-Marinated Chicken Breast

A flavorful main dish, this chicken may also be cut into strips and served on mixed greens with chopped green onions, snow peas, crisp chow mein noodles, and sesame dressing.

Yield: 1 serving
Prep time: 3 minutes
Chill time: 30 minutes
Cook time: 5 or 6 minutes
Each serving has:
150 calories
52 calories from fat
6 g fat
1 g saturated fat
21 g protein
3 g carbohydrates

1 TB. reduced-sodium soy sauce

½ TB. extra-virgin olive oil

¾ tsp. granulated sugar

¼ tsp. garlic powder

⅛ tsp. dry mustard

Pinch ground ginger

1 (3-oz.) boneless, skinless chicken breast half

1. In a quart-size resealable plastic bag, combine soy sauce, olive oil, sugar, garlic powder, dry mustard, and ginger. Seal the bag and gently shake to mix.

2. Trim fat from chicken breast half. Add chicken to the plastic bag, forcing out air and sealing it shut. Turn the bag to coat chicken. Lay flat in the refrigerator and *marinate* for at least 30 minutes.

3. Transfer chicken breast half to a small casserole dish with rounded corners large enough to hold chicken flat, allowing excess marinade to drip into the bag. (Discard the bag.)

4. Cook on high power for 3 or 4 minutes, rotating halfway through cooking time if needed. Remove from the microwave and let stand, covered, for 2 minutes. Check for doneness with a food thermometer reading of 170°F. (If necessary, return to the microwave, covered and vented, for 30-second intervals, allowing to stand for a minute.)

Variation: To grill or broil chicken breast half, coat the grill rack or broiler pan with nonstick cooking spray. Heat the grill or broiler until hot, and grill or broil about 4 to 6 inches from the heat for 4 minutes. Turn chicken breast half, and cook for 2 or 3 minutes on the other side or until done. Let stand for 1 or 2 minutes.

Class Notes

Marinate
means to soak meat, seafood, or other food in a seasoned sauce, called a marinade, which is high in acid content. The acids break down the tissue of the meat, making it tender and adding flavor.

Sweet-and-Sour Vegetarian Noodles $$

The flavors of sweet and sour meld in a slow cooker while you're off doing something else.

½ medium green bell pepper

1 (12-oz.) pkg. frozen ready-to-use veggie crumbles to replace ground beef

1 TB. reduced-sodium soy sauce

¼ tsp. garlic powder

1 (8-oz.) can crushed pineapple in its own juice, undrained

½ cup firmly packed light brown sugar

1 TB. white vinegar

4 cups hot water

4 oz. uncooked Chinese noodles

Yield: 3 servings
Prep time: 3 minutes
Cook time: 3 to 5 hours
Serving size: ¼ cup noodles with 1 cup sweet-and-sour mixture
Each serving has:
272 calories
8 calories from fat
1 g fat
0 g saturated fat
8 g protein
60 g carbohydrates

1. On a cutting board with a sharp knife, coarsely *chop* green bell pepper. Add to a 3½- to 4-quart slow cooker coated with nonstick cooking spray. Add veggie crumbles, soy sauce, garlic powder, pineapple with juice, brown sugar, and vinegar. Stir until thoroughly combined, scraping down sides as necessary. Cover and cook on low heat for 3 to 5 hours.

2. Meanwhile, just before sweet-and-sour mixture is done, pour hot water into a 1½-quart microwave-safe glass bowl. Cook on high power for 8 or 9 minutes or until boiling. Add Chinese noodles, breaking up as needed to fit into the bowl. Cook on high power for 5 or 6 minutes or until done. Drain.

3. Serve sweet-and-sour mixture over Chinese noodles.

Variation: For an economical substitute, prepare 1 package ramen noodles without the seasoning packet to use in place of Chinese noodles. You could serve the sweet-and-sour mixture over rice instead.

Class Notes

Chop tells you to cut a food into pieces. The size is usually qualified by an adverb such as *coarsely* or by a measurement, as in *chop into ½-inch pieces.*

Easy Egg Drop Soup $

Easy to fix, filling, and inexpensive, this hot soup makes a good snack or first course.

Yield: *2 servings*
Prep time: 1 minute
Cook time: 10 minutes
Serving size: ¾ cup
Each serving has:
59 calories
22 calories from fat
2.5 g fat
1 g saturated fat
6 g protein
3 g carbohydrates

1 (14-oz.) can fat-free, less-sodium chicken broth

1 large egg, at room temperature

1 TB. cold water

½ TB. cornstarch

1. Pour broth into a 6-quart nonstick electric wok. Heat to high heat until boiling.

2. Meanwhile, crack egg into a small bowl. Beat with a fork or a whisk until blended. Set aside.

3. In another small bowl, stir cold water into cornstarch just until smooth. Set aside.

4. When broth reaches a boil, reduce heat to medium-low. Briefly stir cornstarch mixture again to blend and add to broth. Stir. Briefly beat egg again to blend. Gradually add egg to broth mixture a little at a time, stirring after each addition to break egg into threads and returning to a simmer before adding more egg. Cook, stirring occasionally, for 1 or 2 minutes or until slightly thickened. Turn off heat and serve hot.

Variation: For stovetop preparation, follow the directions given using a heavy-bottomed, medium saucepan.

Learning Curve _____

If your eggs are past their sell-by date, you might still be able to use them by testing their freshness. Add the egg you plan to use to a deep cup or bowl of tap water. If the egg sinks to the bottom, it's safe to use. If it floats on the water, discard it and test another. Remember sinks = safe but floats = foul.

Indian Golden Chicken Curry ⚡

Spoon this thick curry over brown rice and garnish with crushed cashews, almonds, or peanuts for an added crunch.

1 TB. extra-virgin olive oil

1 tsp. curry powder

1 TB. all-purpose flour

¾ cup fat-free, less-sodium chicken broth

3 TB. golden raisins

½ cup ½-in.-cubed cooked chicken breast

Pinch each salt and ground black pepper

Yield: 1 serving
Prep time: 1 minute
Cook time: 13 or 14 minutes
Each serving has:
258 calories
58 calories from fat
6 g fat
1 g saturated fat
24 g protein
28 g carbohydrates

1. Heat an 11-inch nonstick electric skillet to 200°F. Add olive oil and heat for 1 minute. Sprinkle curry powder and flour over olive oil, stir to blend, and cook for 3 minutes or until well blended and beginning to bubble at the edges.

2. Slowly add broth, stirring to blend. Add raisins and simmer for 7 or 8 minutes or until sauce is thickened and raisins are tender, stirring occasionally.

3. Stir in chicken, salt, and pepper, and cook for 2 minutes or until heated through.

Learning Curve _____

Keeping cooked chicken on hand allows for many quick-fix meals. You can cook plain chicken breasts by your favorite cooking method ahead of time, or you can keep ready-to-use chicken pouches or cans in your pantry. To prepare extra chicken breast halves while you bake dinner, see the recipe for Crunchy Dijon Chicken Breasts in Chapter 9.

Cooling Cucumber Raita $

Serve this tongue-calming accompaniment with spicy Indian curries or other highly seasoned dishes sprinkled with a little chopped cilantro to garnish.

Yield: 5 servings
Prep time: 25 minutes
Chill time: 1 hour
Serving size: 2 tablespoons
Each serving has:
16 calories
0 calories from fat
0 g fat
0 g saturated fat
1 g protein
3 g carbohydrates

½ **medium cucumber**

½ **tsp. salt**

½ **cup fat-free plain yogurt**

¼ **tsp. drained minced garlic**

⅛ **tsp. ground cumin**

1. On a cutting board with a sharp knife, peel cucumber and cut lengthwise into quarters. With a metal spoon, remove the seeds by running the bowl of the spoon along the flesh and scooping out the seeds. Discard seeds. With a grater, finely *grate* cucumber. Transfer cucumber to a fine colander over the sink, sprinkle with salt, and let stand for 15 minutes.

2. Meanwhile, combine yogurt, garlic, and cumin in a small bowl with a lid. Stir until blended.

3. Rinse cucumber mixture. Using your hands, press out as much water as possible. Transfer cucumber to paper toweling and press out as much water as possible.

4. Add cucumber to yogurt mixture, and stir until blended. Cover and chill for at least 1 hour to allow flavors to blend.

Class Notes

Grate is a cooking directive that indicates the food should be cut into very thin strips. For this recipe, you can use a grater—a tool with various sharp blades. To finely grate the cucumber, rub the flesh across the collection of fine-hole rasps.

15

Mediterranean Flavors

In This Chapter

- ◆ Choosing oils for cooking
- ◆ Storing oils to maintain quality
- ◆ Mediterranean-inspired recipes that will whisk you away

Prized for its health-boosting benefits, Mediterranean food has enjoyed the recent spotlight on functional-foods diets. Part of its popularity can be attributed to the delicious tastes, including sharp-flavored lemon, salty feta cheese, meaty olives, and the olive's oil that is high in heart-healthy mono-unsaturated fat.

Oil Orientation

Olive oil lends its fruity flavor to many Mediterranean dishes. A look through this cookbook shows that I call for extra-virgin olive oil in many recipes. You might not use enough oil in your cooking to make it worth buying several varieties of oil. Oils turn rancid over time if they're not used, so if you only have one oil on your shelf, my choice is extra-virgin olive oil. It is flavorful and well suited for salad dressings, marinades, and cold dishes.

Lecture Hall

Don't heat your oil until you're ready to cook or heat over a too-hot temperature. Heating oil to the smoke point breaks it down and leaves it unfit to eat. The smoke point is followed by the flash point, when the oil's vapors can ignite. You can't put out oil fires with water, so learn where the nearest fire extinguisher is located and how to use it.

You may prefer pure olive oil, canola oil, safflower oil, general vegetable oil, or another oil for cooking, sautéing, and baking. These oils are less expensive and may provide a higher smoke point.

Whichever oils you choose, be sure to check the use-by date. If a bottling date is provided, buy the freshest oil possible. Choose oils sold in tins, if available, as they'll shield the contents from light exposure. Still, buy only the quantity of oil you'll use within a year. Store oil in a cool, dark place, away from the stove and all other heat sources. After each use, immediately recap or cork the oil to limit its exposure to the air and return it to storage out of the light. Avoid heat, air, and light, and your oils should provide you many months of tasty cooking.

Of Higher Learning

The Food and Drug Administration allows olive oil manufacturers to claim on the labels: "Limited and not conclusive scientific evidence suggests that eating about 2 tablespoons (23 grams) of olive oil daily may reduce the risk of coronary heart disease due to the monounsaturated fat in olive oil. To achieve this possible benefit, olive oil is to replace a similar amount of saturated fat and not increase the total number of calories you eat in a day."

Countryside No-Cook Chunky Tuna Sauce with Penne Pasta $$

Salty and sweet, the flavors in this dish have great depth and great taste.

4 cups hot water

1½ cups uncooked whole-wheat penne pasta

2 medium tomatoes

1 (3-oz.) pouch ready-to-use light tuna in water

3 TB. drained sliced green olives with pimientos

3 TB. drained chopped black olives

2 TB. golden raisins

½ TB. drained small capers

2 TB. extra-virgin olive oil

1 tsp. drained minced garlic

1 tsp. dried parsley flakes or 1 TB. chopped fresh parsley

Pinch ground black pepper

Yield: 3 servings
Prep time: 2 minutes
Cook time: 18 to 20 minutes
Serving size: 1¾ cups
Each serving has:
273 calories
71 calories from fat
8 g fat
1 g saturated fat
13 g protein
39 g carbohydrates

1. Pour hot water into a 1½-quart microwave-safe glass bowl. Cook on high power for 8 or 9 minutes or until boiling. Add pasta, and cook on high power for 10 or 11 minutes or until done. Drain pasta and set aside.

2. Meanwhile, on a cutting board with a sharp knife, coarsely chop tomatoes. In a serving bowl, combine tomatoes, tuna, green olives with pimientos, black olives, golden raisins, capers, olive oil, garlic, parsley flakes, and pepper. Stir to thoroughly combine.

3. Add pasta to tomato mixture, stirring to combine. Serve immediately.

Learning Curve

Ready-to-use minced garlic can be stored in the refrigerator for easy recipe preparation. If you prefer to use fresh garlic cloves, you would mince 2 cloves for this recipe, as about ½ teaspoon minced garlic equals 1 garlic clove.

Mediterranean Grilled Chicken Salad $$

Drizzle on a balsamic vinaigrette or a simple dressing of extra-virgin olive oil and lemon juice to enjoy this well-seasoned chicken breast on a bed of traditional salad fixings with a Mediterranean flavor.

Yield: 1 serving
Prep time: 5 minutes
Chill time: 30 minutes
Cook time: 8 minutes
Each serving has:
197 calories
52 calories from fat
6 g fat
1 g saturated fat
26 g protein
11 g carbohydrates

1 (3-oz.) boneless, skinless chicken breast half

1 TB. lemon juice

½ TB. extra-virgin olive oil

¼ tsp. dried oregano or ¾ tsp. chopped fresh oregano

⅛ tsp. ground cinnamon

Pinch ground black pepper

1½ cups mixed salad greens

¼ cup coarsely chopped tomatoes

4 black olives or pitted kalamata olives

3 thin strips green bell pepper, halved

1 thin slice red onion, halved

2 TB. shredded fat-free mozzarella cheese

1. On a cutting board with a sharp knife, trim fat from chicken. Place in a quart-size resealable plastic bag. Add lemon juice, olive oil, oregano, cinnamon, and pepper. Close the bag and shake to blend ingredients. Lay the bag flat in the refrigerator and marinate for at least 30 minutes or overnight.

2. Spray a grill rack or broiler pan with nonstick cooking oil spray, and heat a grill or a broiler to high.

3. Remove chicken from marinade, allowing excess marinade to drip into the bag. (Discard the bag.) Grill or broil for 4 minutes on each side, turning once, or until done (170°F on a food thermometer). Let stand for 1 minute before cutting into thin slices.

4. Meanwhile, line a serving plate with salad greens. Scatter tomatoes, olives, green bell peppers, and red onions over top. Arrange chicken breast half over salad, and sprinkle with mozzarella cheese.

Variation: To prepare the chicken breast half in the microwave, place it in a microwave-safe glass dish with rounded corners just large enough to hold the chicken comfortably. Cover with plastic wrap, venting. Cook on high power for 3½ to 4½ minutes. Let stand, covered, for 2 minutes. Check for doneness with a food thermometer (170°F); if needed, return chicken to the microwave on high power for 30-second intervals until done.

Learning Curve

If your chicken breast half is particularly plump, you might find the cooking time is too long. To keep the thinner portion from drying out before the breast is done, pound the chicken to an even thickness. Place the chicken between two pieces of waxed paper and pound with the flat side of a meat mallet—or any heavy, flat utensil you have on hand.

Grecian Pasta Salad $$$$

This cold pasta salad, chock-full of Mediterranean flavors, is a great make-ahead carry-in dish to take along to a potluck.

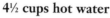

Yield: 10 servings
Prep time: 3 minutes
Cook time: 23 to 27 minutes
Chill time: 6 to 8 hours
Serving size: 1 cup
Each serving has:
195 calories
66 calories from fat
7 g fat
2 g saturated fat
7 g protein
25 g carbohydrates

4½ cups hot water

3 cups uncooked whole-wheat penne pasta

1 (7-oz.) jar whole roasted red peppers packed in olive oil, drained

1 (13.75-oz.) can quartered artichoke hearts packed in brine, drained

1 cup chopped button mushrooms

1 (2.25-oz.) can sliced black olives, drained

1 (4-oz.) pkg. reduced-fat crumbled feta cheese (1 cup)

½ tsp. dried oregano

¼ tsp. ground black pepper

1¼ cups low-fat Greek salad dressing or low-fat Italian salad dressing

1. Pour hot water into a 1½-quart microwave-safe glass bowl. Cook on high power for 10 to 12 minutes or until boiling. Add pasta and cook on high power for 13 to 15 minutes or until done. Drain and rinse pasta in cold water.

2. Meanwhile, on a cutting board with a sharp knife, coarsely chop roasted red peppers into bite-size pieces. In a 2-quart dish with a lid, combine roasted red peppers, artichoke hearts, mushrooms, olives, feta cheese, oregano, and pepper. Add pasta, and gently stir.

3. Pour salad dressing over all, and gently stir until evenly coated. Cover and chill overnight or for 6 to 8 hours. Stir again before serving.

Lecture Hall

Don't use fresh herbs in this dish. Dried are better here because the long standing time will wilt delicate fresh herbs.

Spinach and Feta Orzo $$

This skillet casserole of harmonizing flavors makes a meal easy with the addition of a tossed green salad and maybe a crusty bread.

4 cups hot water

1 cup uncooked orzo pasta

2 tsp. extra-virgin olive oil

1 tsp. drained minced garlic

1 (28-oz.) can crushed tomatoes

1 (15.5-oz.) can cannellini beans, rinsed and drained

1 TB. dried basil or 3 TB. chopped fresh basil

½ tsp. dried oregano or ½ TB. chopped fresh oregano

4 cups packed fresh spinach, rinsed and drained

1 (5-oz.) pkg. reduced-fat crumbled feta cheese (1¼ cups)

Yield: 5 servings
Prep time: 1 minute
Cook time: 18 or 19 minutes
Serving size: 1½ cups
Each serving has:
365 calories
61 calories from fat
7 g fat
3 g saturated fat
22 g protein
58.5 g carbohydrates

1. Pour hot water into a 1½-quart microwave-safe glass bowl. Cook on high power for 8 or 9 minutes or until boiling. Add pasta, and cook on high for 9 minutes or until done. Drain.

2. Meanwhile, heat olive oil in an 11-inch nonstick electric skillet set at 250°F for 1 minute. Add garlic and sauté for 1 minute or until colored. Stir in tomatoes, beans, basil, and oregano. Bring to a boil.

3. Reduce heat and simmer for 5 minutes, stirring frequently. Add spinach, and increase heat to 300°F. Stir spinach into tomato mixture for 2 or 3 minutes or until wilted.

4. Reduce heat to low, and stir in pasta. Stir in cheese, turn off heat, and serve.

Learning Curve

Dried herbs are convenient because they keep well. Fresh herbs can be substituted when available, and many cooks prefer their bright flavor in foods. Use a 3:1 ratio for fresh herbs to dried herbs, adjusting to taste. That makes 1 tablespoon fresh equal 1 teaspoon dried.

Lemon-Kissed Wilted Greens $$

Good for you and delicious, this quick-fix side dish can complement any entrée.

Yield: 3 servings
Prep time: 2 minutes
Cook time: 7 to 9 minutes
Serving size: ½ cup
Each serving has:
52 calories
43 calories from fat
5 g fat
1 g saturated fat
1 g protein
2 g carbohydrates

4 cups packed torn mixed greens (spinach, chard, kale, etc.)

2 TB. extra-virgin olive oil

½ TB. lemon juice

¼ tsp. drained minced garlic

Pinch salt and ground black pepper

1. In a large colander, wash greens and drain loosely. Transfer greens including water that clings to leaves to an 11-inch non-stick electric skillet. Set the skillet to 250°F, and gently stir as greens *wilt*, cooking for 5 or 6 minutes until the skillet is nearly dry.

2. Drizzle olive oil and lemon juice over greens. Add garlic, salt, and pepper. Cook and stir for 2 or 3 minutes or until heated through and greens are tender.

 Class Notes _____

Wilt is a visual clue that refers to the ingredient becoming limp from the heat.

Minty Rice $

A flavorful rice, this fast side dish goes with most meats and fish. Try it with Lemon-Butter Tilapia or Chive and Garlic Tilapia (recipes in Chapter 10), as the fish has time to cook while the rice stands.

½ cup uncooked instant brown rice

1 cup water

1 tsp. chicken bouillon granules

1 tsp. lemon juice

⅛ tsp. garlic powder

¼ tsp. dried mint or ¾ tsp. chopped fresh mint

Yield: 2 servings	
Prep time: 3 minutes	
Cook time: 12 to 14 minutes	
Serving size: ½ cup	
Each serving has:	
99 calories	
7 calories from fat	
1 g fat	
0 g saturated fat	
2 g protein	
22 g carbohydrates	

1. In a 3-cup microwave-safe glass bowl, combine rice, water, bouillon granules, lemon juice, and garlic powder. Stir to mix. Cover with plastic wrap, venting, and cook on high power for 7 to 9 minutes or until most of liquid is absorbed.

2. Remove the bowl from the microwave, and quickly stir in mint. Cover tightly with plastic wrap, and let stand, tightly covered, for 5 minutes. Fluff with a fork before serving.

Variation: If you don't have mint on hand, you can substitute basil or another favorite herb.

Learning Curve _____

If you're using a fresh lemon, bring it to room temperature and roll it gently under your palm on the counter before squeezing—you'll extract more juice.

Hummus in Minutes $

With a bit of heart-healthy omega-3 essential fatty acids from the walnuts, this hummus is perfect paired with warmed pita wedges.

Yield: 6 servings
Prep time: 5 minutes
Serving size: ¼ cup
Each serving has:
118 calories
36 calories from fat
4 g fat
0 g saturated fat
4 g protein
17 g carbohydrates

1 (15-oz.) can garbanzo beans

¼ cup unsalted walnut halves and pieces

2 TB. lemon juice

½ TB. drained minced garlic

½ tsp. ground cumin

1. Drain garbanzo beans into a small dish, reserving liquid. Combine garbanzo beans, walnuts, lemon juice, garlic, cumin, and ¼ cup reserved liquid in a blender or a food processor. Cover the blender or food processor, and blend on high speed for 1 or 2 minutes or until desired consistency is reached. Add additional reserved liquid if the mixture is too stiff.

2. If needed, stop the blender or food processor to scrape down the sides and redistribute ingredients to blend well.

Lecture Hall _____

Never place any utensil—or finger!—into a running blender or food processor. Always take the time to turn off the appliance before uncovering and scraping down the sides.

Part 5

Great Go-Withs

At most meals, we tend to focus on the entrée. But without the wonderful foods served on the side, eating just wouldn't be as pleasurable. Beyond their great taste contribution, side dishes also provide fiber, vitamins, minerals, and antioxidants for your diet.

Take the time to round out your meals with any of the great recipes in the following chapters. You're sure to find just the right accompaniments to your best main dishes.

"A little off-topic, Professor Gilbert, but, what exactly is couscous?"

Chapter 16

Superb Side Salads

In This Chapter

- Valuing the nutritious, economical bean
- Proper storage and preparation of beans
- Light and refreshing side salads to star alongside main dishes

When you need to stretch your grocery budget while maintaining good nutrition, point your cart to the bean aisle. Dried beans are very affordable and provide lots of protein and fiber, as well as vitamins and minerals. They're also low-fat and great replacements for higher-fat (including saturated fat) meats and cheeses in your diet.

Bean Abstract

Buy only dried beans that look clean and not shriveled. When you get them home, keep them in a cool, dry place in their plastic bag, or transfer them to an airtight container. Dried beans can be stored for 1 year, although older beans require a longer cooking time and more water to reconstitute.

To prepare dried beans, begin by sorting or "picking over" the beans. In previous years, cooks had to be careful to remove any stray stones or other debris from dried beans, but now you're more likely to find empty shells or shriveled and darkened beans to discard. You can do the sorting while you have them in a colander to rinse under cool water.

Lentils and split peas don't require soaking, but all other dried beans do. You can use the no-hassle long-soak method, or if you're short on time or forgot to soak the beans the night before, do the quick-soak method.

The Long-Soak Method

This can be done in the large pot with a lid that you'll use to cook the beans. Place the desired amount of beans in the pot. (Remember that the beans will swell to at least three times their dried volume when cooked. Preparing the entire bag is time-saving if you plan to use all those beans or if you plan to freeze the cooked beans for longer storage and convenience.) Cover the beans with water by 3 or 4 inches. Place the lid on the pot to keep out foreign matter—gnats, dust, your roommate's contact lens, you never know. Then, go to bed. Or head off to class.

Fresher beans probably need only 4 hours or so to soften, but they'll be fine if you soak them overnight or all day. Then, you also take the guesswork out of how old any particular bag of beans is.

When the beans are reconstituted and plump, drain the soaking water and rinse the beans. Return the beans to the pot, cover well with water, and cook.

The Quick-Soak Method

If you're really hungry for beans or don't have the time to spare, the quick-soak method is for you. Measure the beans into a large pot with a lid and cover with water by several inches. Set the pot on the stove over high heat and bring to a boil. Boil for 2 minutes. Turn off the heat and remove the pot. Cover the pot and let stand for 1 hour. Drain and rinse the beans. Return them to the pot, cover well with water, and cook.

Let's Get Cookin'

Dried beans have cooking directions on the package that you should follow, as different beans require different cooking times. For best results, cover the beans with the lid ajar while cooking. The beans will cook more evenly, and the water will evaporate less quickly. It's important that the beans remain covered with water while soaking and cooking.

If you don't have access to a stove, you can cook beans in a slow cooker. Soak a 1-pound bag of beans using the long-soak method. In the morning, drain and rinse the beans (and rinse the slow cooker's pot). Return the beans to the slow cooker and cover with water twice as deep. Cover and cook on low heat for 8 to 10 hours or until done.

To freeze any beans you won't be using immediately, drain cooled beans, reserving the cooking liquid. Place 1½ cups cooked beans in a resealable plastic freezer bag, covering with a portion of the reserved cooking liquid. These frozen beans can be used to replace a 14- or 15-ounce can of beans called for in a recipe. Frozen beans keep for up to 6 months.

Lecture Hall

You can cook soaked beans in broth or stock, adding onions, garlic, or other seasonings, but do not add acidic ingredients. Acidic additions, such as tomatoes and vinegar, at the beginning of cooking may prevent the beans from softening. You should also wait until the beans are soft to add salt or sugar.

Of Higher Learning

Canned beans are certainly convenient. While not as inexpensive as dried beans, they require little preparation time and are still budget-friendly.

Veggie-Packed Rice Salad $

A tasty use for leftover rice or a great make-ahead side dish for a nutritious lunch, this salad is packed with nutrients.

½ cup cooked brown rice, cooled or chilled	2 TB. drained sliced green olives with pimiento
¼ cup frozen whole-kernel corn	2 TB. diced celery
	1 TB. diced yellow onions
¼ cup frozen green peas	2 TB. low-fat Italian salad dressing
2 TB. diced green bell pepper	

1. In a 1½-cup or larger bowl with a lid, combine brown rice, corn, peas, green bell pepper, green olives with pimiento, celery, and onions, and stir to mix. Pour salad dressing over rice mixture, and stir until evenly coated.

2. Cover and chill for at least 1 hour. Stir again before serving.

> **Yield: 2 servings**
>
> **Prep time:** 3 minutes
> **Chill time:** 1 hour
> **Serving size:** ⅔ cup
>
> **Each serving has:**
> 129 calories
> 37 calories from fat
> 4 g fat
> 0.5 g saturated fat
> 3 g protein
> 21 g carbohydrates

Of Higher Learning

If you have access to a stovetop and plan to be nearby for 35 to 50 minutes—studying or whatever—regular long-grain brown rice is simple: boil, cover, cook.

Grandma's Best Coleslaw $

Stir together this quick mix before you start to cook dinner, and you've got a creamy, low-fat slaw to accompany nearly any meal.

½ (16-oz.) pkg. shredded green cabbage with carrots coleslaw mix	¼ cup low-fat slaw dressing
	¼ cup reduced-fat mayonnaise

1. In a medium to large bowl with a lid, combine coleslaw mix, slaw dressing, and mayonnaise. Stir well until evenly coated.

2. Cover and chill for at least 30 minutes. Stir again before serving.

> **Yield: 4 servings**
>
> **Prep time:** 3 minutes
> **Chill time:** 30 minutes
> **Serving size:** ½ cup
>
> **Each serving has:**
> 72 calories
> 37 calories from fat
> 4 g fat
> 1 g saturated fat
> 1 g protein
> 9 g carbohydrates

Too-Good Two-Bean Salad ⚡

The dressing for this bean salad imparts a slight kick to your taste buds, making this salad my personal favorite—I'm not kidding; no one else got to taste-test this recipe.

½ small yellow onion

¼ rib celery

1 (14.5-oz.) can cut green beans, rinsed and drained

1 (15-oz.) can dark red kidney beans, rinsed and drained

¼ cup cider vinegar

2 TB. extra-virgin olive oil

½ TB. granulated sugar

¼ tsp. dry mustard

⅛ tsp. garlic powder

⅛ tsp. onion powder

⅛ tsp. ground black pepper

⅛ tsp. ground *cayenne*

Yield: 7 servings
Prep time: 8 minutes
Chill time: 1 hour
Serving size: ½ cup
Each serving has:
90 calories
21 calories from fat
2 g fat
0 g saturated fat
4 g protein
14 g carbohydrates

1. On a cutting board with a sharp knife, cut onion into thin slices and cut in half. Dice celery. Combine onion, celery, green beans, and kidney beans in a 4-cup or larger bowl with a lid.

2. In a small bowl, combine cider vinegar, olive oil, sugar, dry mustard, garlic powder, onion powder, pepper, and cayenne. Stir with a fork until blended. Pour over bean mixture, stirring until coated.

3. Cover and chill for at least 1 hour. Stir again before serving.

Class Notes

Cayenne, sometimes referred to as ground red pepper, is a fiery spice ground from hot chili peppers, especially the cayenne chili, which is a slender, red, very hot pepper.

Easy-Mix Carrot Salad ⚡

Yield: 2 servings
Prep time: 3 minutes
Chill time: 30 minutes
Serving size: ½ cup
Each serving has:
98 calories
16 calories from fat
2 g fat
0 g saturated fat
1 g protein
22 g carbohydrates

Delight in this classic, quick-mix salad, knowing you're getting plenty of vitamin A from the carrots and iron from the raisins.

1 cup shredded carrots
¼ cup raisins

1½ TB. reduced-fat mayonnaise
½ tsp. lemon juice

1. In a medium bowl with a lid, combine carrots, raisins, mayonnaise, and lemon juice. Stir until blended.

2. Cover and chill for at least 30 minutes. Stir again before serving.

Rosy Beet Salad ⚡

Yield: 3 servings
Prep time: 2 minutes
Chill time: 30 minutes
Serving size: ½ cup
Each serving has:
62 calories
2 calories from fat
0 g fat
0 g saturated fat
3 g protein
13 g carbohydrates

This colorful salad will brighten up any meal—as well as your health, as beets are a good source of folate.

1 (15-oz.) can shoestring beets, rinsed and drained
½ cup fat-free plain yogurt

⅛ tsp. ground cloves (optional)
Pinch each salt and ground black pepper

1. In a 3-cup bowl with a lid, combine beets, yogurt, cloves (if using), salt, and pepper. Stir to mix.

2. Cover and chill for at least 30 minutes. Stir again before serving.

Lecture Hall

Beet juice easily stains surfaces, so be sure to wipe up any spots and rinse any utensils and containers immediately. Try to avoid splattering to prevent unnoticed stains. (You won't want to store this salad in your good plastic storage containers either.)

Make-Ahead Creamy Fruit Salad $$

This dish is so simple to make, you'll want to mix it up the night before if you've invited people to dinner. It's one less thing you have to worry about.

1 (16-oz.) pkg. frozen unsweetened sliced peaches

1 (16-oz.) pkg. frozen unsweetened strawberries

1 (16-oz.) pkg. frozen unsweetened mango chunks

1 (20-oz.) can crushed pineapple in its own juice, undrained

1 (6-serving-size) pkg. vanilla sugar-free or regular instant pudding mix

Yield: 12 servings
Prep time: 12 minutes
Chill time: 10 to 12 hours
Serving size: ¼ cup
Each serving has:
92 calories
1 calorie from fat
0 g fat
0 g saturated fat
1 g protein
23 g carbohydrates

1. On a cutting board with a sharp knife, cut peaches into bite-size pieces. Cut strawberries in half.

2. In a 3-quart or 13×9×2-inch container with a lid, combine peaches, strawberries, mango, and pineapple. Sprinkle pudding mix over top, and stir until mixture is evenly distributed and pudding mix is absorbed.

3. Cover and chill for 10 to 12 hours or until fruit is thawed. Stir again before serving.

Variation: You can substitute your favorite unsweetened frozen fruits for the peaches, strawberries, and mango.

Learning Curve

To help make cutting the frozen fruits easier, periodically run the knife blade under warm water. Turn the peach slices on their sides and keep your fingers out of the way to avoid injury.

Fluffy Pistachio Salad ⚡

This mint-green combination is a sweet side salad or a great dessert dish that's nice for carry-in dinners. Plus, it keeps well.

Yield: 10 servings
Prep time: 5 minutes
Chill time: 1 hour
Serving size: ½ cup
Each serving has:
126 calories
49 calories from fat
5 g fat
1 g saturated fat
1 g protein
19 g carbohydrates

1 (20-oz.) can crushed pineapple in its own juice, undrained

1 (4-serving-size) pkg. pistachio sugar-free or regular instant pudding mix

½ cup unsalted chopped pecans

½ cup miniature marshmallows

1 (8-oz.) container fat-free frozen whipped topping, thawed

1. In a large bowl with a lid, combine pineapple and pudding mix until blended. Stir in pecans and marshmallows. Fold in whipped topping until well blended.

2. Cover and chill for at least 1 hour before serving.

Learning Curve

Canned goods are often packed with liquids, such as water, oil, or fruit juices. Watch recipes for directives indicating whether the liquid should be drained or not. Some recipes, such as this one, use the packing liquids and call for *undrained* ingredients.

Chapter 17

Eat Your Veggies

In This Chapter

- ◆ Selecting the freshest vegetables
- ◆ Veggie storing and cooking tips
- ◆ Vegetable side dishes you'll be proud to serve

Vegetables are good for you—usually low in calories, low in fat, high in vitamins and minerals, and a good source of fiber. Without all the fattening additions we too often like to slather on, you can eat vegetables to your heart's content.

Vegetables are at their best quality, as well as least expensive, when they're in season. To save money and get the veggie's best flavor, try to plan your fresh vegetable dishes around seasonable produce.

Vegetable Survey

Perhaps the first matter I must clear up is what is a vegetable. Scientifically speaking, many foods we consider vegetables—bell peppers, squash, cucumbers, tomatoes, avocados—are really seed-bearing fruits. Still, according to the United States Department of Agriculture, vegetables are defined by how they're used, not how they grow. Vegetables are served with the main meal and not as dessert, as fruits are.

Of Higher Learning

The question of fruit versus vegetable actually went before the U.S. Supreme Court. *Nix* v. *Hedden* disputed an 1883 tariff act on imported vegetables. The Nix family fought for reimbursement of unjustly collected taxes on their import of tomatoes, which are botanically fruits. In the 1893 decision, the Supreme Court unanimously ruled that tomatoes, in common language, were considered vegetables.

Now here's a quick synopsis of veggies and what to look for when shopping. You will be quizzed on this. (Just kidding.)

Asparagus have tightly closed tips and newly cut stems when freshest. Buy a bunch with stems of even thickness for even cooking, but you needn't be concerned about searching out pencil-thin spears; asparagus can be tender at any size. Look for even green coloring down the spears (unless you're buying white or purple varieties); you'll snap off a bit of white near the base during preparation. If you won't be cooking the asparagus soon, wrap damp paper towels around the stem ends and store the spears in a sealed plastic bag for a few days in the refrigerator. Rinse asparagus under cool, running water before cooking and snap off the stem ends where they naturally break to discard the fibrous, woody portions.

Avocados should have blemish-free skins that are dimpled dark green or smooth green. Pick avocados that are heavy for their size. Yielding to gentle pressure indicates ripeness. Store at room temperature for 1 to 2 days or in the refrigerator for a week. If you don't use the entire avocado, you can prevent discoloration by keeping the pit with the unused portion, rubbing lemon juice on the cut surfaces and directly covering the surfaces with plastic wrap.

Bell peppers are available in a rainbow of colors. Green bell peppers are commonly available and generally lower priced than red, yellow, orange, or other colors. The green, immature bell peppers have a more intense taste, while red, yellow, and orange varieties have a sweeter flavor. Look for firm, smooth, fresh peppers. Store in the refrigerator in the produce bag for up to a week. To eliminate waste, prepare peppers as they'll be used and freeze in plastic freezer bags.

Broccoli at its best has tight green to purplish buds atop smooth, blemish-free, freshly cut stems. Avoid yellowing buds or leaves and woody stems that are dried out where cut. Keep refrigerated in the produce bag and use within a week.

Carrots called for in this cookbook are ready-to-eat baby carrots. If you like to utilize your vegetable peeler and contemplate thesis themes as you peel, look for crisp, bright carrots. Reject cracked or limp carrots, as well as those with roots sprouting. If the green tops are still on, cut them off before storing the carrots in a plastic bag for 2 weeks or longer. If the carrots have begun to go limp on you, soak them in ice water for 30 to 60 minutes before using.

Cauliflower heads should have compact, creamy-white florets free of discoloration and bright green leaves that aren't wilting or browning. Keep refrigerated in the produce bag and use within a week. Discard the stem end with its leaves, separating the cauliflower into florets. Rinse under cold, running water.

Celery stalks should look crisp and freshly cut. If the leaves are still present, they should look fresh, not yellowed or wilted. Store celery in the produce bag in the refrigerator for up to 2 weeks. Remove individual ribs as needed, trim the ends, and rinse under cold, running water. Should celery begin to go limp, refresh it in ice-cold water for 30 to 60 minutes before using.

Cucumbers for slicing should be bright green, smooth, and slender without yellowing or withering. Store in the produce bag on a top refrigerator shelf. Cucumbers don't have to be peeled before eating. Many times, cucumbers are waxed for sale; if yours is (it'll be shiny and slick-feeling), wash it with a commercially sold fruit and vegetable wash to remove residue.

Of Higher Learning

A stalk? A rib? Just what in the celery are you talking about? Let's keep it simple. Celery grows, the stalk is cut, and it's slipped into a plastic bag to sell at your supermarket. When you follow a recipe, you break off a rib of celery. Got it?

Mushrooms are available in a number of varieties. The mushrooms called for in these recipes are the common, inexpensive button mushrooms. They should have smooth, closed caps; if the gills are showing, they're old. Sliced mushrooms are time-savers when a recipe specifies them. Mushrooms can be stored for several days in a brown paper bag in the refrigerator. Just before using, brush them clean with a mushroom brush or a soft-bristled, clean toothbrush. If needed, you can quickly rinse mushrooms and dry them with paper towels. Trim the stem ends or remove them.

Onions are a kitchen staple available in several forms—green onions, sweet onions, red onions, and yellow onions are called for in this book. Fresh onions should appear

Lecture Hall

Storing potatoes and onions near each other is often a common practice, but don't do it. Fresh produce emits gases, and while it's sometimes beneficial as when ripening an avocado with an apple, potatoes and onions don't play nice. Stored together, potatoes and onions will rot quickly and their flavors will be affected.

just that way, not slimy or moldy. Dried onions should have clean, dry skins without cracks, bruises, wrinkles, mold, or sprouts. Green onions will keep for 2 weeks in the produce bag in the refrigerator. Other onions can be stored in a cool, dark place with circulating air (not near the potatoes).

Potatoes can be brown, gold, red-skinned, or even blue. The recipes in these pages call for general, all-purpose potatoes. They should be free of sprouting eyes, cracks, mold, wrinkles, and green skins while being firm. Potatoes should be stored in a cool, dark place with circulating air (not near the onions) for up to 2 weeks. Just before using, scrub potatoes well under cool, running water with a brush, if you like.

Squash are of two kinds—summer squash and winter squash. Summer squash, such as crookneck squash and zucchini, should be small and smooth-skinned. Keep them in the produce bag in the refrigerator's crisper drawer for several days. Trim the ends and rinse under running water before using. Winter squash, such as acorn and butternut squash, should have clean, thick skins and be firm and full for their size. Keep in a cool, dark place for several months. A large, sharp knife can cut the thick skins. Scoop out and discard the seeds with a metal spoon.

Sweet potatoes may be identified as yams, but you're likely just getting the reddish-skinned, orange-fleshed type of sweet potato. The skins should be unmarked and the potatoes firm, not soft. Store them in a cool, dark, ventilated place, and use within a week. Wash under cool, running water to clean just before preparing.

Tomatoes should be smooth-skinned and appear plump, not wrinkled or bruised. Store them stem side down at room temperature. Refrigerate any cut or very ripe tomatoes that won't be used immediately. Bring them to room temperature again before using, and wash under running water to clean. Cut out the stem end to core a tomato before using; slice off the blossom end, if preferred.

Slow-Baked Potatoes $

When you don't have access to an oven or if you won't have an hour or so to wait by the oven, preparing baked potatoes in your slow cooker is the solution.

6 medium all-purpose potatoes

Yield: 6 servings	

Prep time: 8 minutes
Cook time: 6 to 8 hours
Serving size: 1 potato

Each serving has:
94 calories
1 calorie from fat
0 g fat
0 g saturated fat
2.5 g protein
21 g carbohydrates

1. Scrub potatoes well. Prick all over with the tines of a fork, and wrap in aluminum foil. Place in a 3½- to 4-quart slow cooker.

2. Cover and cook on low for 6 to 8 hours or until tender.

Variation: The potato skins won't dry out in the slow cooker, but if you like them to have a buttery taste, you can lightly spray each potato with a buttery spray (two or three sprays) before wrapping in the foil.

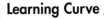

Learning Curve

To get the most out of your roll of foil, tear off small pieces of foil and then cover the potatoes on the diagonal, folding the ends over to enclose the potatoes.

Cinnamon-Sugar-Sprinkled Sweet Potato $$

Full of beta carotene and great taste, this side dish is a welcome change from everyday white potatoes.

1 large sweet potato or yam	**½ tsp. ground cinnamon**
1 TB. firmly packed light brown sugar	**1 TB. light butter with canola oil**

Yield: 2 servings
Prep time: 4 minutes
Cook time: 11 to 13 minutes
Serving size: ½ potato
Each serving has:
108 calories
27 calories from fat
3 g fat
0.5 g saturated fat
1 g protein
20 g carbohydrates

1. Scrub sweet potato and poke all over with the tines of a fork. Place sweet potato on a double layer of paper towels. Cook on high power for 4 or 5 minutes. Turn potato over, rotating if needed. Cook on high power for 4 or 5 minutes more, or until fork-tender. Wrap potato inside paper towels, and let it stand for 3 minutes.

2. Meanwhile, stir together brown sugar and cinnamon in a small bowl.

3. Split sweet potato and fluff pulp with a fork. Work light butter into pulp with the fork, and sprinkle cinnamon-sugar mixture over sweet potato, working into pulp as desired.

Variation: To prepare sweet potato in the oven, scrub and poke all over with the tines of a fork. Lightly coat with a no-calorie buttery spray, wrap in foil, and place on the oven rack in the center of the oven. Bake in a preheated 400°F oven for 1 to 1¼ hours or until fork-tender. Season with cinnamon-sugar and light butter as directed.

Learning Curve

A true yam is a tropical tuber seldom available in the United States. Unless you're in a Latin, Asian, or African market-place, you're probably looking at an orange-fleshed variety of sweet potato, which is good for this recipe.

Glazed Baby Carrots $

A speedy single-serve side dish, sweet glazed carrots go well with almost any entrée.

2 cups hot water

½ cup baby carrots

½ TB. firmly packed light brown sugar

1 tsp. light butter with canola oil

Yield: 1 serving
Prep time: 2 minutes **Cook time:** 9 to 11 minutes
Each serving has: 61 calories 18 calories from fat 2 g fat 0 g saturated fat 1 g protein 11 g carbohydrates

1. Pour hot water into a 3-cup microwave-safe glass bowl. Cook on high power for 5 or 6 minutes or until boiling. Add carrots, and cook on high power for 4 or 5 minutes or until tender. Drain and return carrots to the bowl.

2. Stir brown sugar and light butter into carrots until melted and carrots are evenly coated. Serve hot.

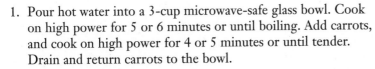

Learning Curve _____

Unless otherwise noted, brown sugar should always be firmly packed for measuring. That means the brown sugar should release from the measuring spoon or measuring cup having taken on its shape.

Pecan-Studded Green Beans $$

This quick side dish is easy to make, yet it makes you feel like you're eating an elegant vegetable accompaniment.

Yield: 3 servings
Prep time: 2 minutes
Cook time: 4 to 6 minutes
Serving size: ½ cup
Each serving has:
68 calories
43 calories from fat
5 g fat
1 g saturated fat
2 g protein
7 g carbohydrates

1½ TB. light butter with canola oil

1½ TB. chopped unsalted pecans

1 (14.5-oz.) can whole or cut green beans, rinsed and drained

Pinch salt and ground black pepper or to taste

1. Place light butter in a small, wide-bottomed microwave-safe glass dish. Sprinkle pecans over top, and cook on high power for 45 to 90 seconds or until butter is bubbling and pecans are fragrant.

2. Stir green beans into pecans until evenly coated. Cook on high power for 3 or 4 minutes or until heated through.

3. Season with salt and pepper, and stir again before serving.

Learning Curve

When a recipe calls for a chopped ingredient, the placement of the directive dictates the measuring. In this recipe, the pecans should be chopped before measuring out the 1½ tablespoons. (Purchase the pecans chopped to save time.) Sometimes a recipe calls for something such as 1 cup seedless grapes, chopped. In that case, the grapes should be measured first and then chopped.

Lemon-Pepper Asparagus ♫♫♫

Savor the early spring taste of asparagus enhanced with lemon juice for a fat-free side dish.

3 cups water

1 lb. fresh asparagus

1½ to 2 tsp. lemon juice

½ tsp. lemon-pepper seasoning or ground black pepper

Yield: 4 servings
Prep time: 1 minute
Cook time: 9 to 11 minutes
Serving size: ½ cup
Each serving has:
23 calories
1 calorie from fat
0 g fat
0 g saturated fat
2.5 g protein
5 g carbohydrates

1. Pour water into a 1-quart microwave-safe glass dish. Cook on high power for 6 or 7 minutes or until boiling.

2. Meanwhile, snap ends off asparagus spears. On a cutting board with a sharp knife, cut spears into 1- to 1½-inch pieces. Carefully add asparagus to boiling water. Let stand for 3 or 4 minutes or until crisp-tender. Drain and return asparagus to the dish.

3. Splash on lemon juice and sprinkle on lemon-pepper seasoning. Stir until evenly coated, and serve immediately.

Learning Curve

To trim asparagus spears, hold a spear's end with one hand and about halfway or so down the spear with the other hand. Bend gently until the spear naturally breaks off its woody end, and discard it.

Summer Squash Medley $$

This side dish is quick to make, tastes great, and will leave no left-overs.

Yield: 1 serving
Prep time: 3 minutes
Cook time: 5 or 6 minutes
Each serving has:
65 calories
20 calories from fat
2 g fat
1 g saturated fat
5 g protein
8 g carbohydrates

½ **very small yellow summer squash, trimmed**

½ **very small zucchini squash, trimmed**

1 **large button mushroom, trimmed**

1 **thin slice yellow onion**

¼ **tsp. dried Italian seasoning**

2 **TB. 2 percent-milk shredded cheddar cheese**

1. On a cutting board with a sharp knife, cut yellow summer squash and zucchini squash into thin slices. Cut mushroom into slices. Cut onion slice in half and separate into half rings.

2. Combine yellow summer squash, zucchini squash, mushroom, and onion in a 2-cup microwave-safe glass dish. Sprinkle Italian seasoning on top. Cover with plastic wrap, venting, and cook on high power for 4 or 5 minutes or until vegetables are tender, stirring halfway through cooking time and rotating if needed.

3. Uncover and stir squash mixture. Sprinkle cheese over top, and cook on high power for 30 to 45 seconds or until cheese starts to melt.

Learning Curve

Watch for ingredient directions such as "trimmed." In this recipe, the squashes should have either the stem ends or the blossom ends cut off, depending on which halves of the squashes are being used. The mushroom should have its stem freshly cut; the portion with the old cut should be discarded.

Sweet and Easy Acorn Squash $

This easy side dish provides its own serving dish, perfect for impressing your guest.

1 small acorn squash (about the size of a large grapefruit)	2 TB. firmly packed light brown sugar
2 tsp. light butter with canola oil	

Yield: 2 servings
Prep time: 5 minutes
Cook time: 8 to 10 minutes
Serving size: 1 half squash
Each serving has:
133 calories
11 calories from fat
1 g fat
0 g saturated fat
2 g protein
32.5 g carbohydrates

1. Wash and dry acorn squash. On a cutting board with a large, sharp knife, cut squash in half lengthwise from stem end to blossom end. With a metal spoon, scoop out and discard seeds and strings.

2. Arrange each squash cut side down in a microwave-safe glass dish large enough to hold them comfortably. Add about 1 inch water to the dish, and cook on high power for 6 or 7 minutes or until nearly tender. Remove the dish and carefully turn over each squash half. Add 1 teaspoon light butter and 1 tablespoon brown sugar to the cavity of each squash half. Return the dish to the microwave, and cook on high power for 2 or 3 minutes or until tender.

3. Stir sauce and lightly coat squash flesh, allowing the remainder to pool in cavities for dipping. Carefully remove squash halves with tongs or 2 spoons. Scoop squash flesh from shells to eat.

Lecture Hall _____

Use extra caution when cutting any hard-shelled winter squash. Keep your fingers out of the way, as the rounded acorn squash is prone to rolling.

Cheesy Dijonnaise Cauliflower $$

If you're not partial to its characteristic flat flavor, use this side dish as a tasty way to serve cooked cauliflower.

Yield: 4 servings
Prep time: 5 minutes
Cook time: 8 to 10 minutes
Serving size: 1 cup
Each serving has:
78 calories
33 calories from fat
4 g fat
2 g saturated fat
3.5 g protein
5 g carbohydrates

1 medium head cauliflower	3 TB. Dijon mustard
¼ cup water	½ cup 2 percent-milk shredded sharp cheddar cheese
⅓ cup reduced-fat mayonnaise	

1. On a cutting board with a sharp knife, cut off dark green leaves from cauliflower and discard. Cut cauliflower into *florets*, discarding the core. Place florets in a 1-quart microwave-safe glass dish. Pour in water. Cover with plastic wrap, venting, and cook on high power for 6 or 7 minutes or until cauliflower is tender. Drain.

2. Meanwhile, combine mayonnaise and Dijon mustard in a small bowl. Stir until blended. Spoon into cauliflower and stir to coat.

3. Sprinkle cheese over top, and cook on high power for 1½ to 2½ minutes or until cheese is melted.

Class Notes

Florets are the flower or bud ends of cauliflower and broccoli. Cut off these ends with only a small amount of the stems. You can discard the stems or reserve them for other recipes to stretch your dollar. Cream soups and vegetable medleys make good use of tender broccoli and cauliflower stems.

Chapter 18

Using Your Noodle

In This Chapter

- ◆ Supermarket time- and money-savers
- ◆ Help avoiding impulse buys
- ◆ Neat noodle dishes you'll crave

Food shopping is easy if you have an unlimited grocery budget. You buy what you want when you want it. Most shoppers, however—likely you included—have to watch what they spend. With a few tips, hints, and supermarket secrets revealed, you can eat well all week for less dough.

One great way to stretch your food budget is to plan dishes using noodles. Inexpensive and filling, a variety of noodles can round out your meals deliciously.

Smart Supermarket Strategies

Saving time and money when grocery shopping starts well before you set foot in the supermarket. A little planning saves you time in the long run, and it definitely saves you money.

Start by looking at your local supermarket's circular if it has one, whether you nab it from your neighbor's newspaper or check it out online. Use the flier to create a grocery list. Scan the sale items for your staples, special buys, and foods you can create meals around. If you're familiar with the store's layout, it's helpful to arrange the list as you will navigate the aisles. If you have coupons for those items, attach them directly to the list. I also make a note—a simple circled "c"—by items I have a coupon for so I don't forget.

With your list prepared, clean out your refrigerator and toss anything past its use-by date, too old leftovers, and everything you no longer recognize. If you throw out anything you thought was okay and planned to use, you need to add it to your shopping list. And now your refrigerator is spacious and ready to accept all the great foods that need refrigeration immediately upon your arrival home.

> **Learning Curve**
>
> Use a "disposable" e-mail address to subscribe to newsletters offered by the brands you often buy. Many communications from these companies include product coupons you can print. Check with your local supermarket to be sure it accepts online coupons, as some won't.

> **Lecture Hall**
>
> Do not, I repeat, do not go grocery shopping on an empty stomach. When you're hungry, resisting impulse buying is even harder, and you can end up spending more money. Also avoid shopping when you're rushed. When you're in a hurry, you won't take time to compare prices fairly. Packaging isn't necessarily equal among different brands. To know how much you're really paying, look for the per-unit price and compare ounces to ounces.

Be sure to always check the sell-by, use-by, and best-by dates in the store. Coming home to find your turkey pepperoni expired last month means at least time spent collecting the package and your receipt so you can stand in line at the store's customer service department.

When you shop, look above and below your eye level. The store places the best-selling, more expensive items at eye level. Bargains can be found when you search outside this zone. Less popular brands and store brands are most often just as good as the name-brand version. Read the food label to ensure similar quality and nutrition. Try them once. If you aren't satisfied with the store brands, many supermarkets will offer you your money back.

Also look into getting the supermarket's loyalty-program card if your supermarket offers one. You can usually apply for a store's card at the customer service counter. This often helps you save money.

Before you leave the store, you might also want to double-check that the cashier took off any coupons you had before completing the transaction. (I was sent to the customer service line a few times to settle my coupons before I learned this time-saving tip.)

Learning Curve

Comparison shopping, bargain hunting, and label reading are more easily accomplished when few shoppers are in the store. If you can, shop early in the morning on a weekday. Most supermarkets are busiest on weekends and in late afternoon.

Golden Mushroom Noodles $

A flavorful side dish good for accompanying meat entrées, you can make this noodle recipe heartier by using crimini (baby portobello) mushrooms.

Yield: 1 serving
Prep time: 1 minute
Cook time: 13 to 16 minutes
Each serving has:
209 calories
33 calories from fat
4 g fat
0.5 g saturated fat
9 g protein
35 g carbohydrates

3 cups hot water

¾ cup uncooked yolk-free whole-wheat extra-wide egg noodles

1 TB. light butter with canola oil

1 cup sliced button mushrooms

½ TB. prepared steak sauce

1. Pour hot water into a 1-quart microwave-safe glass bowl. Cook on high power for 6 or 7 minutes or until boiling. Add egg noodles, and cook on high power for 6 to 8 minutes or until done. Drain.

2. Meanwhile, add ½ tablespoon light butter to an 11-inch non-stick electric skillet. Set the skillet at 300°F, and cook light butter for 30 seconds or until melted and bubbly at edges. Add mushrooms, and cook and stir for 5 or 6 minutes or until colored and tender. Add egg noodles and remaining ½ tablespoon light butter, stirring until evenly coated.

3. Turn off heat, stir in steak sauce until evenly coated, and serve hot.

Variation: For stovetop preparation, cook egg noodles in a saucepan according to the package directions. In a small skillet or saucepan over medium-low to medium heat, melt ½ tablespoon light butter. Add mushrooms and cook, stirring frequently, for 5 or 6 minutes or until colored and tender. Add drained egg noodles and remaining ½ tablespoon light butter, stirring until evenly coated. Turn off heat, stir in steak sauce until evenly coated, and serve.

Learning Curve

Be sure to read over all the information printed on an ingredient's packaging. Many times you'll find cooking directions, serving suggestions, recipes, and more useful details.

Creamy Poppy Seed Noodles $

Subtle tasting, this creamy dish can be served alongside nearly any fish, poultry, or meat entrée.

3 cups hot water

1½ cups uncooked yolk-free whole-wheat extra-wide egg noodles

1 tsp. light butter with canola oil

½ tsp. poppy seeds

⅛ tsp. garlic pepper

Pinch salt

¼ cup fat-free sour cream

Yield: 2 servings		
Prep time: 2 minutes		
Cook time: 12 to 15 minutes		
Serving size: ¾ cup		
Each serving has:		
188 calories		
16 calories from fat		
2 g fat		
0 g saturated fat		
7 g protein		
35 g carbohydrates		

1. Pour hot water into a 1-quart microwave-safe glass bowl. Cook on high power for 6 or 7 minutes or until boiling. Add egg noodles, and cook on high power for 6 to 8 minutes or until done. Drain egg noodles and return to the bowl.

2. Stir light butter, poppy seeds, garlic pepper, and salt into hot noodles. Add sour cream and stir until evenly coated. Serve immediately.

Variation: If you don't have garlic pepper on your spice rack, substitute a pinch of garlic powder plus a pinch of ground black pepper.

Learning Curve

Starting with hot water reduces the cooking time needed for the water to reach a boil. Still, if you have to stand at the faucet for several minutes before the water gets hot, you haven't saved any time and probably wasted a good amount of water.

Dilly Cottage Noodles $

Highly flavored and textured, this side dish can be spooned up with bold beef or pork dinners.

Yield: 2 servings	

Prep time: 1 minute

Cook time: 12 to 15 minutes

Serving size: ¾ cup

Each serving has:

194 calories

7 calories from fat

1 g fat

0 g saturated fat

13 g protein

33 g carbohydrates

3 cups hot water

1½ cups yolk-free whole-wheat extra-wide egg noodles

½ cup fat-free small-curd cottage cheese

1 tsp. dried dill weed or 1 TB. chopped fresh dill

Pinch ground black pepper

1. Pour hot water into a 1-quart microwave-safe glass bowl. Cook on high power for 6 or 7 minutes or until boiling. Add egg noodles, and cook on high power for 6 to 8 minutes or until done. Drain egg noodles and return to the bowl.

2. Meanwhile, combine cottage cheese, dill weed, and pepper in a small bowl. Stir well. Add to egg noodles, stirring until evenly coated. Serve immediately.

Learning Curve

Noodles are available in a variety of sizes from very delicate thin strands to extra-wide ribbons. Substantial sauces need the support of wider noodles while thinner sauces can be paired with finer cuts.

Garlic-Butter Orzo

When you need a generally pleasing side dish to accompany a bold-flavored spotlighted main course, this dish is perfect.

3 cups hot water

⅓ cup uncooked *orzo*

1 TB. light butter with canola oil

¾ tsp. lemon juice

¼ tsp. Worcestershire sauce

½ to 1 tsp. drained minced garlic

Dash hot pepper sauce

Yield: 2 servings
Prep time: 1 minute
Cook time: 16 to 19 minutes
Serving size: ½ cup
Each serving has:
122 calories
20 calories from fat
2 g fat
0 g saturated fat
4 g protein
22 g carbohydrates

1. Pour hot water into a 1-quart microwave-safe glass bowl. Cook on high power for 6 or 7 minutes or until boiling. Add orzo, and cook on high power for 9 or 10 minutes or until done. Drain.

2. Meanwhile, combine light butter, lemon juice, Worcestershire sauce, garlic, and hot pepper sauce in a 1½-cup microwave-safe glass bowl. Cover with plastic wrap, venting, and cook on high power for 45 to 90 seconds or until butter is melted and sauce is bubbly. Stir sauce, add orzo, and stir until evenly coated. Serve hot.

Class Notes

Orzo isn't a noodle strictly speaking, but a long-grained rice-shape pasta. You'll find it in a small package along-side other pasta shapes.

Speedy Soy-Sauced Rice Noodles $

These chewy noodles make an unassuming side dish for Asian entrées.

Yield: 4 servings
Prep time: 2 minutes
Cook time: 20 minutes
Serving size: ½ cup
Each serving has:
133 calories
25 calories from fat
3 g fat
0 g saturated fat
2 g protein
25 g carbohydrates

6 cups hot water

4 oz. rice noodles

1 green onion

1 TB. extra-virgin olive oil

½ to 1 tsp. drained minced garlic

2 TB. reduced-sodium soy sauce

½ TB. hot pepper sauce

1. Pour hot water into a 6-quart nonstick electric wok to high heat. Cook for 15 minutes or until boiling. Add rice noodles, covering with boiling water, and cook for 3 minutes or until done. Unplug the wok and drain rice noodles. Return rice noodles to the wok, pushing to one side, and replug in, and set to medium heat.

2. Meanwhile, on a cutting board with a sharp knife, finely chop green onion. Set aside.

3. Add olive oil to the wok. Stir garlic into olive oil and cook for 30 seconds or until golden. Reduce heat to low, and stir rice noodles and garlic together. Stir in soy sauce and hot pepper sauce until noodles are evenly coated.

4. Turn off heat, sprinkle green onion over individual servings, and serve.

Learning Curve _____

If your measuring spoon set doesn't have a ½-tablespoon measure, remember that ½ tablespoon is equal to 1 ½ teaspoons.

Broccoli and Sesame Soba Noodles $$

A cold side dish with Asian flavor, these noodles can be served along-side the Teriyaki-Marinated Chicken Breast (recipe in Chapter 14) or Hot Grilled Thighs (recipe in Chapter 9). They're also hearty enough to serve as a vegetarian entrée.

4 cups hot water

4 oz. dried soba noodles

2 medium stalks broccoli

2 green onions

¼ cup Asian sesame with gin-ger salad dressing

½ tsp. drained minced garlic

2 TB. toasted sesame seeds

Yield: 4 servings		
Prep time: 5 minutes		
Cook time: 12 to 14 minutes		
Serving size: 1 cup		
Each serving has:		
180 calories		
60 calories from fat		
7 g fat		
1 g saturated fat		
7 g protein		
27 g carbohydrates		

1. Pour hot water into a 1½-quart microwave-safe glass bowl. Cook on high power for 8 or 9 minutes or until boiling. Add soba noodles, breaking as needed to fit, and cook on high power for 4 or 5 minutes or until done. Drain. Rinse noodles thoroughly in cold water and drain again.

2. Meanwhile, on a cutting board with a sharp knife, cut broc-coli into florets. (Discard stalks or reserve for use in another recipe.) Coarsely chop green onions.

3. In a small bowl, stir together salad dressing, garlic, and green onions. Transfer soba noodles to a serving bowl. Pour salad dressing mixture over soba noodles, and stir until evenly coated. Add sesame seeds, and stir until evenly distributed. Add broccoli, and stir until evenly distributed. Serve at room tem-perature or cold.

Learning Curve

If you can't find toasted sesame seeds, buy regular sesame seeds and toast them yourself. You might find toasting instruc-tions given on the package, but if not: pour the sesame seeds into a small, dry skillet over medium-low to medium heat. Toast sesame seeds for 6 to 8 minutes or until golden brown. Shake the skillet and stir the sesame seeds frequently, watching care-fully, as sesame seeds are quick to burn.

Cabbage and Ramen Noodles $

This easy-to-make noodle dish is a great way to use up leftover coleslaw mix.

Yield: 5 servings
Prep time: 3 minutes
Cook time: 16 to 18 minutes
Serving size: ½ cup
Each serving has:
85 calories
24 calories from fat
3 g fat
1 g saturated fat
2.5 g protein
13 g carbohydrates

½ (16-oz.) pkg. shredded green cabbage with carrots coleslaw mix

4 cups plus 2 TB. hot water

1 (3-oz.) pkg. chicken-flavor ramen noodle soup

1. Place coleslaw mix in a 6-cup microwave-safe glass bowl. Cover with plastic wrap, venting, and cook on high power for 5 or 6 minutes or until cooked through and tender, stirring and rotating if needed halfway through cooking time. Let stand, covered, while preparing noodles.

2. Pour 4 cups hot water into a 1½-quart microwave-safe glass dish. Cook on high power for 8 or 9 minutes or until boiling. Add ramen noodles, breaking up, and cook on high power for 3 minutes or until done. Drain and return noodles to the dish. Stir in coleslaw mix.

3. In a small bowl, stir the contents of ramen noodle seasoning packet into 2 tablespoons hot water until blended. Pour over noodle mixture, stirring to coat evenly.

Variation: You can substitute your favorite ramen noodle soup flavor.

Learning Curve

When you're in a hurry, you can cut the cooking time to boil the water by 1 or 2 minutes. The water will be hot enough to cook the pasta or noodles just before it actually begins to boil.

Chapter 19

Grains That Make the Grade

In This Chapter

- ◆ Choosing nutritious grains
- ◆ Storing and cooking grains for flavor and health benefits
- ◆ Grain dishes to tempt your taste buds

Grains are the basic foundation of eating. Finely ground into flours, processed for quicker cooking, and left whole for optimal nutrition, grains feed us as breakfast cereals, in soups and salads, baked into desserts and breads, as foundations for side dishes and casseroles, and even as fillers for entrées.

Grains provide various nutrients, including fiber, protein, vitamins, amino acids, and more. As with any foods, eating a wide variety supplies a compilation of health benefits.

Grain Honor Roll

Supermarket aisles offer a selection of grains in various forms. A number of the grains you may find are ...

Barley is most often called for in soups. It may also be used in cold salads and rice-type dishes. Pearled barley, with its bran removed and polished, is the most common type of this nutty-tasting, chewy grain that's available in both regular and instant versions.

Bulgur is processed from wheat and nutty in flavor. Used similarly to rice, bulgur can also be used in cold salads, such as tabbouleh, a Middle Eastern recipe with parsley, tomatoes, onions, and mint in olive oil and lemon juice.

Cornmeal is ground from yellow, white, or even blue corn. Commonly, you'll find yellow or white enriched degerminated cornmeal on supermarket shelves. If you want a whole grain, look for stone-ground cornmeal. Blue cornmeal is a specialty item with a nutty taste.

Couscous, while used as a grain, is actually a tiny pasta that's a staple ingredient in North African cuisine and is typically made from traditional semolina flour. The recipes here call for the whole-grain, quick-cooking variety of instant whole-wheat couscous.

Hominy is processed from corn kernels, and is puffed and soft after the hulls and germs are removed. The ground meal is referred to as "grits" and is most popular in the South.

Millet is a small, pale, round grain with little flavor. Toast it before cooking for a nuttier taste. Millet is most commonly used as birdseed.

Learning Curve

Don't forget to check in the organic and ethnic sections of your supermarket as well, as some of the specialty grains may well be stocked there. If your area is home to Asian, Latin American, or other kinds of markets, shop those stores, too.

Oats are a flavorful grain commonly enjoyed for breakfast as well as in baked goods. Steel-cut, old-fashioned rolled, quick-cooking, and instant varieties are available.

Quinoa (KEEN-wah) is a nutritious grain high in calcium, B vitamins, and protein. The taste is slightly nutty; it can be toasted before cooking for a deeper color and flavor. A naturally occurring bitter-tasting residue may need to be removed first by rinsing the raw grains under running water; check your package directions.

Rice is available in a number of varieties. The recipes included in this cookbook call for instant brown rice. It cooks quickly while still retaining its outer bran layers, lending to its nutty taste and more chewy consistency. When cooked rice is called for in a recipe, you can choose regular long-grain brown rice. The cooking time is long, but the preparation is easy and the price is very affordable.

Wild rice is the seed of a marsh grass and not truly a rice. The seed is long, pointed, deep brown in color, and firm and chewy with a rich nutlike flavor.

Of Higher Learning

The publication of Dietary Guidelines for Americans is a joint venture by the Department of Health and Human Services and the Department of Agriculture every 5 years. The most recent release advises consuming at least half, or three, of your recommended daily grains as whole grains. For a complete copy of Dietary Guidelines for Americans 2005 or various related articles, visit www.healthierus.gov/dietaryguidelines.

Keep highly processed, degerminated grains in a cool, dry, dark place in an airtight container. Grains that still contain their germ contain oils that may cause rancidity in time. Store these grains in the refrigerator if they won't be used in a short period of time. Check package directions for best-by dates and storage recommendations.

The package directions will also provide cooking instructions for that grain, or follow recipe directions for the called-for ingredient. Whole grains that retain their natural nutrients typically take longer to cook, but because they're less processed, they're usually less expensive. Which grains you choose may be a balance between cost, time, availability, and existing kitchen appliances.

Effortless Salsa Rice $

Try this super-easy alternative to Spanish rice when you're in the mood for Mexican.

1 cup water	**¼ cup prepared salsa**
½ cup uncooked instant brown rice	

1. Combine water and brown rice in a 3-cup microwave-safe glass bowl. Cover with plastic wrap, venting, and cook on high power for 7 or 8 minutes or until most of water is absorbed, rotating if needed. Remove the bowl from the microwave and cover tightly with plastic wrap. Let stand for 5 minutes.

2. Fluff rice with a fork, and stir in salsa until evenly coated.

Variation: For stovetop preparation, follow the package directions to cook instant brown rice or regular long-grain brown rice, as desired. When rice is done, stir in salsa.

Yield: 2 servings

Prep time: 2 minutes

Cook time: 12 or 13 minutes

Serving size: ½ cup

Each serving has:

104 calories

7 calories from fat

1 g fat

0 g saturated fat

2.5 g protein

23 g carbohydrates

Learning Curve

Microwave cooking typically speeds up the cooking process so you can finish faster. This rule doesn't hold true for rice and pasta, as they need time to absorb liquid to become rehydrated.

Crunchy Cashew Rice $

An unassuming yet tasty side dish, this rice can complement almost any entrée.

1 cup fat-free, less-sodium chicken broth	½ cup uncooked instant brown rice
2 TB. diced celery	2 TB. finely chopped unsalted cashews
2 TB. diced yellow onions	
Pinch ground black pepper	

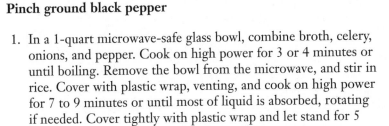

Yield: 2 servings
Prep time: 2 minutes
Cook time: 15 to 18 minutes
Serving size: ½ cup
Each serving has:
158 calories
43 calories from fat
5 g fat
1 g saturated fat
5 g protein
25.5 g carbohydrates

1. In a 1-quart microwave-safe glass bowl, combine broth, celery, onions, and pepper. Cook on high power for 3 or 4 minutes or until boiling. Remove the bowl from the microwave, and stir in rice. Cover with plastic wrap, venting, and cook on high power for 7 to 9 minutes or until most of liquid is absorbed, rotating if needed. Cover tightly with plastic wrap and let stand for 5 minutes or until liquid is absorbed and rice is tender.

2. Fluff rice with a fork before serving, and sprinkle 1 tablespoon cashews over top of each serving.

Learning Curve

If you can only find whole cashews and don't have a nut mill, place a handful of cashews in a resealable plastic bag and close the bag. Pound cashews into pieces using a meat mallet, rolling pin, or other heavy, solid object. (Take care not to puncture the bag.)

Cranberry and Walnut Wild Rice $$$

A lightly sweet, bold side dish, this chewy wild rice mixture livens up the simplest of main dishes.

Yield: 3 servings
Prep time: 1 minute
Cook time: 65 to 80 minutes
Serving size: ½ cup
Each serving has:
234 calories
55 calories from fat
6 g fat
0 g saturated fat
8 g protein
38 g carbohydrates

¼ cup chopped unsalted walnuts

½ heaping cup wild rice

1 (14-oz.) can fat-free, less-sodium chicken broth

¼ tsp. onion powder

¼ cup dried cranberries

1. Add walnuts to an 11-inch nonstick electric skillet set at 300°F. *Toast*, stirring often, for 2 minutes or until fragrant. Add wild rice and toast, stirring often, for 2 more minutes. Slowly pour in broth. Stir in onion powder. Stir in dried cranberries. Increase heat to highest setting, and bring to a boil.

2. Reduce heat, cover, and simmer for 1 to 1¼ hours or until wild rice is tender and liquid is absorbed.

3. Fluff with a fork before serving.

Class Notes

Toast is a directive to heat an ingredient until it's browned and crisp, or in the case of nuts, fragrant and flavorful. Nuts should carefully be watched while toasting, as they can quickly burn.

Goldens and Cherries Couscous $$

When you want a side dish with a touch of sweet, pop this combination into the microwave.

⅔ cup fat-free, less-sodium chicken broth

¼ cup dried golden raisin and sour cherry mixture

⅛ tsp. ground black pepper

½ cup instant whole-wheat couscous

Yield: 4 servings
Prep time: 2 minutes
Cook time: 4 to 6 minutes
Serving size: ½ cup
Each serving has:
144 calories
5 calories from fat
1 g fat
0 g saturated fat
5 g protein
32 g carbohydrates

1. In a 3-cup microwave-safe glass bowl, stir together broth, dried goldens and cherries, and pepper. Cook on high power for 2 or 3 minutes or until fully boiling. Remove the bowl from the microwave. Stir in couscous, cover tightly with plastic wrap, and let stand for 2 or 3 minutes or until liquid is absorbed.

2. Fluff couscous with a fork before serving.

Variation: If you can't find dried goldens and cherries mixed, you can combine whatever proportions you prefer for ¼ cup total golden raisins or even dark raisins and dried sour cherries.

Learning Curve

These directions call for you to fluff with a fork before serving to separate the grains without damaging them and making them mushy.

Sautéed Vegetable Medley Couscous $

An aromatic side dish that's quick and easy, this couscous can complete nearly any meal without overpowering it.

Yield: 2 servings
Prep time: 2 minutes
Cook time: 10 to 13 minutes
Serving size: ⅔ cup
Each serving has:
160 calories
24 calories from fat
3 g fat
0 g saturated fat
6 g protein
28 g carbohydrates

2 tsp. extra-virgin olive oil

¼ cup chopped yellow onions

¼ cup shredded carrots

¼ cup sliced small button mushrooms

½ tsp. drained minced garlic

Pinch ground ginger

½ cup fat-free, less-sodium chicken broth

¾ tsp. reduced-sodium soy sauce

¾ tsp. lemon juice

⅓ cup uncooked whole-wheat couscous

1. Set an 11-inch nonstick electric skillet to 325°F. Add olive oil, and heat for 30 seconds. Add onions and sauté for 2 or 3 minutes or until softened. Add carrots, mushrooms, garlic, and ginger. Cook and stir for 3 to 5 minutes or until mushrooms are colored.

2. Add broth, soy sauce, and lemon juice, and bring to a boil. Stir in couscous, turn off heat, and cover and let stand for 5 minutes or until liquid is absorbed.

3. Fluff with a fork before serving.

Learning Curve

Reduced-sodium soy sauce is often labeled "lite" soy sauce. Different brands vary in the sodium content, which is still quite high. If you have regular soy sauce, you can substitute half water plus half soy sauce in the recipes, and you'll actually be saving on some milligrams of sodium.

Toasted Millet with Herbs $

Prepare this flavor-infused grain dish with any combination of herbs you have in your spice rack. Experiment to find your favorite blend.

½ cup whole millet

1 cup fat-free, less-sodium chicken broth

½ tsp. dried parsley flakes

¼ tsp. dried marjoram

¼ tsp. dried thyme

⅛ tsp. garlic powder

⅛ tsp. onion powder

Yield: 3 servings
Prep time: 1 minute
Cook time: 31 to 33 minutes
Serving size: ½ cup
Each serving has:
133 calories
13 calories from fat
1 g fat
0 g saturated fat
5 g protein
25 g carbohydrates

1. Heat an 11-inch nonstick electric skillet to 250°F. Add millet to the dry skillet and spread into a single layer. Toast for 6 to 8 minutes, stirring often, or until golden and fragrant. Slowly pour in broth. Increase heat to the highest setting and bring to a boil. Stir, reduce heat, cover, and simmer for 20 minutes or until most of liquid is absorbed.

2. Stir in parsley flakes, marjoram, thyme, garlic powder, and onion powder. Cover and cook over low heat for 5 minutes or until liquid is absorbed and millet is tender.

Learning Curve

Whenever a recipe calls for fat-free, less-sodium chicken broth, you can always substitute vegetable broth for a vegetarian dish.

Southwestern-Style Quinoa $

Complement your Tex-Mex entrées with this hearty side dish.

Yield: 5 servings
Prep time: 3 minutes
Cook time: 32 minutes
Serving size: ¾ cup
Each serving has:
160 calories
19 calories from fat
2 g fat
0 g saturated fat
8 g protein
29 g carbohydrates

½ medium yellow onion

1 tsp. extra-virgin olive oil

1 tsp. drained minced garlic

½ cup uncooked quinoa

1 cup fat-free, less-sodium chicken broth

½ tsp. ground cumin

¼ tsp. ground cayenne

Pinch salt

⅔ cup frozen whole-kernel corn

1 (15-oz.) can black beans, rinsed and drained

1 TB. dried cilantro or 3 TB. chopped fresh

Learning Curve

Quinoa is a good substitute when cooking for those who have a wheat allergy.

1. On a cutting board with a sharp knife, chop onion into ½-inch squares.

2. In an 11-inch nonstick electric skillet set at 325°F, heat olive oil for 30 seconds. Add onions and sauté for 2 minutes. Add garlic and sauté for 1 minute or until onions and garlic are golden. Stir in quinoa until evenly distributed. Slowly pour in broth. Add cumin, cayenne, and salt, and stir. Bring to a boil, reduce heat, cover, and simmer for 20 minutes or until most of liquid is absorbed.

3. Add corn to quinoa mixture and stir. Cover and cook over low heat for 5 minutes or until corn is heated through. Uncover and stir in black beans and cilantro. Cook for 2 minutes or until heated through.

Part 6

Something More

In addition to eating three nutritious meals a day, you're going to want to nosh. Finding health-conscious desserts, sweets, beverages, and snacks can be a challenge. But with a few mindful substitutions, you can delight in all the mouth-watering recipes featured in Part 6.

Snacks, sweets, and beverages add variety to your diet in smaller portions. Plus, they're delicious and refreshing when you need a between-meal pick-me-up.

"I never could've done it without my roommate's study-break smoothies."

Chapter 20

Study-Time Snacks

In This Chapter

- Dipping to your health with vegetables
- Swirling about sweet dips with healthful fruits
- Flavorful dips to scoop up with chips, crackers, and breads

If you're a finger-food junkie when it comes time to study, you can use that habit to put more variety and nutrients into your diet. Veggies and fruits become delicious treats when paired with tasty dips. Even traditional snack dippers can be chosen with both good taste and good health in mind.

Dean's List Dippers

When you throw a party, they're crudités. When you're buying and preparing them, you can call them vegetables. Whatever the moniker, bite-size veggies can cling to any number of tongue-tantalizing dips. Here are some raw vegetables perfect for dipping:

- Bell pepper strips
- Broccoli florets

- Carrot sticks or baby carrots
- Cauliflower florets
- Celery sticks
- Cucumber rounds or spears

- Grape tomatoes
- Mushroom caps
- Radishes

Some vegetables should be briefly blanched before serving alongside dips. Blanching slightly tenderizes the vegetables and helps the vegetables hold their color. To blanch vegetables, place them in boiling water for 30 seconds. Remove the vegetables and plunge them into a prepared bowl of ice water. Here are some good blanching candidates:

- Asparagus spears
- Broccoli florets
- Brussels sprouts
- Cauliflower florets

- Green beans
- Snow peas
- Yellow squash rounds or spears
- Zucchini rounds or spears

Fruits become a special treat when prepared for dipping. Again with time-saving convenience in mind, your local supermarket probably offers precut fruits. They might be a little more costly for the volume, but then you might not want to buy a whole watermelon, cantaloupe, and honeydew to make a melon medley for yourself. Tasty fruits for sinking into scrumptious dips include these:

- Apple slices
- Cherries (pitted)
- Grapes (seedless)
- Kiwi slices
- Melon balls or chunks

- Orange sections
- Peach slices
- Pear slices
- Pineapple chunks
- Strawberries

Some fruits are prone to oxidation after they're cut. To keep your apples, peaches, and pears from browning too quickly, immerse them in a solution of 4 cups water with 1 tablespoon lemon juice.

Some savory dips and especially spreads call for chips, crackers, and breads. Make smart choices when purchasing these dippers and you can enjoy your snacking without guilt. Look for baked, low-fat, whole-grain, and/or low-sodium dippers. Baked tortilla chips, whole-grain crackers, and pretzels can scoop up great taste without wrecking your good intentions.

Kickin' Southwestern Chip Dip $$

Provide hearty baked tortilla chips to scoop up this chunky dip with an addictive flavor.

1 TB. red wine vinegar

1 medium ripe tomato

1 ripe avocado

½ tsp. extra-virgin olive oil

½ TB. hot pepper sauce

1 tsp. drained minced garlic

1½ TB. dried cilantro or ¼ cup chopped fresh

⅔ cup diced green onions

⅔ cup drained canned or cooked black-eyed peas

⅔ cup frozen whole-kernel corn

Yield: 10 servings
Prep time: 8 minutes
Chill time: 30 minutes
Serving size: ⅓ cup
Each serving has:
58 calories
28 calories from fat
3 g fat
0 g saturated fat
2 g protein
7 g carbohydrates

1. Pour red wine vinegar into a 4-cup or larger container with a lid.

2. On a cutting board with a sharp knife, core and dice tomato.

3. Cut avocado in half lengthwise and twist the halves to separate. Using a metal spoon, slip the bowl of the spoon between skin and flesh to scoop out flesh without pit. Dice avocado, adding and stirring into red wine vinegar as you go. To remove pit, carefully push the back of the knife blade into pit and gently twist to pull free. Remove skin and dice avocado as with the first half.

4. Add olive oil, hot pepper sauce, garlic, and cilantro to avocado mixture, and stir. Add green onions, tomato, black-eyed peas, and corn, and stir until mixed.

5. Cover and chill for at least 30 minutes before serving. Stir again before serving.

Learning Curve

If you'll be holding this dip for a time, reserve the avocado pit after removing. Place the pit atop the dip mixture before covering. It might help retard discoloration of the avocado. Remove the pit before serving.

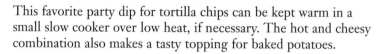

Easy Beefy Nacho Dip $$$

This favorite party dip for tortilla chips can be kept warm in a small slow cooker over low heat, if necessary. The hot and cheesy combination also makes a tasty topping for baked potatoes.

Yield: 18 servings
Prep time: 6 minutes
Cook time: 8 to 12 minutes
Serving size: ¼ cup
Each serving has:
96 calories
33 calories from fat
4 g fat
2 g saturated fat
10 g protein
6 g carbohydrates

1 lb. ground round

1 (16-oz.) pkg. 2 percent-milk pasteurized processed cheese product

1 (16-oz.) jar salsa

1. Place ground round in a 6-cup microwave-safe glass bowl. Cook on high power for 2 to 2½ minutes. Stir to break up meat and redistribute, and cook on high power for 1 or 2 minutes more or until meat is nearly browned. (You should still see some pink when you remove it from the microwave.) Stir to break up meat and until browned. Drain well. Pat dry with paper towels, and set aside, checking for doneness (160°F on a food thermometer).

2. Place cheese in a 1½-quart microwave-safe glass dish. Using a butter knife or spoon, cut cheese into chunks for easier melting. Cook on high power for 3 or 4 minutes, stirring every minute until melted.

3. Stir in salsa, and cook on high power for 2 or 3 minutes, stirring every minute until cheese is well melted and mixture is well blended.

4. Stir in ground round until evenly distributed, and serve hot.

Variation: You can omit the ground round when you need a true pantry-shelf recipe.

Learning Curve

Unless a recipe indicates a particular heat for salsa, you can use what you like best—mild, medium, or hot. If you'll be sharing the recipe with others, you may want to take the group's general heat tolerance into consideration, too.

Boston Baked Beany Dip 💲

Baked chips or crackers can rake through this flavorful bean dip.

1 small yellow onion

1 (16-oz.) can vegetarian beans in tomato sauce or pork and beans

3 TB. molasses

2 TB. prepared yellow mustard

Yield: 10 servings
Prep time: 2 minutes
Serving size: ¼ cup
Each serving has:
69 calories
3 calories from fat
0 g fat
0 g saturated fat
2.5 g protein
14 g carbohydrates

1. On a cutting board with a sharp knife, very coarsely chop onion.

2. In a blender, combine beans, onion, molasses, and mustard. Cover and blend at high speed for 30 to 45 seconds or until desired consistency is reached. Refrigerate any leftovers.

Lecture Hall _____

If you need to scrape down the sides of a blender to incorporate all the ingredients, always turn it off and wait for the blades to stop before removing the cover and inserting anything into the blender container.

Wilted Spinach Salad Dip 💲💲

Take your favorite veggie crudités, crackers, or chips for a spin through this zesty dip.

1 cup reduced-fat mayonnaise

1 cup fat-free sour cream

1 (.6-oz.) pkg. zesty Italian salad dressing mix

1 (10-oz.) pkg. frozen chopped spinach, thawed and drained

½ cup finely chopped mushrooms

¼ cup 50 percent-less-fat bacon pieces or imitation bacon bits

Yield: 12 servings
Prep time: 3 minutes
Chill time: 30 minutes
Serving size: ¼ cup
Each serving has:
67 calories
30 calories from fat
3 g fat
1 g saturated fat
2 g protein
8 g carbohydrates

1. In a medium bowl with a lid, combine mayonnaise, sour cream, and salad dressing mix, and stir until blended. Stir in spinach, mushrooms, and bacon pieces until evenly distributed.

2. Cover and chill for at least 30 minutes. Stir again before serving.

Seasoned Veggie Dip $

Keep this deliciously simple dip on hand for healthy veggie snacking, along with baby carrots, celery sticks, cherry tomatoes, broccoli florets, or other bite-size vegetables.

Yield: 4 servings
Prep time: 2 minutes
Chill time: 30 minutes
Serving size: 2 tablespoons
Each serving has:
38 calories
18 calories from fat
2 g fat
0.5 g saturated fat
1 g protein
5 g carbohydrates

¼ cup fat-free sour cream

¼ cup reduced-fat mayonnaise

¾ tsp. dried parsley flakes or 2 tsp. chopped fresh parsley

¾ tsp. dried chives or 2 tsp. chopped fresh

½ tsp. dried dill weed or 1½ tsp. chopped fresh

½ tsp. curry powder

⅛ tsp. garlic powder

⅛ tsp. onion powder

1. In a small bowl with a lid, combine sour cream, mayonnaise, parsley flakes, chives, dill weed, curry powder, garlic powder, and onion powder. Stir until blended.

2. Cover and chill for at least 30 minutes. Stir again before serving.

Learning Curve _____

Storage bowls with lids are great kitchenware. Still, whenever a recipe calls for a bowl with a lid so the dish can be covered, any container can always be covered with plastic wrap or foil if you don't have a lid.

Sunny Spinach Dip $$

Veggie dippers are perfectly paired with this ranch-flavored blend, or dip into it with your favorite crackers.

2 green onions

1¾ cups fat-free or low-fat ranch salad dressing

1 cup fat-free sour cream

1 (10-oz.) pkg. frozen chopped spinach, thawed and drained

1 cup unsalted roasted sunflower seeds

¼ cup diced celery

1 (2-oz.) jar diced pimientos, drained

Yield: 18 servings
Prep time: 5 minutes
Chill time: 30 minutes
Serving size: ¼ cup
Each serving has:
76 calories
40 calories from fat
4 g fat
1 g saturated fat
2 g protein
8.5 g carbohydrates

1. On a cutting board with a sharp knife, finely chop green onions.

2. In a large bowl with a lid, combine salad dressing, sour cream, spinach, sunflower seeds, green onions, celery, and pimientos. Stir until well blended.

3. Cover and chill for at least 30 minutes. Stir again before serving.

Learning Curve _____

To drain frozen spinach thoroughly, press out as much liquid as possible. When well drained, press out the last of the liquid with layers of paper towels.

So-Simple Spice and Cream Cracker Spread *$$*

Let your guests spread this duo over an assortment of hearty crackers.

Yield: 8 servings
Prep time: 1 minute
Serving size: 2 tablespoons (1 ounce) cream cheese
Each serving has:
45 calories
3 calories from fat
0 g fat
0 g saturated fat
4 g protein
6 g carbohydrates

1 (8-oz.) pkg. fat-free cream cheese   ¾ cup steak sauce

1. Place cream cheese block on a small serving platter or in a shallow serving dish.

2. Pour steak sauce evenly over the top, allowing it to run down the sides.

Of Higher Learning

King George IV of England pronounced a new table sauce prepared by his chef, Henderson William Brand, to be "A1." The label is now synonymous with steak sauce in North America.

Loaded Potato Skins $

This recipe is also great for using up leftovers from Slow-Baked Potatoes (recipe in Chapter 17) by starting with hot potatoes at the third step of the directions.

1 medium all-purpose potato

1 green onion or to taste

2 TB. 2 percent-milk shredded cheddar cheese

1 tsp. 50 percent-reduced-fat bacon pieces

1 TB. fat-free sour cream (optional)

Yield: 1 serving
Prep time: 3 minutes
Cook time: 9 or 10 minutes
Each serving has:
135 calories
22 calories from fat
2.5 g fat
1.5 g saturated fat
5.5 g protein
23 g carbohydrates

1. Scrub potato and prick all over with the tines of a fork. Place potato between 2 white paper towels. Cook on high power for 4 or 5 minutes or until fork tender, turning over and rotating if needed halfway through cooking time. Let stand, covered, for 4 minutes.

2. Meanwhile, on a cutting board with a sharp knife, finely chop green onion.

3. Cut potato in half lengthwise. Using a small metal spoon, scoop out pulp from potato halves, leaving a ½-inch shell with skin. Sprinkle cheese into hollows of potato halves. Sprinkle bacon pieces and green onion over cheese.

4. Cook on high power for 30 to 60 seconds or until cheese melts. Serve with sour cream (if using).

Variation: Personalize these potato skins with your favorite toppings and dips. Try provolone or mozzarella cheese with bacon pieces dipped in fat-free Russian or Catalina salad dressing. Or use a Mexican blend cheese with jalapeño slices topped with a dollop of sour cream or dipped in salsa. Or maybe sprinkle on mozzarella cheese and chopped turkey pepperoni and dip in pizza sauce.

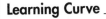

Learning Curve

The bane of every cook's kitchen—what to do with the scooped-out potato pulp? Once I was hungry so I ate the potato pulp—with my fingers, no less—while I melted the cheese. Should you be more civilized, you could refrigerate the pulp to use the next time you want mashed potatoes. Or stir in a little to thicken a soup or stew.

Anywhere Energy-Boosting Trail Mix
$$$

Carry this handy snack pack in your backpack, and you'll never be caught without a sweet and crunchy snack that's good for you and keeps you away from the vending machines.

Yield: 8 servings
Prep time: 2 minutes
Serving size: ¼ cup
Each serving has:
152 calories
77 calories from fat
9 g fat
1 g saturated fat
4 g protein
17 g carbohydrates

⅓ **cup dried sour cherries**

⅓ **cup dried cranberries**

⅓ **cup raisins**

⅓ **cup unsalted, dry-roasted cashews**

⅓ **cup unsalted, dry-roasted peanuts**

⅓ **cup unsalted, roasted sunflower seeds**

1. In a sandwich-size resealable bag, combine dried sour cherries, dried cranberries, raisins, cashews, peanuts, and sunflower seeds.

2. Seal the bag, forcing out all the air. Shake to distribute evenly. Eat within a month or 2.

Of Higher Learning

Fiber, protein, iron, vitamin A, vitamin B₆, vitamin C, vitamin E, vitamin K, folate, potassium, and zinc are just a handful of the nutrients well represented in this mix.

21

Sweet Treats

In This Chapter

- ◆ Choosing chocolate for good taste
- ◆ Quick and easy fruit desserts
- ◆ Heavenly chocolate treats

Dessert can make your life a little sweeter, but as chocoholics around the world will tell you, nothing is as decadent as chocolate. Knowing the kinds of chocolate available and how they can be used makes cooking with them even sweeter. Indulge well!

Chocolate Research

Chocolate is sold in several varieties, as you'll witness on a trip down the baking aisle. If you're a chocolate aficionado, you can skip this section and take off for your favorite specialty shop. But any supermarket should provide the chocolates needed for your everyday needs. Some of the chocolates you should find include these:

Milk chocolate is perhaps the most recognizable chocolate in the United States. Containing milk solids and sugar with the cocoa butter, milk chocolate is typically enjoyed in candy bars. Not often used in baking, you can usually substitute the chip form for semi-sweet chocolate chips in recipes if you prefer the milder, sweeter flavor.

Semi-sweet chocolate can be used in baked goods, candies, sauces, frostings, and more. Having at least 35 percent chocolate liquor in its makeup, it also contains sugar and cocoa butter. The European version is referred to as bittersweet chocolate, and you can use either in recipes.

Unsweetened chocolate is also known as baking chocolate or bitter chocolate. The chocolate liquor doesn't have sugar added to it, allowing the cook to adjust the sweetness as desired.

White chocolate doesn't contain any chocolate liquor, but is a blend of milk solids, sugar, and cocoa butter. If a white chocolate seems very inexpensive, it's likely a vanilla coating made with vegetable shortening, which isn't as flavorful as the cocoa butter chocolate variety.

Chocolate chips are available in semi-sweet, milk, and white chocolate varieties. Chocolate chips contain a little less cocoa butter than blocks of chocolate to help them retain their familiar droplet shape.

Cocoa powder has much of the cocoa butter removed from the chocolate liquor before it's ground into a powder. Typically, you'll find nonalkalized cocoa powder. Some recipes call for Dutched cocoa powder, which is a special alkalized version.

Class Notes

Bloom refers to the grayish haze that appears on the surface of chocolate that has been held in warm or humid conditions, causing sugar or fat to come to the surface. It might not look appetizing, but you can use the chocolate as normal.

Store your chocolate in its packaging in a cool, dry, dark place. Dark chocolates (semi-sweet and unsweetened) keep for up to a year. Milk chocolate and white chocolate should be used within 6 months. Check the packages of all chocolates for best-by dates. If chocolates are stored in a warmer or humid area, they may develop *bloom*. These chocolates are still safe to use.

Many recipes call for the chocolate to be melted before incorporating. Perhaps the safest way to melt chocolate is in the microwave. Place the chocolate in a microwave-safe bowl, chopping it into chunks as needed. Follow the package or recipe directions, or cook on high power, stirring after the first minute and every 30 seconds thereafter. Don't cook the chocolate until completely melted; rather, stir it until smooth. Be careful not to introduce water into the melting chocolate. Be sure the spoon you use to stir it is dry, or it may seize or become stiff and lumpy.

Shortcut Cinnamon Rolls $

Warm and gooey is sometimes just what you need.

¼ **cup light butter with canola oil**

¼ **cup firmly packed light brown sugar**

1 tsp. ground cinnamon

1 (8-count) pkg. refrigerated reduced-fat big buttermilk biscuit dough

Yield: 8 servings
Prep time: 5 minutes
Cook time: 11 or 12 minutes
Serving size: 1 biscuit
Each serving has:
191 calories
63 calories from fat
7 g fat
2 g saturated fat
4 g protein
29 g carbohydrates

1. Measure light butter into an 8×2-inch round microwave-safe glass dish. Have brown sugar and cinnamon measures ready. Open biscuit dough.

2. Cook light butter on high power for 30 to 60 seconds or until melted. Sprinkle brown sugar and cinnamon evenly over melted butter. Arrange biscuit dough pieces in the dish, starting with the center biscuit and tightly fitting remaining 7 biscuit dough pieces around the outside edge. Cook on high power for 5 or 6 minutes or until biscuits are done.

3. Remove the dish from the microwave, and carefully invert onto a large serving plate by placing the serving plate upside down on top of the dish and then turning both plate and dish over together. Allow the dish to stand inverted on the serving plate for 5 minutes. Remove the dish. Serve individual biscuits hot with a drizzling of cinnamon sauce.

Variation: These cinnamon rolls are also terrific iced. In a small bowl, add 1 teaspoon fat-free milk to ½ cup confectioners' sugar. Stir until smooth, dribbling in additional milk if needed to moisten completely. Using a spoon, drizzle icing over cinnamon rolls while hot on the serving plate.

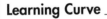

Learning Curve

By cooking these biscuits in the microwave, you won't be able to check for doneness by visible browning. The biscuits will visually rise and lose their shiny raw dough appearance. To confirm doneness, pull one biscuit apart to see if the inside is airy and cooked.

Candy Apple Fluff $$$

If your sweet tooth craves big bowls of cloudlike concoctions, this candy-bar-sweet, apple-crunchy jumble should satisfy it.

Yield: 12 servings
Prep time: 10 minutes
Chill time: 30 minutes
Serving size: ½ cup
Each serving has:
95 calories
25 calories from fat
3 g fat
2 g saturated fat
1 g protein
17 g carbohydrates

1 (20-oz.) can crushed pine-apple in its own juice, drained

2 medium eating apples (Granny Smith, Gala, Braeburn, etc.)

1 (8-oz.) pkg. fat-free frozen whipped topping, thawed

1 (3.5-oz.) pkg. caramel-filled milk chocolate candy bar sticks such as Hershey's Sticks (9 sticks)

1. In a large bowl with a lid, add drained pineapple.

2. On a cutting board with a sharp knife, finely chop apples, stirring into pineapple as you cut to prevent discoloration. (Discard cores.)

3. Stir whipped topping into pineapple mixture.

4. On a cutting board with a sharp knife, finely chop each candy bar stick. Stir into whipped topping mixture until evenly distributed.

5. Cover and chill for at least 30 minutes. Stir again before serving.

Learning Curve _____

Many recipes direct you to stir the dish again before you serve it. This ensures that all the ingredients are blended together and evenly distributed for the best taste in each serving.

Just-Stir Fruit Dip $

If you need an incentive to eat more fruit in your diet, whip up this creamy concoction that livens up fresh strawberries, apple slices, bananas, cherries, melon chunks, grapes, kiwi slices, oranges, peaches, pears, pineapple—pretty much any fruit other than a lemon.

1 (8-oz.) pkg. fat-free cream cheese, at room temperature

1 (7-oz.) jar marshmallow créme

1. In a medium bowl, combine cream cheese and marshmallow créme. Stir together until well blended and smooth.

2. Cover and chill, if desired.

Learning Curve _____

Fat-free cream cheese is naturally soft so you can really blend it straight from the fridge. If you use reduced-fat or regular cream cheese, you'll want to set it out for about 30 minutes.

Yield: 8 servings
Prep time: 5 minutes
Serving size: ¼ cup
Each serving has:
102 calories
3 calories from fat
0 g fat
0 g saturated fat
4 g protein
20 g carbohydrates

Caramel-Coated Pretzel Rods $$

Sweet, salty, crunchy, and chocolaty—everything you're looking for in a treat.

Yield: *14 servings*
Prep time: 25 minutes
Cook time: 2 or 3 minutes
Set time: 1 hour
Serving size: 2 pretzels
Each serving has:
257 calories
77 calories from fat
9 g fat
2 g saturated fat
6 g protein
43 g carbohydrates

1 cup miniature semi-sweet chocolate chips

1 cup chopped unsalted walnuts

1 (14-oz.) pkg. traditional caramels, unwrapped

1 TB. water

1 (12-oz.) pkg. pretzel rods (about 28 whole rods)

1. On a large work surface, arrange sheets of wax paper for drying coated pretzel rods. On 1 sheet of wax paper, combine chocolate chips and walnuts, mixing until evenly distributed.

2. In a 4-cup microwave-safe measuring cup or other deep microwave-safe bowl, combine unwrapped caramels and water. Cook on high power for 2 or 3 minutes or until melted, stirring and rotating if needed after each minute of cooking time. Let stand for 1 or 2 minutes to cool slightly.

3. Tipping the measuring cup as needed, coat each pretzel rod with caramel about halfway up rod. Allow excess caramel to drip back into the measuring cup. Roll pretzel rod in chocolate chip–walnut mixture to cover caramel. Place on wax paper to set. Repeat until ingredients are used.

4. Let pretzel rods stand for at least 1 hour or until set. Store in an airtight container between layers of wax paper.

Lecture Hall _____

> Don't let the caramel become too cool, or the pretzel rods will begin to break off in the caramel. Reheat it on high power for 20 to 30 seconds to keep it warm enough for dipping.

Easy Peanut Butter Chocolate Fudge $

This rich chocolate fudge has undertones of peanut butter and the crunch of peanuts.

1 (12-oz.) pkg. semi-sweet chocolate chips

1 (10-oz.) pkg. peanut butter chips

1 (14-oz.) can fat-free sweetened condensed milk

1 tsp. light butter with canola oil

1 tsp. vanilla extract

1 cup chopped unsalted peanuts

Yield: 32 servings
Prep time: 8 minutes
Cook time: 2 or 3 minutes
Chill time: 1 hour
Serving size: 2 pieces
Each serving has:
137 calories
71 calories from fat
8 g fat
4 g saturated fat
3 g protein
13 g carbohydrates

1. In a 6-cup microwave-safe glass bowl, combine chocolate chips and peanut butter chips. Cook on high power for 2 or 3 minutes, stirring every 30 seconds until melted.

2. Stir sweetened condensed milk into chocolate mixture. Stir in light butter and vanilla extract. Stir in peanuts until evenly distributed.

3. Turn chocolate mixture into a wax paper–lined 8×8×2-inch dish. Smooth out top and push evenly into corners. Cover and chill for at least 1 hour or until firm.

4. Remove the wax paper from the dish, and turn out fudge onto a cutting board, pulling off the wax paper. Cut into 1×1-inch pieces with a sharp knife. Refrigerate any leftovers.

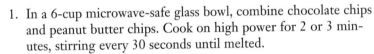

Learning Curve

When you line the dish with wax paper, leave enough overhang past the edges of the dish so you can remove the wax paper with the fudge easily when it's firm.

Easy Iced Chocolate Brownies $

When your only cooking appliance is a microwave and you're craving chocolaty brownies, this recipe answers your stomach's call.

Yield: 16 servings	

Prep time: 6 to 8 minutes

Cook time: 11 to 14 minutes

Serving size: 2×2-inch square

Each serving has:

115 calories

30 calories from fat

3 g fat

1 g saturated fat

2 g protein

19 g carbohydrates

½ cup light butter with canola oil

¼ cup cocoa powder

2 large eggs, at room temperature

1 cup granulated sugar

1 cup all-purpose flour

1 tsp. vanilla extract

¼ tsp. salt

½ cup miniature semi-sweet chocolate chips (optional)

1. In a medium bowl, combine light butter and cocoa powder, and stir with a rubber spatula until well blended. Add eggs, sugar, flour, vanilla extract, and salt. Stir until dry ingredients are moistened and mixture is well blended.

2. Turn batter into an 8×8×2-inch microwave-safe glass dish with rounded corners. Cook on high power for 1 to 1½ minutes. Using a rubber spatula, stir batter well to redistribute. Cook on high power for 1 to 1½ minutes more, and stir again to redistribute, pulling out any batter that's beginning to set in the corners. Cook on high power for 4 to 6 more minutes or until edges are set and center is just tacky. Cool on a wire rack for 5 minutes or until center is dry to the touch.

3. Sprinkle chocolate chips (if using) across top of warm brownies. Let stand for 1 or 2 minutes and then spread melting chips evenly over top with a butter knife or icing spatula. Cool slightly before cutting into squares.

Learning Curve

Microwave ovens cook the corners and outside edges of foods faster than the centers. Selecting a square dish with rounded corners and stirring the cooking batter helps even out the cooking of this recipe. If you're cooking unevenly shaped foods in the microwave, such as broccoli spears, arrange them in a circle with the more delicate parts, the florets, in the center for the best results.

Chilly Cocoa No-Cook Cookies ✦

These little chocolaty bites quiet your cookie craving when you can't bake up a batch.

¾ cup granulated sugar

¾ cup light butter with canola oil

3 TB. cocoa powder

1 TB. water

½ tsp. vanilla extract

2 cups uncooked quick oats

2 TB. confectioners' sugar (optional)

Yield: 32 servings
Prep time: 10 minutes
Chill time: 3 hours
Freeze time: 1 hour
Serving size: 1 cookie
Each serving has:
57 calories
20 calories from fat
2 g fat
0.5 g saturated fat
1 g protein
8 g carbohydrates

1. In a large bowl, combine sugar and light butter, and stir until sugar is incorporated. Add cocoa powder, water, and vanilla extract, and stir until blended and smooth. Stir in oats until evenly coated. Cover and chill for 3 hours or until mixture is firm.

2. Working quickly, drop mixture from a small spoon onto a wax paper–lined tray, baking sheet, or cookie sheet. Sprinkle confectioners' sugar (if using) lightly over tops of cookies.

3. Freeze cookies on the tray for 1 hour or until firm. Transfer to a wax paper–lined container in a single layer. Cover and freeze until serving. Enjoy cold from the freezer.

Learning Curve

Because light butter with canola oil is soft from the refrigerator, these cookies need to be frozen to keep from getting "melty." If you're not concerned with the fat content, you can substitute regular butter. Drop the cookies just after mixing, and chill in the refrigerator.

No-Bake Peanut Butter Apple Cookies $$

When you need a little something after dinner, this chewy, peanut-buttery tidbit might do the trick.

½ **cup chopped dried apples**	½ **cup corn flakes cereal**
¼ **cup apple juice or apple cider**	1 **cup peanut butter chips**

Yield: 12 servings

Prep time: 8 to 10 minutes

Soak time: 1 hour

Set time: 10 to 15 minutes

Serving size: 1 cookie

Each serving has:

129 calories

48 calories from fat

5 g fat

4 g saturated fat

3 g protein

16 g carbohydrates

1. In a small bowl, soak dried apples in apple juice for 1 hour. Drain, and lightly pat dry with a paper towel. Transfer apples to a 3-cup microwave-safe bowl, and add cereal.

2. Cook peanut butter chips in a small microwave-safe bowl on high power for 1 minute. Stir until melted, returning to the microwave for 20- to 30-second intervals and stirring until melted if needed.

3. Pour peanut butter over apple mixture, and stir until all ingredients are evenly coated. Working quickly, drop mixture by spoonfuls onto a sheet of wax paper. Cool until set. Store leftovers in the refrigerator in a single layer or between layers of wax paper.

Learning Curve

If the melted peanut butter chips start to set before you've dropped all the cookies, place the mixture in the microwave and cook on high power for 20 to 30 seconds. Stir mixture again and resume dropping cookies.

Chapter 22

Delectable Desserts

In This Chapter

- ◆ Fruit 101
- ◆ Cakes to soothe your sweet tooth
- ◆ Fruity dessert treats

Fruits may be the best foods. They're full of nutrients and sweet enough to enjoy for dessert, whether out of hand or incorporated into delectable concoctions. Choosing and handling good fruit makes for good eating. When you peruse the produce aisle, keep your nose open; your sense of smell can be a great advantage in picking the freshest, tastiest fruits, whether you're going to use them in a dessert or not.

Even if you're not a big fan of fruits, this chapter has something sweet I'm sure you'll like.

Fruit Composition

Knowing how to choose, store, and prepare fresh fruits allows you to enjoy the health benefits and get the most out of the money you spend. Plus, you can purchase many fruits in single servings—maybe perfect for your current needs. Keep the following tips in mind as you shop.

Apples are grown in thousands of varieties, but you'll probably find only the same several commercially grown ones at the market. Good eating apples are subjective to taste, of course, but you might want to try Cortland, Fuji, Gala, Granny Smith, Jonathan, or Red Delicious. Apples that retain their shape when heated are good for cooking and baking—Golden Delicious, Granny Smith, Ida Red, Northern Spy, or Rome Beauty.

Choose apples with unbroken skin, no bruises, and no "scabby" branch marks. Smell the stem end for a ripe, apple-y aroma. Handle them gently on the trip home so as not to cause bruising.

Lecture Hall _____

Don't cut apples too soon before you'll use them, or they'll turn brown. To avoid this, toss sliced apples with a little lemon juice, or other acidic citrus juice. Or you can submerge the apple slices in acidulated water—4 cups water with 1 tablespoon lemon juice.

For long storage, keep apples in the refrigerator, as they'll continue to ripen at room temperature. Retain the skin, and much of the apple's nutrients, whenever possible.

Bananas are harvested while unripe for better shipping. They ripen if left at room temperature, and bananas separated from the hand, or the bunch, ripen a bit faster. Buy green bananas if you want to hold them for a few days. Yellow bananas and those with some brown flecks are sweet for eating. Very ripe bananas and those overripe for eating are best for baked goods and puréeing. To stop the ripening process, you can store the bananas in the refrigerator; the peels will turn black, but that's okay.

Cherries sold fresh are generally sweet cherries you can eat out of hand. Cherries should be plump, unblemished, and deeply colored. (Royal Anne cherries are naturally golden. Cherries just shouldn't be pale compared to their peers.) Should you find cherries with their stems, buy those, because they'll stay fresh a bit longer. Store cherries in a plastic bag in the refrigerator. Wash them when you're ready to use them, and use within a week.

Because cherries have a short harvesting season, you'll find both sweet and sour cherries in several canned and frozen versions. The upside is that these are already pitted.

Grapes are categorized as red or green and can be seedless or seeded. Whichever type you choose, the grapes should be plump, unblemished, and secured to a fresh, unwithered vine. Store them in the produce bag in the crisper drawer. You can add a dry paper towel to absorb any moisture to maintain freshness longer. Pick and wash grapes when ready to use, using in a week or so.

You can freeze grapes in a cleaned and dried single layer on a tray and then transfer them to a plastic freezer bag to use within 6 months. Enjoy the grapes frozen, or thaw at room temperature.

Lemons are prized for their juice and peel. Look for unblemished, firm skin on a lemon that's heavy for its size. You can store lemons for weeks at room temperature (they make practical and pretty decorations), or place them in plastic bags in the refrigerator. Bring them to room temperature before squeezing; you can warm them in the microwave for about 20 seconds if you're in a rush. Wash the skin well, especially if you'll be grating the *zest*. Rolling a whole lemon under your palm on the counter yields more juice once cut. You should be able to get 2 or 3 tablespoons juice from each lemon.

> **Class Notes**
>
> **Zest** is the small slivers of peel from citrus fruits such as lemons, limes, oranges, or grapefruits. The zest is the outer skin of the fruit and not the underlying white pith, which is often bitter-tasting. The kitchen tool used to grate the peel is referred to as a *zester*.

Oranges you'll be picking up for eating will probably be Valencias or navel oranges, the latter being nearly seedless. The skin should be smooth but can be blemished or green; just avoid cuts and mold. The orange should be fragrant, firm, and heavy for its size. Store oranges for a week or so at room temperature or for 3 or 4 weeks in the refrigerator. Wash the skin well, especially if you're zesting the orange. Bring an orange to room temperature before juicing, and roll it under your palm on the countertop to elicit the most juice.

Peaches can be found in two varieties, cling and freestone. Freestone peaches have pits that are easily removed, and they're usually preferable for eating out of hand. Choose plump peaches with unblemished skins. Store them at room temperature in a bowl or other smooth-sided container, as they bruise easily. If soft, peaches can be stored in a plastic bag in the refrigerator for several days. Wash before eating, rubbing gently to remove any fuzz. To remove the skin for cooking, cut an X at the bottom and *blanch* for about 30 seconds for easy removal. Toss cut peaches with lemon juice to retard browning.

> **Class Notes**
>
> **Blanch** directs you to place foods in boiling water briefly and then submerge or rinse in cold water to stop the cooking process. Blanching foods such as peaches and tomatoes makes peeling easier.

Pears you'll typically find in supermarkets are Bartlett, Bosc, and D'Anjou. All will likely be hard. Buy them well before you plan to eat them (look for unblemished skins), and keep them at room temperature to ripen. Bartletts will turn light green and then yellow when ripe. Bosc pears will yield to light pressure and hold up well to cooking. D'Anjou pears are also good for baking and hold their shape when sliced for salads. They should be tinged yellow when ripe. Handle pears gently, as they bruise easily. Ripe pears can be held in plastic bags in the refrigerator for several days. Wash before eating. You can core pears with a melon baller or a small spoon.

Pineapples should be plump and heavy for their size. Choose fruit with fresh green leaves, a sweet aroma, and no molding at the base. To prepare a pineapple for eating, remove the crown of leaves by twisting and pulling it free. Use a sharp, sturdy knife to cut off the skin around the pineapple from top to bottom. If you don't need slices, I find it easiest to quarter the pineapple. Cut down the pineapple just inside the core to remove and then slice down the skin to remove. Store cut pineapple in an airtight container in the refrigerator for up to several days. Fresh precut pineapple is available, although you'll usually pay for the service.

Strawberries should be evenly red colored and firm, with fresh green hulls. Reject any packages with visible mold, dry brown hulls, bruised berries, moisture, or off odors. Store in the open plastic container they come in or in a colander in the refrigerator. Plan to use them within a couple days. Wash just before eating or using. Remove the hulls with a strawberry huller or a paring knife.

Speedy Pineapple Upside-Down Cake $

You can serve this candied cake warm from the microwave or cold from the fridge.

3 TB. light butter with canola oil

½ cup firmly packed light brown sugar

½ (20-oz.) can pineapple slices in their own juice, ½ cup juice reserved

5 whole maraschino cherries

1 (9-oz.) pkg. lemon cake mix

1 large egg, at room temperature

Yield: 8 servings
Prep time: 5 minutes
Cook time: 11 to 13 minutes
Serving size: 1 slice
Each serving has:
252 calories
43 calories from fat
5 g fat
2 g saturated fat
1.5 g protein
51 g carbohydrates

1. Measure light butter into an 8×2-inch round microwave-safe dish. Cook on high power for 20 to 30 seconds or until melted. Sprinkle brown sugar evenly over melted butter. Arrange 5 pineapple slices around the edge of the dish. Add maraschino cherries in centers of pineapple slices.

2. In a medium bowl, combine cake mix, egg, and ½ cup reserved pineapple juice, and stir until well blended. Pour evenly over pineapple slices. Cook on high power for 10 to 12 minutes or until just the very center of cake still looks tacky, rotating half-way through cooking time if needed.

3. Cool on a wire rack for 10 to 15 minutes before inverting onto a serving plate. (Place the serving plate upside down atop the cake dish. Turn the plate and the dish over together, releasing cake onto the serving plate.) Refrigerate any leftovers.

Variation: If you can't find a 9-ounce package of cake mix, you can use half of an 18.25-ounce package.

Learning Curve

Because firmly packing brown sugar to measure results in a measuring cup–shaped chunk of brown sugar in your bowl, you'll need to use a spoon or your fingertips to break it up.

Cherry-Topped Pineapple Cheesecake Dessert $$

When you need something as pretty as it is delicious, try this recipe.

Yield: 24 servings	
Prep time: 15 minutes	
Chill time: 8 hours	
Serving size: 2¼×2⅛-inch pieces	
Each serving has:	
170 calories	
54 calories from fat	
6 g fat	
3.5 g saturated fat	
4 g protein	
25 g carbohydrates	

3 (8-oz.) pkg. reduced-fat cream cheese or Neufchâtel cheese, at room temperature

1½ cups confectioners' sugar

1 (20-oz.) can crushed pineapple in its own juice, drained

1 (8-oz.) pkg. fat-free frozen whipped topping, thawed

2 cups miniature marshmallows

1 cup plus 2 TB. graham cracker crumbs

1 (20-oz.) can lite reduced-calorie cherry pie filling

1. In a large bowl with a spoon, combine cream cheese and confectioners' sugar, chopping cream cheese into chunks and working in confectioners' sugar, smoothing with the back of the spoon until blended thoroughly. Add pineapple, whipped topping, and marshmallows, and stir until well blended and evenly distributed.

2. Coat a 13×9×2-inch dish with nonstick cooking spray. Evenly sprinkle 1 cup graham cracker crumbs across the bottom of the dish. Shake the dish, if needed, to distribute crumbs across the bottom, and smooth and even out with the back of a spoon.

3. Spoon cream cheese mixture evenly over graham cracker crumbs, smoothing out the top with the back of the spoon. Evenly cover the top with cherry pie filling, leaving 1-inch margins around the edges. Sprinkle remaining 2 tablespoons graham cracker crumbs across the top. Cover and chill for at least 8 hours or overnight or until set.

4. Cut into squares to serve, using a small spatula to remove pieces from the dish. Refrigerate any leftovers.

Variation: If you need a lower-fat dessert, you can prepare this recipe as a trifle. Substitute fat-free cream cheese for reduced-fat cream cheese. Blend fat-free cream cheese and confectioners' sugar as directed. Blend in pineapple, whipped topping, and marshmallows as directed. Line the bottom of a large bowl with low-fat graham crackers. Spoon ½ of cream cheese mixture over top. Arrange a second layer of low-fat graham crackers and then spoon remaining cream cheese mixture over top. Evenly cover the top with cherry pie filling as directed. Crush 1 or 2 low-fat graham crackers to sprinkle the crumbs across the top. Cover and chill until serving time. Spoon into dessert dishes or bowls to serve.

Learning Curve

Frozen whipped topping is easily thawed in the refrigerator. The whipped topping will be thawed enough to incorporate into a recipe in just a couple hours, or it can wait in the refrigerator until you're ready for it.

Pretty Lemon Cream Angel Cake $$$

You can garnish this pretty cake with fresh raspberries, fanned strawberries, sliced kiwi, blueberries, cherries, or any decorative combination.

Yield: 8 servings
Prep time: 10 minutes
Serving size: 1 slice
Each serving has:
238 calories
11 calories from fat
1 g fat
0 g saturated fat
3 g protein
53 g carbohydrates

1 (16-oz.) prepared large round angel food cake

1 (15.75-oz.) can lemon pie filling

½ (8-oz.) pkg. fat-free frozen whipped topping, thawed

1. On a cutting board with a large, serrated knife, cut angel food cake into 3 horizontal layers. Remove the top 2 layers together, keeping them aligned in placement with the bottom layer.

2. Spoon lemon pie filling into a medium bowl. With a rubber spatula, fold whipped topping into lemon pie filling until blended.

3. Spoon ⅓ of mixture or so onto the cut surface of the bottom angel food cake layer, and spread smooth. Replace middle layer atop bottom layer. Spread ½ of remaining mixture over middle layer. Replace top layer over middle layer. Spread remaining mixture on the top of cake. Cover and refrigerate if not serving immediately. Refrigerate any leftovers.

 Lecture Hall _____

If you don't have a serrated knife, find one you can borrow for this recipe. Angel food cake is airy and very delicate. A heavy hand with a regular knife blade can smash it into a dense, tear-worthy state.

Apple-Nut Slow Cooker Cake $$

This dense, coffeecakelike dessert is delightful served warm, and it's yummy topped with a scoop of reduced-fat vanilla ice cream.

1 cup all-purpose flour

1 cup granulated sugar

2 tsp. baking powder

1 tsp. ground cinnamon

¼ tsp. salt

4 cooking apples (Granny Smith, Golden Delicious, Gala, etc.)

2 large eggs, at room temperature

2 tsp. vanilla extract

½ cup chopped unsalted walnuts or pecans

Yield: 8 servings
Prep time: 10 minutes
Cook time: 2 to 2½ hours
Serving size: 1 slice
Each serving has:
244 calories
41 calories from fat
4.5 g fat
1 g saturated fat
5 g protein
48 g carbohydrates

1. In a large bowl, combine flour, sugar, baking powder, cinnamon, and salt. Stir to blend.

2. On a cutting board with a sharp knife, chop apples into ½-inch pieces, stirring each apple or two into flour mixture as you chop to prevent discoloration. Stir apples in flour mixture to coat completely. Add eggs and vanilla extract, and stir until dry ingredients are incorporated. Stir in walnuts until evenly distributed.

3. Turn mixture into a 3½- to 4-quart slow cooker that's been coated with nonstick cooking spray. Using the back of the spoon, smooth out the top for even thickness.

4. Cover and cook on high for 2 to 2½ hours or until done (outer edge will be browned and a cake tester, toothpick, or strand of uncooked spaghetti when poked through the center of the cake will come out clean). Cut into wedges and serve warm.

Variation: If you don't care for nuts, you can substitute raisins.

 **Learning Curve** _____

When recipes call for apples, you aren't limited to using just one variety. You can mix and match apples appropriate for the recipe—eating, cooking, or baking apples.

Cherry Cola Gels $

Top these very cherry gelatin dishes with a dollop of fat-free whipped topping for an easy-to-make dessert.

Yield: 4 servings
Prep time: 5 minutes
Chill time: 4 hours
Serving size: 1 dish
Each serving has:
97 calories
0 calories from fat
0 g fat
0 g saturated fat
2 g protein
21 g carbohydrates

1 (15-oz.) can pitted dark sweet cherries in heavy syrup

1 cup water or as needed

1 (4-serving-size) pkg. cherry sugar-free or regular gelatin

1 cup diet or regular cola

1. Drain syrup from cherries into a microwave-safe 4-cup liquid measure or other liquid measuring cup. Add enough water to measure 1 cup. Cook on high power for 2 or 3 minutes or until boiling. Stir in gelatin until dissolved. Slowly stir in cola until blended. (It will foam.) Chill for 1 hour or until slightly thickened. (Refrigerate opened cherries.)

2. Gently stir in cherries, and divide mixture among 4 dessert dishes. Cover and chill for 3 hours or until set.

Lecture Hall _____

If you've grabbed a can of Diet Coke or other cola for this recipe, don't forget to measure out 1 cup. A can is 12 ounces, or 1½ cups.

Maple-Sweet Stuffed Apples $

When it's dinner for one, this sweet ending is worth taking the time to prepare (although it's really not that long!).

1 large cooking apple (Fuji, Gala, Rome Beauty, etc.)

1 tsp. light butter with canola oil

1 TB. dried cranberries or raisins

1 TB. maple syrup

Yield: 1 serving
Prep time: 4 minutes
Cook time: 10 or 11 minutes
Each serving has:
135 calories
14 calories from fat
1.5 g fat
0 g saturated fat
0 g protein
32 g carbohydrates

1. On a cutting board with an *apple corer* or a sharp knife, core apple without pushing core out through the bottom. With a paring knife, peel apple about ⅓ of the way down from the stem end.

2. Place apple in a small, deep, microwave-safe bowl. Fill hollow of apple with light butter and cranberries. Pour maple syrup over apple, allowing it to run down sides. Cover with plastic wrap, venting, and cook on high power for 5 or 6 minutes or until tender. Let stand, covered, for 5 minutes before serving.

Class Notes _____

An **apple corer** is a kitchen tool used to remove the core of a whole apple. It has a long, round blade to slice through the apple from the stem end to the blossom end, cutting out the centered core.

Single-Serving Toasted Angel Sandwich 💲

Indulge in this fast-and-easy meal-ender when it's dinner for one.

Yield: 1 serving
Prep time: 2 minutes
Cook time: 1 to 3 minutes
Each serving has:
198 calories
6 calories from fat
1 g fat
0 g saturated fat
6 g protein
43 g carbohydrates

1 TB. fat-free cream cheese, at room temperature

2 (¾-in.-thick) slices prepared angel food cake loaf

2 tsp. raspberry fruit spread or jam

4 to 6 sprays buttery spray

Confectioners' sugar to taste (optional)

1. Spread cream cheese evenly over 1 cake slice. Spread fruit spread evenly over other cake slice. Sandwich cake slices together to enclose fillings. Lightly coat outside of sandwich slices with buttery spray.

2. Coat an 11-inch nonstick electric skillet with nonstick cooking spray and heat to 300°F. Toast sandwich on each side for 30 to 90 seconds or until golden as desired. Sprinkle on a little confectioners' sugar (if using). Serve warm.

Variation: Use your favorite flavors of cream cheese and fruit spreads for variety.

Learning Curve

Confectioners' sugar is also known as powdered sugar or 10X sugar. The package will probably have a little cornstarch added to prevent caking.

Sweet and Creamy Double-Banana Pudding ⸖

For a pretty presentation, crumble a couple vanilla wafers and sprinkle the crumbs across the top of the pudding.

2 small bananas, peeled

2 cups fat-free milk, cold

1 (4-serving-size) pkg. banana créme sugar-free or regular instant pudding mix

12 to 15 reduced-fat vanilla wafer cookies, or as needed

Yield: 4 servings
Prep time: 7 minutes
Serving size: 1 cup
Each serving has:
239 calories
20 calories from fat
2 g fat
1 g saturated fat
5 g protein
52 g carbohydrates

1. On a cutting board with a butter knife, thinly slice bananas. Set aside.

2. Pour milk into a 1-quart serving bowl. Sprinkle pudding mix over milk. With a fork or a whisk, vigorously beat for 2 minutes or until smooth and mixture is beginning to thicken. Stir in bananas until evenly distributed. Smooth out top of pudding.

3. Arrange vanilla wafers around the outside edge of the serving bowl, tops facing in and pushing about halfway down into pudding. Serve immediately, or cover and chill until serving time.

Learning Curve

If you want to garnish this dish with banana slices, rub a little lemon juice over the cut surfaces to prevent discoloration if you need to hold dessert. Or slice and arrange bananas atop the pudding just before carrying it to the table.

Sunshine and Snow Sweet Fluff Pie $

The tangy taste of pineapple and lemon float in creamy whipped topping grounded in a graham cracker crust—*yum!*

Yield: 8 servings
Prep time: 8 minutes
Chill time: 1 hour
Serving size: 1 slice
Each serving has:
183 calories
44 calories from fat
5 g fat
1 g saturated fat
2 g protein
34.5 g carbohydrates

1 (20-oz.) can crushed pineapple in its own juice

1 (4-serving-size) pkg. lemon sugar-free instant pudding mix

1 (8-oz.) pkg. fat-free frozen whipped topping, thawed

1 (9-in.) prepared reduced-fat graham cracker crust

1. In a medium bowl, combine pineapple and pudding mix. Stir for 2 minutes or until pudding mix is incorporated and mixture begins to thicken. *Fold* in whipped topping with a rubber spatula or a spoon until thoroughly combined.

2. Spoon pineapple mixture into graham cracker crust, mounding as needed. Place pie in a pie carrier or cover with a plastic bowl large enough to invert over pie without touching. Chill for at least 1 hour. Cut into wedges to serve.

Class Notes

Fold instructs you to combine a dense and light mixture with a circular action from the middle of the bowl. Run the spatula down the back side of the bowl to the bottom of the bowl and then circle it up toward the front of the bowl; turn the bowl to incorporate all the ingredients. Folding prevents the light mixture from getting stirred down into the dense mixture, keeping the overall mix light.

Chapter 23

Pleasurable Sippers

In This Chapter

- ◆ Making good food choices
- ◆ Trimming fat wherever you can
- ◆ Understanding serving sizes for portion control
- ◆ Tasty drinks to quench your thirst

With so many food and drink temptations swirling about you, it's easy to give in to the high-fat, high-calorie, ready-made consumables that offer little nutritional value. With a little know-how and a little planning, you can make the best food choices. And good foods and beverages keep you satisfied and feeling strong and healthy. You feel better when you eat better. It's really that simple. More good news—more ready-made foods are now health focused.

As I hope you've noticed, perhaps especially here in Part 6, eating responsibly isn't about deprivation. Everything in moderation, as the adage goes. Plus, choosing more healthful ingredients can make traditionally decadent dishes no less delicious, yet they'll be less fat-, cholesterol-, sugar-, and calorie-laden.

Eating for Your Best You

Sometimes making good food choices is as simple as learning what it is you're eating. If you've been eating without paying attention to much more than taste, looking to a food label to see exactly the makeup of the food you consume may be eye-opening. (For information on understanding food labels, see Chapter 2.)

Start with the foods you have in your pantry and refrigerator right now. These items are likely your staples and regularly consumed foods. When you find a food too high in fat, saturated fat, cholesterol, sodium, or sugars—or too low in dietary fiber, protein, vitamins, or minerals—search out alternatives. Pick up a gallon of 2 percent milk instead of whole milk. Substitute leaner ground turkey breast for ground beef. Look for fruits canned in their own juices or water instead of heavy syrup. Some changes will be painless; others might be more difficult. Take on these changes gradually—perhaps only one at a time or over a long adjustment period. If you love regular mayonnaise but don't like the taste of the fat-free version, make a plan. Make a half-and-half mixture of regular and lite mayonnaise until you're ready to phase out the regular mayo. Then mix lite mayonnaise with a reduced-fat version. Perhaps you'll decide that reduced-fat mayonnaise is as far as you need to reduce the fat. That's okay. Just know that taste buds can be retrained. This is true for fat and sodium content, as well as learning to like a nuttier, whole-grain texture.

If you're choosing all the best ingredients for your needs, you'll want to check your portion sizes. The number of calories, grams of fat, and percentage of calcium doesn't mean a thing if you don't know the serving size. Measure at least once to see how much that serving is. You may discover you've been eating two servings of your breakfast cereal. Having a visual cue to estimate serving size is helpful. Keep the following comparisons in mind as you put together your meals and snacks.

Food	Visual Cue
3 ounces meat	deck of cards
1 medium fruit	baseball
1 cup salad greens	baseball
1 cup pasta	tennis ball
¼ cup dried fruits or nuts	golf ball
2 tablespoons peanut butter	ping-pong ball
2 tablespoons sour cream	ping-pong ball

Food	Visual Cue
1 cup flakes cereal	fist
1 medium potato	computer mouse
1½ ounces cheese	4 dice
1 teaspoon light butter	1 die

Leading a busy life can lead to absentminded eating. I know how easy it is to be rushed and scarf down an entire meal without realizing it or finish off an entire family-size bag of chips while you study. Eating slowly and enjoying the taste of your food can keep you from eating too much.

You'll also eat less if you only eat when you're hungry. At times, it's easier said than done. Think back to all the times you ate because everyone else was eating, because there was food at the party, because you paid for the buffet, because you were bored, because you blew the exam, because you spotted the cake on the counter, because …. When you're hungry, eat; when you're full, stop.

Learning Curve

If you tend to eat whatever's in front of you, invest in snack-size resealable plastic bags. When you bring home a family-size package of any snack food, check the serving size listed in the nutrition facts panel. Then, separate the package into individual servings, using the snack-size bags. Take just one bag when you want a snack. If you want more, you'll consciously have to pull out another serving.

Hawaiian Island Shake $

Sip this quick-blend tropical treat to relax and let it take you away to the islands ….

Yield: 2 servings	
Prep time: 2 minutes	
Serving size: 1 cup	
Each serving has:	
135 calories	
11 calories from fat	
1 g fat	
1 g saturated fat	
5 g protein	
25 g carbohydrates	

½ **cup fat-free milk**

½ **cup fat-free plain yogurt**

1 **TB. sweetened shredded coconut**

1½ **tsp. granulated sugar**

⅛ **tsp. vanilla extract**

¾ **cup undrained pineapple chunks in their own juice**

1. Pour milk and yogurt into a blender. Add coconut, sugar, and vanilla extract. Carefully spoon in pineapple with juice.

2. Blend on high speed for 20 to 30 seconds or until desired consistency is reached. Serve cold.

Learning Curve _____

Fat-free milk is also known as skim milk. Many cartons carry both terms because "fat-free" is a more consumer-friendly label.

Applenana Smoothies $

Enjoy a serving of this fruity, refreshing blend with one fruit serving toward your daily recommendation.

1 medium banana   **1 cup fat-free plain yogurt**

1 cup apple juice, chilled

1. In a small bowl, coarsely chop banana and mash with a fork.

2. Pour apple juice, yogurt, and banana into a blender.

3. Blend on high speed for 10 to 20 seconds or until desired consistency is reached. Serve cold.

Yield: 2 servings
Prep time: 2 minutes
Serving size: 1⅓ cups
Each serving has:
179 calories
5 calories from fat
0.5 g fat
0 g saturated fat
8 g protein
37 g carbohydrates

Learning Curve _____

If you'd like to enjoy recipes that should be served cold without waiting, place the individual ingredients in the refrigerator ahead of time to chill. Canned goods, juices, and the like can be chilled before being blended into a recipe.

Mocha Smoothie $

Blend up this delicious duo for a cool treat or a great use of leftover coffee.

½ **cup prepared coffee, cooled**   **1 cup 50 percent-less-fat chocolate ice cream**

1. Pour coffee into a blender. Add ice cream.

2. Cover and blend on high speed for 10 seconds or until blended.

Yield: 1 serving
Prep time: 1 minute
Each serving has:
241 calories
81 calories from fat
9 g fat
6 g saturated fat
6 g protein
34 g carbohydrates

Of Higher Learning _____

Hawaii is the only state in the United States where coffee bean are commercially grown. (Puerto Rico, a U.S. territory, also grows coffee.)

Sugar and Spice Hot Chocolate $

A wintry day's indulgence, this hot chocolate can float mini marsh-mallows or be stirred with a candy cane.

Yield: 1 serving
Prep time: 2 minutes
Cook time: 2 or 3 minutes
Each serving has:
193 calories
61 calories from fat
7 g fat
4 g saturated fat
9 g protein
26.5 g carbohydrates

1 cup fat-free milk

2 TB. semi-sweet chocolate chips or milk chocolate chips

¼ tsp. vanilla extract

¼ tsp. ground cinnamon

Pinch ground nutmeg

1. Pour milk into a microwave-safe mug. Cook on high power for 2 or 3 minutes or until hot.

2. Stir in chocolate chips until melted and blended. Stir in vanilla extract, cinnamon, and nutmeg until blended. Cool as desired.

Learning Curve

Preparing hot chocolate with milk makes a richer, creamier drink while adding calcium to your diet.

Morning Sunrise Juice $$

Wake up to this breakfast juice with a twist.

Yield: 1 serving
Prep time: 1 minute
Each serving has:
117 calories
0 calories from fat
0 g fat
0 g saturated fat
1 g protein
28 g carbohydrates

⅔ cup home-style orange juice, chilled

⅓ cup cranberry juice, chilled

1. Pour orange juice into a glass. Pour in cranberry juice.

2. Stir and serve cold.

Learning Curve

Orange juice is now available in any number of varieties that tout specialized dietary benefits. Choose the orange juice that meets your needs—calcium-supplemented, cholesterol-reducing, low-acid, etc.

Appendix A

Glossary

al dente   Italian for "against the teeth." Refers to pasta or rice that's neither soft nor hard but just slightly firm against the teeth.

all-purpose flour   Flour that contains only the inner part of the wheat grain. Usable for all purposes from cakes to gravies.

almonds   Mild, sweet, and crunchy nuts that combine nicely with creamy and sweet food items.

apple corer   A kitchen tool with a long, round blade to cut out the core of a whole apple.

artichoke hearts   The center part of the artichoke flower, often found canned in grocery stores.

arugula   A spicy-peppery garden plant with leaves that resemble a dandelion and have a distinctive—and very sharp—flavor.

at room temperature   A directive often given for eggs, butter, cream cheese, and other ingredients that should not be incorporated into a mixture while cold.

au gratin   The quick broiling of a dish before serving to brown the top ingredients. When used in a recipe name, the term often implies cheese and a creamy sauce.

bake   To cook in a dry oven. Dry-heat cooking often results in a crisping of the exterior of the food being cooked. Moist-heat cooking, through methods such as steaming, poaching, etc., brings a much different, moist quality to the food.

balsamic vinegar   Vinegar produced primarily in Italy from a specific type of grape and aged in wood barrels. It is heavier, darker, and sweeter than most vinegars.

barbecue   To quick-cook over high heat, or to cook something long and slow in a rich liquid (barbecue sauce).

basil   A flavorful, almost sweet, resinous herb delicious with tomatoes and used in all kinds of Italian or Mediterranean-style dishes.

baste   To keep foods moist during cooking by spooning, brushing, or drizzling with a liquid.

beat   To quickly mix substances.

Belgian endive   A plant that resembles a small, elongated, tightly packed head of romaine lettuce. The thick, crunchy leaves can be broken off and used with dips and spreads.

black pepper   A biting and pungent seasoning, freshly ground pepper is a must for many dishes and adds an extra level of flavor and taste.

blanch   To place a food in boiling water for about 1 minute (or less) to partially cook the exterior and then submerge in or rinse with cool water to halt the cooking.

blend   To completely mix something, usually with a blender or food processor, more slowly than beating.

bloom   The grayish haze that appears on the surface of chocolate that has been held in warm or humid conditions, causing sugar or fat to come to the surface.

blue cheese   A blue-veined cheese that crumbles easily and has a somewhat soft texture, usually sold in a block. The color is from a flavorful, edible mold that is often added or injected into the cheese.

boil   To heat a liquid to a point where water is forced to turn into steam, causing the liquid to bubble. To boil something is to insert it into boiling water. A rapid boil is when a lot of bubbles form on the surface of the liquid.

bouillon   Dried essence of stock from chicken, beef, vegetable, or other ingredients. This is a popular starting ingredient for soups as it adds flavor (and often a lot of salt).

breadcrumbs   Tiny pieces of crumbled dry bread, often used for topping or coating.

brine   A highly salted, often seasoned, liquid used to flavor and preserve foods. To brine a food is to soak, or preserve, it by submerging it in brine. The salt in the brine penetrates the fibers of the meat and makes it moist and tender.

broil   To cook in a dry oven under the overhead high-heat element.

broth   *See* stock.

brown   To cook in a skillet, turning, until the food's surface is seared and brown in color, to lock in the juices.

brown rice   Whole-grain rice including the germ with a characteristic pale brown or tan color; more nutritious and flavorful than white rice.

bulgur   A wheat kernel that's been steamed, dried, and crushed and is sold in fine and coarse textures.

cake flour   A high-starch, soft, and fine flour used primarily for cakes.

cannellini beans   A type of white bean of an ivory coloring with a velvety texture.

capers   Flavorful buds of a Mediterranean plant, ranging in size from *nonpareil* (about the size of a small pea) to larger, grape-size caper berries produced in Spain.

caramelize   To cook sugar over low heat until it develops a sweet caramel flavor. The term is increasingly gaining use to describe cooking vegetables (especially onions) or meat in butter or oil over low heat until they soften, sweeten, and develop a caramel color.

caraway   A distinctive spicy seed used for bread, pork, cheese, and cabbage dishes. It's known to reduce stomach upset, which is why it's often paired with, for example, sauerkraut.

carbohydrate   The basic nutritional component of starches, sugars, fruits, and vegetables that causes a rise in blood sugar levels. Carbohydrates supply energy and many important nutrients, including vitamins, minerals, and antioxidants.

cayenne   A fiery spice made from (hot) chili peppers, especially the cayenne chili, a slender, red, and very hot pepper.

cheddar   The ubiquitous hard cow's milk cheese with a rich, buttery flavor that ranges from mellow to sharp. Originally produced in England, cheddar is now produced worldwide.

chili powder   A seasoning blend that includes chili pepper, cumin, garlic, and oregano. Proportions vary among different versions, but they all offer a warm, rich flavor.

chilies (or **chiles**)   Any one of many different "hot" peppers, ranging in intensity from the relatively mild ancho pepper to the blisteringly hot habañero.

chives   A member of the onion family, chives grow in bunches of long leaves that resemble tall grass or the green tops of onions and offer a light onion flavor.

chop   To cut into pieces, usually qualified by an adverb such as "*coarsely* chopped," or by a size measurement such as "chopped into ½-inch pieces." "Finely chopped" is much closer to mince.

cider vinegar   Vinegar produced from apple cider, popular in North America.

cilantro   A member of the parsley family and used in Mexican cooking (especially salsa) and some Asian dishes. Use in moderation, as the flavor can overwhelm. The seed of the cilantro is the spice coriander.

cinnamon   A sweet, rich, aromatic spice commonly used in baking or desserts. Cinnamon can also be used for delicious and interesting entrées.

clove   A sweet, strong, almost wintergreen-flavor spice used in baking and with meats such as ham.

count   In terms of seafood or other foods that come in small sizes, the number of that item that compose 1 pound. For example, 31-to-40-count shrimp are large appetizer shrimp often served with cocktail sauce; 51-to-60 are much smaller.

couscous   Granular semolina (durum wheat) that is cooked and used in many Mediterranean and North African dishes.

crimini mushrooms   A relative of the white button mushroom but brown in color and with a richer flavor. The larger, fully grown version is the portobello. *See also* portobello mushrooms.

croutons   Chunks of bread, usually between ¼ and ½ inch in size, sometimes seasoned and baked, broiled, or fried to a crisp texture and used in soups and salads.

crudités   Fresh vegetables served as an appetizer, often all together on one tray.

cumin   A fiery, smoky-tasting spice popular in Middle-Eastern and Indian dishes. Cumin is a seed; ground cumin seed is the most common form used in cooking.

curd   A gelatinous substance resulting from coagulated milk used to make cheese. Curd also refers to dishes of similar texture, such as dishes made with egg (lemon curd).

curry   Rich, spicy, Indian-style sauces and the dishes prepared with them. A curry uses curry powder as its base seasoning.

curry powder   A ground blend of rich and flavorful spices used as a basis for curry and many other Indian-influenced dishes. Common ingredients include hot pepper, nutmeg, cumin, cinnamon, pepper, and turmeric. Some curry can also be found in paste form.

dash   A few drops, usually of a liquid, released by a quick shake of, for example, a bottle of hot sauce.

devein   The removal of the dark vein from the back of a large shrimp with a sharp knife.

dice   To cut into small cubes about ¼-inch square.

Dijon mustard   Hearty, spicy mustard made in the style of the Dijon region of France.

dill   An herb perfect for eggs, salmon, cheese dishes, and, of course, vegetables (pickles!).

dollop   A spoonful of something creamy and thick, like sour cream or whipped cream.

double boiler   A set of two pots designed to nest together, one inside the other, and provide consistent, moist heat for foods that need delicate treatment. The bottom pot holds water (not quite touching the bottom of the top pot); the top pot holds the ingredient you want to heat.

dredge   To cover a piece of food with a dry substance such as flour or corn meal.

drizzle   To lightly sprinkle drops of a liquid over food, often as the finishing touch to a dish.

dry   In the context of wine, a wine that contains little or no residual sugar, so it's not very sweet.

entrée   The main dish in a meal. In France, however, the entrée is considered the first course.

extra-virgin olive oil   *See* olive oil.

feta   A white, crumbly, sharp, and salty cheese popular in Greek cooking and on salads. Traditional feta is usually made with sheep milk, but feta-style cheese can be made from sheep, cow, or goat milk.

fillet   A piece of meat or seafood with the bones removed.

flake   To break into thin sections, as with fish.

floret   The flower or bud end of broccoli or cauliflower.

flour   Grains ground into a meal. Wheat is perhaps the most common flour. Flour is also made from oats, rye, buckwheat, soybeans, etc. *See also* all-purpose flour; cake flour.

fold   To combine a dense and light mixture with a circular action from the middle of the bowl.

garbanzo beans (or **chickpeas**)   A yellow-gold, roundish bean used as the base ingredient in hummus. Chickpeas are high in fiber and low in fat.

garlic   A member of the onion family, a pungent and flavorful element in many savory dishes. A garlic bulb contains multiple cloves. Each clove, when chopped, provides about 1 teaspoon garlic. Most recipes call for cloves or chopped garlic by the teaspoon.

garnish   An embellishment not vital to the dish but added to enhance visual appeal.

ginger   Available in fresh root or dried, ground form, ginger adds a pungent, sweet, and spicy quality to a dish.

gnocchi   Small dumplings made of potatoes, ricotta cheese, or semolina flour that may have eggs and other ingredients added. They are prepared and served similarly to pastas.

grate   To shave into tiny pieces using a sharp rasp or grater.

grind   To reduce a large, hard substance, often a seasoning such as peppercorns, to the consistency of sand.

grits   Coarsely ground grains, usually corn.

handful   An unscientific measurement; the amount of an ingredient you can hold in your hand.

hors d'oeuvre   French for "outside of work" (the "work" being the main meal), an hors d'oeuvre can be any dish served as a starter before the meal.

hummus   A thick, Middle Eastern spread made of puréed garbanzo beans, lemon juice, olive oil, garlic, and often tahini (sesame seed paste).

Italian seasoning   A blend of dried herbs, including basil, oregano, rosemary, and thyme.

julienne   A French word meaning "to slice into very thin pieces."

kalamata olives   Traditionally from Greece, these medium-small, long black olives have a smoky rich flavor.

lentils   Tiny lens-shape pulses used in European, Middle Eastern, and Indian cuisines.

marinate   To soak meat, seafood, or other food in a seasoned sauce, called a marinade, which is high in acid content. The acids break down the muscle of the meat, making it tender and adding flavor.

marjoram   A sweet herb, a cousin of and similar to oregano, popular in Greek, Spanish, and Italian dishes.

meld   To allow flavors to blend and spread over time. Melding is often why recipes call for overnight refrigeration and is also why some dishes taste better as leftovers.

microwave-safe   A description given to dishes, bowls, and other cookware that can safely be used for cooking in a microwave oven.

mince   To cut into very small pieces smaller than diced pieces, about ⅛ inch or smaller.

mold   A decorative, shaped metal pan in which contents, such as mousse or gelatin, set up and take the shape of the pan. Also, a fungus-produced growth on foods resulting from spoilage or dampness.

Napa cabbage   Also called Chinese cabbage, is a member of the cabbage family with thick stems, crisp texture, and fresh, mild flavor. The tight heads are elongated with crinkly edged, pale green leaves.

no salt added   A food label indicating a food was prepared without the salt normally used in processing, although it still contains the sodium that's a natural part of the food itself.

Neufchâtel cheese   A mild, spreadable cheese of Normandy, France. Lower-fat, lower-calorie cream cheese is often labeled Neufchâtel cheese in the United States.

nutmeg   A sweet, fragrant, musky spice used primarily in baking.

olive oil   A fragrant liquid produced by crushing or pressing olives. Extra-virgin olive oil—the most flavorful and highest quality—is produced from the first pressing of a batch of olives; oil is also produced from later pressings.

olives   The fruit of the olive tree commonly grown on all sides of the Mediterranean. Black olives are also called ripe olives. Green olives are immature, although they are also widely eaten. *See also* kalamata olives.

oregano   A fragrant, slightly astringent herb used in Greek, Spanish, and Italian dishes.

orzo   A rice-shape pasta used in Greek cooking.

oxidation   The browning of fruit flesh that happens over time and with exposure to air. Minimize oxidation by rubbing the cut surfaces with a lemon half. Oxidation also affects wine, meats, fish, and whole grains.

paprika   A rich, red, warm, earthy spice that also lends a rich red color to many dishes.

Parmesan   A hard, dry, flavorful cheese primarily used grated or shredded as a seasoning for Italian-style dishes.

parsley   A fresh-tasting green leafy herb, often used as a garnish.

pecans   Rich, buttery nuts, native to North America, that have a high unsaturated fat content.

peppercorns   Large, round, dried berries ground to produce pepper.

pesto   A thick spread or sauce made with fresh basil leaves, garlic, olive oil, pine nuts, and Parmesan cheese. Some newer versions are made with other herbs.

pickle   A food, usually a vegetable such as a cucumber, that's been pickled in brine.

pinch   An unscientific measurement term, the amount of an ingredient—typically a dry, granular substance such as an herb or seasoning—you can hold between your finger and thumb.

pita bread   A flat, hollow wheat bread often used for sandwiches or sliced, pizza style. Terrific soft with dips or baked or broiled as a vehicle for other ingredients.

pizza cutter   A sharp, circular blade at the end of a handle that cuts as it rolls, making quick work of cutting a pizza into slices.

portobello mushrooms   A mature and larger form of the smaller crimini mushroom, portobellos are brownish, chewy, and flavorful. Often served as whole caps, grilled, or as thin sautéed slices. *See also* crimini mushrooms.

preheat   To turn on an oven, broiler, or other cooking appliance in advance of cooking so the temperature will be at the desired level when the assembled dish is ready for cooking.

purée   To reduce a food to a thick, creamy texture, usually using a blender or food processor.

reduce   To boil or simmer a broth or sauce to remove some of the water content, resulting in more concentrated flavor and color.

reserve   To hold a specified ingredient for another use later in the recipe.

rice vinegar   Vinegar produced from fermented rice or rice wine, popular in Asian-style dishes.

ricotta   A fresh Italian cheese smoother than cottage cheese with a slightly sweet flavor.

roast   To cook something uncovered in an oven, usually without additional liquid.

Roma tomato   Also called a plum tomato, a smaller, elongated tomato often used in Italian cooking.

rosemary   A pungent, sweet herb used with chicken, pork, fish, and especially lamb. A little of it goes a long way.

salsa   A style of mixing fresh vegetables and/or fresh fruit in a coarse chop. Salsa can be spicy or not, fruit-based or not, and served as a starter on its own (with chips, for example) or as a companion to a main course.

sauté   To pan-cook over lower heat than used for frying.

sear   To quickly brown the exterior of a food, especially meat, over high heat to preserve interior moisture.

sesame oil   An oil, made from pressing sesame seeds, that's tasteless if clear and aromatic and flavorful if brown.

shellfish   A broad range of seafood, including clams, mussels, oysters, crabs, shrimp, and lobster. Some people are allergic to shellfish, so take care with its inclusion in recipes.

shred   To cut into many long, thin slices.

simmer   To boil gently so the liquid barely bubbles.

skillet (also **frying pan**)   A generally heavy, flat-bottomed metal pan with a handle designed to cook food over heat on a stovetop or campfire.

skim   To remove fat or other material from the top of liquid.

slice   To cut into thin pieces.

stew   To slowly cook pieces of food submerged in a liquid. Also, a dish that has been prepared by this method.

stir-fry   To cook small pieces of food in a wok or skillet over high heat, moving and turning the food quickly to cook all sides.

stock   A flavorful broth made by cooking meats and/or vegetables with seasonings until the liquid absorbs these flavors. This liquid is then strained and the solids discarded. Can be eaten alone or used as a base for soups, stews, etc.

sweetened condensed milk   Evaporated milk with about a 40 percent sugar content.

tarragon   A sweet, rich-smelling herb perfect with seafood, vegetables (especially asparagus), chicken, and pork.

teriyaki   A Japanese-style sauce composed of soy sauce, rice wine, ginger, and sugar that works well with seafood as well as most meats.

thyme   A minty, zesty herb.

toast   To heat something, usually bread, nuts, or grains, so it's browned and crisp.

tofu   A cheeselike substance made from soybeans and soy milk.

translucent   A visual directive that requires the ingredient, such as an onion, to be clear-looking or partially transparent.

vinegar   An acidic liquid widely used as dressing and seasoning, often made from fermented grapes, apples, or rice. *See also* balsamic vinegar; cider vinegar; rice vinegar; white vinegar; wine vinegar.

walnuts   A rich, slightly woody flavored nut.

well   A depression made in the center of dry ingredients into which wet ingredients are added so the dry ingredients can be slowly incorporated.

whisk   To rapidly mix, introducing air to the mixture.

white mushrooms   Button mushrooms. When fresh, they have an earthy smell and an appealing "soft crunch."

white vinegar   The most common type of vinegar, produced from grain.

wild rice   Actually a grass with a rich, nutty flavor, popular as an unusual and nutritious side dish.

wilt   A visual clue that indicates the ingredient, such as a dark leafy green, has become limp from the heat.

wine vinegar   Vinegar produced from red or white wine.

wok   A pan for quick-cooking.

Worcestershire sauce   Originally developed in India and containing tamarind, this spicy sauce is used as a seasoning for many meats and other dishes.

zest   Small slivers of peel, usually from a citrus fruit such as lemon, lime, or orange.

zester   A kitchen tool used to scrape zest off a fruit. A small grater also works well.

Resources

When you need the most up-to-date food and nutrition information available, these websites can help. With a few mouse clicks, you'll learn how to eat well and find food storage and preparation tips. Many sites offer recipes to expand your cooking repertoire. Bookmark your favorites!

The American Dietetic Association
www.eatright.org
Timely, science-based food and nutrition information and much more.

The American Egg Board
www.aeb.org
Recipes, nutrition information, egg industry statistics, and more.

Cattlemen's Beef Board and National Cattlemen's Beef Association
www.beefitswhatsfordinner.com
Recipes, nutrition information, and more.

Department of Health and Human Services
www.healthierus.gov/dietaryguidelines
Complete copy of the Dietary Guidelines for Americans 2005 and related articles.

Federal Citizen Information Center
www.pueblo.gsa.gov
Free publication offers.

National Agricultural Library
www.nutrition.gov
Information on nutrition, healthy eating, and food safety.

National Chicken Council
www.eatchicken.com
Recipes, cooking tips, chicken nutrition, and more.

National Fisheries Institute
www.aboutseafood.com
Recipes, cooking tips, and nutrition and health information on fish and seafood.

National Pork Board
www.otherwhitemeat.com
Recipes, pork cooking basics, and more.

National Turkey Federation
www.eatturkey.com
Everything you want to know about turkey, from recipes and preparation tips to cooking demonstrations.

Nutrition Data
www.nutritiondata.com
Provides complete nutrition analysis for any food or recipe, and helps you select foods that best match your dietary needs.

United States Department of Agriculture
www.mypyramid.gov
Helps you choose the foods and the amounts that are right for you.

Index

W

X–Y–Z

Check out these BEST-SELLERS

READ BY MILLIONS!

Grammar and Style
SECOND EDITION

978-1-59257-115-4
$16.95

Buying & Selling a Home
FIFTH EDITION

978-1-59257-458-2
$19.95

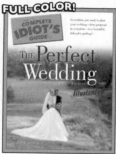

FULL COLOR!

The Perfect Wedding

978-1-59257-566-4
$22.95

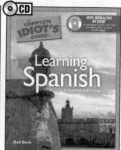

Learning Spanish
FOURTH EDITION

978-1-59257-485-8
$24.95

Investing
THIRD EDITION

978-1-59257-480-3
$19.95

Baby Sign Language

978-1-59257-469-8
$14.95

Total Nutrition
FOURTH EDITION

978-1-59257-439-1
$18.95

Positive Dog Training
SECOND EDITION

978-1-59257-483-4
$14.95

The Bible
THIRD EDITION

978-1-59257-389-9
$18.95

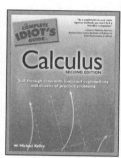

Calculus
SECOND EDITION

978-1-59257-471-1
$18.95

Music Theory
SECOND EDITION

978-1-59257-437-7
$19.95

The Perfect Resume
FOURTH EDITION

978-1-59257-463-6
$14.95

Playing the Guitar
SECOND EDITION

978-0-02864244-4
$21.95

Manga
ILLUSTRATED

978-1-59257-335-6
$19.95

Knitting & Crocheting
THIRD EDITION

978-1-59257-491-9
$19.95

More than **450 titles** available at booksellers and online retailers everywhere

ALPHA

www.idiotsguides.com